The New
Complete
Lurcher

The New
Complete
Lurcher

D. Brian Plummer

SWAN·HILL
PRESS

The Complete Lurcher — a manual
was originally published by the
Woodbridge Boydell Press in 1979

Copyright © 1998 D. Brian Plummer

First published in the UK in 1998
by Swan Hill Press, an imprint of Airlife Publishing Ltd

British Library Cataloguing-in-Publication Data

A catalogue record for this book is available from the British Library

ISBN 1 85310 992 4

Typeset by Phoenix Typesetting, Ilkley, West Yorkshire.
Printed in England by St Edmundsbury Press Ltd, Bury St Edmunds, Suffolk.

Swan Hill Press
an imprint of Airlife Publishing Ltd
101 Longden Road, Shrewsbury, SY3 9EB, England

I dedicate this book to David Hancock of Sutton Coldfield,
one of the few people I have met who justifies the title 'friend'.

Preface

A visitor to a lurcher show, a stranger who is not conversant with the subject of lurchers, might well be forgiven for asking, 'What exactly is a lurcher?' A small, fragile, whippet-like creature, bedecked with a dog rug despite the fact that it is springtime, passes near. Its owner states the dog is not an Italian greyhound but a lurcher. Near the beer tent is tied a giant steel-grey dog, hirsute and archaic enough in appearance to pass as one of the giant Celtic hounds that became extinct in the early 1800s. If its owner can be found amid the bubbling chaos of the refreshments tent he too will proclaim the dog to be a lurcher. Four dogs, indistinguishable from greyhounds, are led by a young lady who would seem more at home among a group of young, upwardly mobile executives than the dicklo wearing group to whom she is speaking, also declares her dogs to be lurchers and seems astonished at being questioned about their claim to the title, as does the owner of the very leggy collie type that is more finely built that any sheep-herding dog seen at the sheepdog trials. This dog too is a lurcher, as is the bizarrely patterned, merle-coloured smooth dog which is eagerly greeting passers-by, stretching and twisting his harlequin-patterned body to make contact with a medium-sized straw-coloured beauty whose ancestors supposedly herded mixed flocks of sheep, cattle and turkeys along the Norfolk roads. This dog too is a lurcher, and by now the newcomer, should he be a thinking person, must be thoroughly confused by the vast array of dogs, as variable in shapes and sizes, colours and types as a pound of Dolly Mixtures.

The purpose of this book is to attempt to define the types of lurcher, to explain their origins, to describe how the types can be bred and to show how lurchers and their close bedfellows can be trained, entered and conditioned to fulfil some kind of function to justify their keep and title. I trust the reader will now bide with me for the next few hundred pages and perhaps even forgive my unfortunate habit of using anecdotes to illustrate certain points.

Contents

1

Lurchers

If asked to define what is meant by the word 'lurcher' and to complete my definition in as few words as possible, I should be obliged to answer 'a mongrelised greyhound' or simply 'a dog with a strong trace of greyhound blood'. Webster's, as might be expected, is a shade more precise and defines the type thus: 'dog of nondescript breed, something between a collie and a greyhound, especially one used by poachers'. Chambers is even more precise – 'a dog with a distinct cross of greyhound, especially a cross of greyhound and collie' – and omits to mention any reference to the poacher – a type of person with whom, or so tradition has it, the lurcher appears to have strong affiliations. However, the expression 'mongrelised greyhound' is a far more accurate description of the types of dog afforded the appellation 'lurcher', though it is fair to state that in some cases at least there has been considerable thought and effort put into the production of these mongrelised greyhounds.

There is some dispute as to the origin of the word 'lurcher'. Phil Drabble, in *Of Pedigree Unknown*, believes the name is derived from the Anglo-Saxon expression 'to lurch' or to steal, and if truth be told the majority of mongrelised greyhounds display a remarkable propensity to consider virtually all organic matter edible and will go to considerable efforts to obtain such organic matter, particularly if such food is placed out of reach. My own opinion is that the name is simply an anglicised corruption of the French 'le chasseur', a dog specifically bred and tailored to be an able catcher of edible game. In this sense I confess I am a heretic for I know of no etymologist who accepts my explanation of the origin of the word 'lurcher'.

Unlike the greyhound, whose advocates claim great antiquity for their dogs, the lurcher is of fairly recent origin. John Caius in his letters to Conrad Gestner makes mention of a small dog much used by warreners, but whether this dog was a lurcher, a whippet or diminutive whippet

Lurchers of very mixed breeding are sometimes useful.

now known as the Italian greyhound is questionable. Legend has it that the lurcher came into being either by producing very leggy hirsute collies and breeding faster-herding dogs by careful selection (though this seems a shade unlikely) or by crossing droving dogs with greyhounds or greyhound types (I'll elaborate on the expression 'greyhound types' later) to produce intelligent fleet hunting dogs. That herding dogs were the ancestors of these early lurchers is beyond dispute, for prior to the nineteenth century England could claim to be home to only a small number of native breed types. Herding dogs of variable type ranging from dogs similar to Border collies to small Old English sheepdogs were common in Scotland, England and Wales. Mastiffs and mastiff derivatives were less common, scenthounds ranging in size from giants of the stature of modern staghounds to diminutive pocket beagles were not readily available, and while breed types used to flush birds – types which would later evolve into spaniels, setters and pointers – might well have provided the base from which lurchers might be bred, herding dogs, curs, call them what you will, were readily available and the obvious candidates for the dogs from which lurchers would have been bred.

It is rather foolish to underestimate the hunting ability of the sundry herding dogs of Britain. Indeed, herding is quite simply an adaptation of hunting where the subordinate animals (the sheepdogs) drive the quarry (the sheep) towards the alpha male (the shepherd). The essential element of restraint stops the collie slaughtering its wards, and when that Spencerian quality is absent collies can, and do, become ferocious killers of livestock. Collies allowed to wander free from the restrictions of chains or kennels often become splendid hunters of small game and one frequently hears of collies being used in the place of lurchers. David Hancock of Sutton Coldfield tells the tale of the collie belonging to Chuck Arrowsmith, a settled ex-itinerant from Harden, Walsall. The collie was not only a ferocious guard but was such a remarkable hunter that the family declined to use a lurcher while the collie lived. Hancock mated the Arrowsmith collie to a fawn greyhound bitch, track-bred and sired by the great hound Jimsun, and bred the lurcher Chuckles, a fine hunter with a splendid nose that has entered into the pedigrees of a great number of lurchers throughout Britain. Nicholas Stevenson of Cumbria can tell a similar tale regarding his bearded collie, a brother–to–sister bred dog inbred to Turnbull's Blue, perhaps the most famous bearded collie ever bred. The puppy, a pale slate blue, became an impressive hunter that easily caught and killed foxes and was almost fleet enough to be able to become a proficient rabbit catcher. Tales of the hunting prowess of collies are in fact legion and it is highly likely that artisan hunters were enthusiastic about exploiting this quality in the production of lurchers.

One of the earliest lurcher types to emerge was the Norfolk lurcher, still popular among the sporting fraternity though now much bastardised by additions of greyhound and deerhound blood to produce more fleet and typey animals. Originally the Norfolk lurcher was supposedly bred from a greyhound sire and a Smithfield collie dam, for it was believed that a collie dam influenced the potential intelligence of the hybrid more than would a collie sire – the excessive importance of maternal inheritance has long been disproved, one should add, though it is still believed by many modern lurcher breeders. The Smithfield collie is, however, a baffling enigma and was supposedly used to drive store cattle from country districts to towns for slaughter. It is highly unlikely that the type was fixed, and smooth and rough, tall and short dogs were often afforded the sobriquet 'Smithfield collie' by the drovers. Frederick Rolfe, the anti-hero of Lilias Rider Haggard's I Walked By Night, makes scant reference to the dog bred from a greyhound/Smithfield collie union and the author in a footnote refers to the type thus: 'The Smithfield Cattle Dog, small collies seen with drovers at all cattle markets etc. They are considered to be the most intelligent, teachable and hardy dogs and largely used as a cross with greyhound for producing lurchers for running rabbits and hares.'

Various forms of the Smithfield persisted in the south of England until relatively modern times. One form, the Blue Shagg sheepdog, was popular in Dorset and Wiltshire and resembled a type that was intermediate in size between the working bearded collie and the old bobtailed sheepdog (the ancestor of the Old English sheepdog). The Blue Shagg was not bobtailed, one should add, but was invariably docked – hence the expression to curtail or stop short an activity (for 'cur' was then used as a synonym for a farm dog). Dogs similar in type to Blue Shagg sheepdogs were until October 1992 regularly bred by Tom Muirhead, the working bearded collie specialist who lived near Wanlockhead, Dumfrieshire. Muirhead was considered a bastion, indeed perhaps the last bastion, of the working bearded collie and sold many excellent working beardies all over the world. He retired in 1992, prematurely aged by arthritis and the hard life a hill shepherd is expected to endure.

Today, the majority of Norfolk lurchers seen at lurcher shows are a spectacular straw colour and resemble the small old-fashioned Scottish deerhounds, or Scottish greyhounds, of yesteryear. No doubt deerhound and greyhound blood has been added to the collie greyhound mix, and the type would bear little resemblance to the dog described by Frederick Rolfe.

Perhaps at this point reference to Frederick Rolfe, the self-styled King of the Norfolk Poachers (a questionable title perhaps), makes it expedient to mention the Webster's reference to the lurcher's connection with the poacher. Curiously there are few references to convicted poachers being accompanied by dogs of any sort during their illegal forays, and certainly not with lurchers. In fact if one considers the nature of the work conducted by poachers of the nineteenth century dogs would be singularly out of place and a decided nuisance should the poacher be pursued by police officers or gamekeepers. Pheasants and partridges constituted the principal quarry of the nineteenth-century poacher and as pheasants roost aloft and partridges are virtually unapproachable after sunset, a lurcher would hardly be a desirable accoutrement for the professional poacher desiring to make a living from this profession. Rabbits and hares were seldom profitable enough quarry to tempt the professional poacher to run the gauntlet of keepers and police. Hence few professional poachers kept, let alone worked, lurchers.

Three-quarter greyhound Bedlington.

The lurcher was, however, the essential accompaniment to that Autolycus figure, that snapper up of ill-considered trifles, the moucher, the village ne'er-do-well, the permanently unemployed rustic. To such a person a lurcher would be a valuable asset and hence the lurcher became the insignia of the village disreputable. Such a dog could slip through hedges and snap up a rabbit feeding too far from home or a hare caught napping and return its catch to its owner. Such a dog would make no great inroads into the game a district held and like its owner would live just outside the law. Farm workers who owned such dogs were regarded with suspicion by landowners and the possession of a lurcher often resulted in dismissal, even though the dog, like its owner, was simply a petty pilferer of game rather than an out and out criminal.

The genetic make-up of these early lurchers has long been debated. Some authorities consider the breed type to be simply a herding dog bred on racy lines, others believe the dog to be a collie with simply a dash of greyhound blood to give the resulting crossbred the necessary speed to come to terms with a rabbit. The svelte, streamlined shape one associates with the modern lurcher, the lurcher winning at country shows, would have been noticeable by its absence in these early running dogs, for cunning, nose and that indefinable quality known as bushcraft were prized more than sheer speed; but changes were already afoot that were to change the shape, size and disposition of the lurcher.

Brian Vesey Fitzgerald, writing of the lurcher in his book 'It's My Delight', admittedly a glorious piece of hokum that glorifies the itinerant and rural misfit, states that he believes the lurcher is one of the most intelligent of dogs, nearly the equal of the poodle in I.Q. and streets ahead of its collie ancestor – though Fitzgerald is of the opinion that the Bedlington terrier and not the collie was possibly the ancestor of the lurcher; however, I will explore his notions at a later date. Truly, in 1948 when Vesey Fitzgerald published his book sagacity and nose were highly prized qualities in a lurcher, and speed of the quality found only in the greyhound was seldom encountered in a proper warrener's lurcher. However, some five years later events were to take place that would cause the lurcher to change greatly.

In 1953 Armand Delille, a French physician, introduced myxomatosis into Europe. Whatever the morality or nature of the introduction the disease wiped out some 95% of the rabbit population and Britain, which once hosted an abundant population of a hundred million rabbits – plague numbers which made Britain one of the most rabbit-infested countries in the world – was rendered virtually rabbit-free. It is estimated only five million rabbits survived the disease and the species was not to

Head study of an attractive type of lurcher.

acquire any level of immunity to myxomatosis for another thirty or so years.

This disease altered both the ecology and the economy of these islands drastically. Rabbit-eating species such as buzzards and stoats became more insectivorous, so it is believed, reverting to the diets they enjoyed before the rabbit arrived in Britain. Black-back gulls gorged on the abundance of putrefying rabbit meat for a season and then suffered greatly when the rabbit population almost disappeared. Carrion abounded during the mid-1950s as blind, emaciated rabbits sat out their last hours on the warm tarmac of roads and were mercifully killed by oncoming vehicles. Then quite suddenly the rabbit virtually disappeared, or became so rare that the appearance of a rabbit would merit a mention in local newspapers.

On the credit side certain pastures took on a new lease of life once the ravages of the rabbit ceased. Crop yields improved by as much as a third and it became profitable to graze sheep on land that was once so undermined with rabbits that sheep found it difficult to forage or walk. Sour pastures riddled with sorrel, dock and spurry, pastures made intensely acidic as the results of excessive quantities of rabbit urine, suddenly flourished and produced different species of edible herbage. It now became profitable to lime and plough land adjacent to ancient warrens – land that had steadfastly refused to yield reasonable crops for two hundred years.

With the virtual extinction of the rabbit the warrener too became superfluous. For two hundred years or so these tradesmen had kept the numbers of rabbits at an acceptable level with snares, ferrets and, perhaps, lurchers. Now the services of these rustic artisans were no longer required; some turned to mole catching, others to rural crafts while others forsook the countryside and sought employment in the towns. For a while *Exchange and Mart*, at one time perhaps the only vehicle to sell ferrets and lurchers, was filled with advertisements selling ferreting lurchers, and then quite suddenly there was a dearth of rabbit-hunting lurchers in the dogs column of the paper for it was no longer practicable or sensible to breed and train rabbit-catching dogs. Hares, however, were unaffected by the disease and for a while at least became more numerous. The warreners' lurchers were seldom fast enough to outstrip a hare afforded fair law: to breed faster dogs the rabbit-catching strains of lurcher were adulterated with the blood of deerhounds and greyhounds. Adulteration accurately describes the process, I'm afraid, for nose and brain were lost at the expense of speed and stamina when more sighthound blood was added to the mix. Prior to myxomatosis warreners' strains of lurcher, fairly true breeding strains at that, were not uncommon, but by 1963 one seldom saw rabbiting dogs advertised in the pages of *Exchange and Mart* and the majority of advertisements extolled only the speed and stamina of the mongrel hounds.

What was advertised were hybrid mixtures that were virtually long-dogs rather than true lurchers – mixtures of sighthounds with such a small percentage of baseline blood that the said hybrids were often difficult to train to a high standard. Deerhound-based crosses were popular and the majority of puppies offered for sale could seldom be considered true lurchers. Horror of horrors, saluki-blooded lurchers began to appear, composites with such a percentage of saluki blood in their make-up that the lurchers cum longdogs would have been precious little use to the warreners of pre-myxomatosis days, but were tailored to chase and catch only hares. Lurchers with the sagacity described by Vesey Fitzgerald in his many books probably belonged in the realms of fiction or fantasy anyway, but the biddable warreners' dogs of wartime years, descended from perhaps a hundred years of lurcher to lurcher breeding bred down from types of long-extinct collie, perhaps became virtually extinct or so diluted with sighthound blood that they were practically useless at the tasks for which true lurchers were intended. Yet such longdog-blooded dogs performed tolerably well in the pursuit of a hare and thus were highly prized by the sporting fraternity, which still kept lurchers. Then quite suddenly the rabbit began to reappear in the British countryside.

Aragao, who had first researched the machinations of myxomatosis, predicted that rabbits would acquire a certain degree of immunity to the disease, and eventually perhaps as few as 25% of the rabbit population would succumb to the infection. For many years naturalists questioned the wisdom of Aragao's prediction and the infrequent population explosions the rabbit experienced were ruthlessly and easily culled by keepers, until for the first time ever naturalists began to question James Edmund Harting's immortal quote, 'One thing is certain, the rabbit will always be with us.' Such is the incredible fecundity of the rabbit that it was only a matter of time before the rabbit became an important pest species yet again.

By the early 1970s they were once more becoming quite a common sight in the British countryside and it became quite a profitable venture to keep and work lurchers. The principal quarry of the lurcher should always be the rabbit, and the hare should always be regarded as a welcome but unexpected bonus by the lurcher owner. Likewise the principal quarry of the longdog or supersaturated lurcher (lurchers with less than 25% baseline blood) is the hare, and the rabbit should always be considered as a welcome but equally unexpected bonus by the longdog keeper. However, long before the rabbit once again became numerous enough to merit the title 'pest species' other events were to take place that would alter the shape, type, size and mental ability of the lurcher still further.

In 1974 a group of coursing enthusiasts based in Berkshire staged the first organised lurcher show at Lambourn, Berkshire. The first show was held as a social event designed to raise a few pounds for the Injured Jockey Appeal, but the popularity the event enjoyed was amazing. Within a few years most country shows staged classes for lurchers and lurcher breeding experienced a boom. Many dealer/breeders made small fortunes during the years immediately after Lambourn, for such was the popularity the lurcher enjoyed that virtually any greyhound-blooded mongrel found a ready sale.

Lurchers were judged according to their aesthetic appeal, and because

A three-quarter bred bearded-collie and greyhound hybrid.

sighthounds are so aesthetically pleasing, so symmetrical and so perfectly balanced, dogs with a strong trace of sighthound were invariably the winners at these shows. Collie-blooded dogs, short of neck and some-what cloddy in shape, were seldom placed except by deliberate iconoclasts who were determined to create a precedent by their selection. Indeed so poorly were collie hybrids represented that certain shows staged special classes for collie lurchers so that true lurchers rather than longdogs stood at least some chance of winning some rosettes, if not the coveted Best In Show award. Thus, to produce good, typey, showable animals breeders added yet more sighthound blood to an already super-saturated sighthound mixture. The results were often pleasing to see but were a star's flight from the type of lurcher desired by the warreners of pre-myxomatosis days, and true lurchers with more than 25% of their lineage made up of base blood not only became extremely rare but also unfashionable. Few breeders maintained the old strains and there certainly were strains of lurcher in the days before myxomatosis, as indeed there are strains today, but few of the modern strains of lurcher have sagacity and nose enough to satisfy professional warreners.

During the early 1960s Phil Drabble published his great book *Of Pedigree Unknown*, a piece of work which, while it eulogises the merits of the deer-hound-bred longdog, made mention of the Bedlington terrier lurcher, and before proceeding further with the evolution of the modern lurcher it is expedient to mention this type of running dog. Vesey Fitzgerald's notions concerning the nature of the lurcher are scarcely scientific, but he did travel amid the itinerant families during the 1930s and saw a great many of the dogs that were, and still are, part and parcel of every itinerant band. Vesey Fitzgerald had always questioned the origin of the lurcher and while he conceded that many of the East Anglian strains were derived from pastoral dogs blended or crossed with greyhounds, he believed that the majority of the lurchers bred by itinerants and warreners had Bedlington terrier ancestors. When Vesey Fitzgerald mingled with what John Pattison called the 'blackfaced tinkers' (the term 'blackfaced' is not derogatory but is derived from the Gallic word 'dhubi' – black or dark of visage, the origin of the clan name McPhee, one of the most populous tinker clans in the Highlands) he observed strains of lurcher with soft blue-black rough jackets and silky topknots, and these he concluded were Bedlington terrier greyhound hybrids – which was a fairly popular hybrid in 1930, one should add. Personally I feel Vesey Fitzgerald may well have been wrong about the origin of these hirsute dogs, for similar coat and colour can be created by mating working bearded collies with greyhounds, and the progeny of such a union would be a great deal more hardy and many times more durable than a modern Bedlington terrier hybrid. Life beneath the vardos was indeed hard and a dog needed to be constitutionally sound to survive such a lifestyle.

However, be that as it may, the revival of the rabbit population brought about a revival of interest in the production of Bedlington lurchers, both the Bedlington greyhound hybrids and the smaller Bedlington whippet lurchers which have always been popular with ferreters, and at the 1980 Lambourn show three quarters of the winning stock were dogs that sported a linty coat similar to that produced by mating Bedlington terriers to greyhounds or whippets. The type is very appealing, quite attractive, and the first-generation Bedlington × greyhound or whippet hybrids appear very true to type.

The qualities this lurcher type is supposed to possess are often debated in the sporting press. It is argued that the hybrid inherits speed from its sighthound ancestor (either whippet or greyhound) and nose and courage from its Bedlington parent. However, in recent years

21

numerous attempts to create a Working Bedlington Terrier Club have received a somewhat mixed response and many declare that the modern Bedlington terrier is a far cry from the desperately game dogs described by Rawdon Lee. Critics of this terrier state that the Bedlington is inert, not simply lacking in courage, and often shows little hunting instinct and even less vitality. A far more serious fault, however, is the fact that many Bedlington terriers are cursed with the problem of copper toxicosis, an inherited malaise that also afflicts Dobermanns and Skye terriers. Claims that certain so-called working strains of Bedlington, namely the Gutch Common strain bred by the late Margaret Williamson, are free of this disease are without foundation and it is accurate to state that the problem is rampant in the breed, though breeders are making stringent efforts to eradicate the complaint.

More insidious still is the fact that first-cross Bedlington terrier/sighthound hybrids (greyhound or whippet bred) do not manifest the disorder (but many certainly carry it) for both the greyhound and the whippet are genetically free of copper toxicosis. Hence even a Bedlington terrier that is destined to die of the disorder will produce lurchers that are not troubled with copper toxicosis. However, when Bedlington terrier lurchers are mated together (when the parents are bred from Bedlington terriers) the disease often appears in the resulting puppies and there are many instances of Bedlington terrier lurcher composites dying from diseases the symptoms of which are virtually identical to those manifested by victims of copper toxicosis.

Yet the crossbreed has its devotees, most of whom swear by the Bedlington lurcher, though it is distressing to see advertisements for stock which is very indiscriminately bred and may well introduce the problems of copper toxicosis into the mongrelised lurcher gene pool. Sufficient to say that despite the problems Bedlington terrier blood may bring, Bedlington lurchers (both greyhound and whippet bred) are extremely attractive dogs and the first-cross hybrids are seldom troubled by disorders that beset the Bedlington terrier.

The return of the rabbit produced a need for lurchers with a strong baseline that could be trained to a high standard to work with ferrets, lamps and even longnets. Despite the claims of longdog aficionados and owners of supersaturated lurchers, dogs with a high proportion of sighthound blood seldom make satisfactory general-purpose hunting dogs.

It would, however, be untrue to state that no one kept alive the traditional strains of lurcher or deliberately bred collie composite hybrids before the return of the rabbit – though buyers would do well to treat advertisements for lurchers from long-established strains with extreme suspicion. Certain breeders, however, specialised in breeding collie lurchers long before the rabbit explosion of the late 1970s. One of these breeders, David James of Bloxwich, has bred a line of collie greyhound hybrids that won well at the early lurcher obedience tests. The line bred by David has been continued by breeders such as Tay and Wright and is still one of the most successful competition strains in Britain today. Later Terry Ahern of Tamworth began breeding collie greyhound hybrids from a first-cross collie greyhound hybrid he purchased from Lutterworth in the late 1970s, and the blend of Ahern's Rusty and bitch line from David James continues to win and work well in the field. Rusty was a very adaptable dog and an extremely easy dog to train. He died quite young from meningitis but not before he mated many bitches, and he did much to revive the cult of the collie greyhound.

It would be impossible to write about the collie greyhound lurcher without mentioning David Hancock of Sutton Coldfield, the world's most successful breeder of the hybrid. Hancock's kennel is little short of

A three-quarter bred Border-collie greyhound.

immense and comprises some fifty greyhound bitches and some seventeen or so collie or collie greyhound stud dogs. Some three hundred or so puppies are produced each year and Hancock-bred lurcher wins at obedience trials and the recent N.L. & R.C. tests are legion.

David began lurcher breeding shortly after the poultry industry experienced a depression and his egg producing and table poultry farm went into liquidation. His first litters of lurchers were three-quarter-bred collie greyhound bred from D. Fish's Merle and Monalee Champ and Jimsun-sired bitches, and because of Hancock's strict breeding plan he achieved success virtually from day one of his venture. Later the same year David acquired Richard Jones, a merle-coloured bearded collie/Border collie hybrid, who was later to become the most important sire in lurcher history. Richard sired several thousand puppies during his long life and produced two famous sons, Taffy and Wendel, to a Minisotta/Linden Eland bitch. Taffy sired an incredible number of puppies and produced the Scottish N.L. & R.C. representatives at the 1992

Border collie stud dog, the sire of excellent lurchers.

Blairgowrie Trials. His stock was gifted with an incredible nose and the thrust one normally associates with longdogs. Various other collie stud dogs reside at Cottage Farm, the most famous of which is Rufus, a red merle Border-type collie, the sire of the 1991 Blairgowrie winner and several national obedience champions. Hancock breeds a variety of collie hybrids ranging from three-quarter collie greyhound hybrids, untypey but easily trained dogs that are prized by lampers and ferreters alike, to three-quarter greyhound collie hybrids, fast, agile dogs that find a ready market among coursers and lampers. Hancock considers this crossbred to be the most versatile of dogs and capable of virtually any feat a lurcher enthusiast could require of a running dog.

The Hancock breeding policy is a strange, and perhaps inflexible, one that has caused considerable interest over the years. He breeds only from greyhound bitches and considers track dogs to be equally as suitable as coursing-bred animals. Indeed some of his very best stock has been produced from fairly small track-bred bitches, particularly bitches sired by So Clever and the explosive stud dog Hit The Lid. He refrains from using his collie stud dogs on visiting lurcher and greyhound bitches and his half-bred stud dogs are allowed to mate only visiting lurchers and not greyhounds. By dint of such methods David has achieved a virtual monopoly of the collie greyhound market. It is of interest to note that most of Hancock's stud dogs are merle, either red or blue merle, and the majority of the spectacular merles seen at shows throughout Britain are descended from dogs bred at Cottage Farm, Sutton Coldfield.

It should be mentioned that other breeds are sometimes used to produce lurchers, and shortly after the publication of Simpson's *Rebecca The Lurcher* a spate of supposedly exotic hybrids was advertised in the pages of *Exchange and Mart*. Foxhound × greyhound hybrids were apparently legion (mention is made in the book of such a crossbred). Supposedly the hybrids would be expected to have some of the nose of the foxhound and some of the speed of the greyhound. The fact that neither breed could be considered either tractable (I have kept foxhounds at walk on numerous occasions) or sagacious was apparently overlooked by the breeders, one should add. Later a litter of otterhound/greyhound puppies was advertised in the pages of the same magazine. It is to be hoped that this experiment was terminated at the first cross and that these hybrids did not enter the mongrel lurcher gene pool. Otterhounds are among the worst carriers or hip dysplasia, and space invader-type hip scores have been recorded when otterhounds have been hip tested.

On the subject of dogs with hip dysplasia, it might be wise to mention the once notorious but often versatile G.S.D. greyhound hybrids, for G.S.D.s too are often cursed with this crippling disorder. Drabble mentions that his hybrid was often produced by scrap dealers – probably by the misalliance of a greyhound with a guard dog, for the type of hybrid produced by the union would seldom be capable of coming to terms with hares. During the 1970s, however, one of these hybrids achieved great notoriety and for a brief while it was even suggested that the hybrid should be outlawed – a ludicrous notion perhaps, but then equally ludicrous notions were to be implemented by the Dangerous Dogs Act some years on. One Geoffrey Battans of Leighton Buzzard shot into the public notice when he pleaded guilty to poaching 216 deer including specimens from a small nucleus produced at Woburn, of the rare Pere David deer that had been extinct in the wild for some three thousand years. Battans' accomplice in the venture or ventures was named as a G.S.D. × greyhound and was much photographed by reporters eager to play up Battans' adventures and to depict him as a latter-day Robin Hood. Closer examination of the dog revealed it to be a large, smooth-coated, prick-eared pedigree unknown type that was almost certainly not a genuine G.S.D. × greyhound. The animal was, however, very versatile and apparently extremely well trained.

Later, in 1980, Hancock produced a litter of genuine G.S.D. × greyhounds using a guard dog mated to a Linden Eland-bred greyhound bitch to satisfy an order from Battans and two of his associates. David failed to sell the rest of the litter and never again attempted to breed a litter of these hybrids. For some reason, perhaps simply coincidence, the majority of the litter was plagued with bone weaknesses and these became very lame after the leg bones were shattered. Other breeders seem to have had better luck with the hybrid, and one of the most successful exponents of the crossbred must surely be Steve Barton of Abergavenny who represented Wales at the N.L. & R.C. finals at Blairgowrie in 1991. This animal was a most impressive lurcher with the most beautiful movement and galloping action. It was superbly trained, had an excellent nose and found well in the rush beds among which it was required to work. If the animal had had more experience one feels it would have been the overall winner at the trials, and in the following year it again represented Wales at Blairgowrie.

Despite the fact that many G.S.D.s are cursed with the affliction of hip dysplasia greyhounds are rarely, if ever, carriers of the disorder, hence the first-cross G.S.D. × greyhound hybrids are dysplasia-free. However, should two lines of lurcher, both carrying lines to G.S.D.s, be mated

Chris Wain's famous collie greyhound Kerry.

together there is a possibility of dysplasia occurring in the resulting litter. Such a disorder was unheard of in lurchers until the late 1980s when two lurcher enthusiasts wrote to *Shooting News* complaining that they had bought two puppies which became crippled with the ailment. Greyhounds are some of the most perfect of dogs and it is a shame that lurchers bred from these physical paragons should be afflicted by the disorders that curse certain other breeds.

During the early 1970s lurchers bred from Airedales or Irish terriers experienced a brief spell of popularity. Some spectacular rough-coated black and tan lurchers were shown at Lambourn in 1977 and while these did not receive a rosette they were extremely interesting and vital-looking animals. They had apparently been produced by mating a Jokyl-bred Airedale male to a black greyhound bitch, flapping track-bred and of dubious pedigree, but the puppies from the union were both distinctive and impressive. Both the owners of these dogs stated they were more than satisfied with the performances of their dogs in the field and neither owner complained that the dogs were in any way aggressive or hostile to other animals.

27

Phillip King of Ballyconnel is one of the last breeders of Irish terrier lurchers and swears by their performance in the field. Phillip, one of the great raconteurs of the lurcher world, believes that the merest dash of Irish terrier blood, a quarter perhaps, gives a lurcher more dash and fire than any other baseline confers. Phillip prizes the endurance of his lurchers and believes that composites of Irish terrier and greyhound provide the ideal ingredients for a lurcher. He is certainly Ireland's largest breeder of lurchers and has an excellent record for producing good coursing and working lurchers.

In the late 1980s and early 1990s a spate of advertisements for Wheaten terrier-bred lurchers appeared in the columns of *Shooting News*. The majority of these hybrids were produced from Wheaten terriers from Peter Gorman's strain – an enigmatic bloodline that is reputed to have J Line Staffordshire bull terrier ancestors. As to whether these lurchers were worth developing by adding another cross of greyhound blood to enhance the type and increase the speed of the lurchers bred from the union has yet to be resolved. Two puppies I have seen sired by Wheaten terriers out of a Sandman-bred greyhound (are any greyhounds free of the influence of Sandman these days?) were interesting but untypey with Norfolk-type coats but very short and rather unsightly backs. Both lurchers were a shade aggressive with other dogs but were a little too young to have achieved any success in the field.

Retriever crosses are rare these days and this is rather a pity for a retriever (Labrador, Chesapeake, golden or flatcoated) makes an admirable base for a lurcher. Curiously such hybrids were fairly commonly produced between the cessation of World War Two and 1953 (the onset of myxomatosis) but for some reason fell out of favour. It is said of Labrador hybrids that they are either very good or very bad, depending on the shape and weight of the hybrids one supposes, but the early agility and obedience tests of the 1980s saw one quite heavy Labrador greyhound hybrid compete with some success. Should an enterprising lurcher breeder choose to start breeding retriever hybrids I am sure a market could be created for the puppies, particularly when clients realise how easy these hybrids are to teach and how strong a hunting instinct retrievers confer on the crossbreds. My own choice would in fact be a line bred from an epilepsy-free golden retriever and a good class greyhound, though golden retrievers have a well earned reputation for being slow to mature.

Spaniel hybrids too are seldom seen and this is a pity because springer spaniel blood has much to offer a lurcher. True, the wilful disposition of the springer, some of which would sooner hunt than eat, might well be inherited by the lurchers bred from springer spaniels, but once a lurcher puppy experiences firm but gentle discipline long before it is taken hunting it might be expected to perform well. One of the best and most versatile lurchers I have encountered was a bitch bred by Don Southerd of Overseal who mated a greyhound bitch to a working springer spaniel. The bitch from this union admittedly lacked the class one might expect from a lurcher with a higher percentage of greyhound blood, but was a wonderfully versatile hunter and quite a successful fox catcher. Walsh (*Lurchers and Longdogs*) mentions the wilful disposition of the bitch when at a coursing meet. Don was fined five pounds for having a loose dog, a heinous sin among the coursing fraternity! Don later mated the bitch to the St Leger dog, Cash For Dan, and further diffused the spaniel blood with a succession of saluki greyhound crosses, but records that most of his strain of longdog (for longdog rather than lurcher they must now be called) will still retrieve a catch to hand as a result of the springer spaniel influence. Personally I have always felt that the puppies from Cash For Dan should have been exploited as lurchers and the line saturated no further with saluki or greyhound blood, but Southerd's interests lie in coursing rather than in pure and simple lurcher work.

During the mid-1960s certain breeders living on smallholdings along the Welsh borders made pin money, if not a living, by breeding bull terrier lurchers, mating English and Staffordshire bull terrier males to greyhound bitches. One advertisement for these hybrids read, 'Lurchers, I've tried them all and the only ones are bull terrier greyhounds', as an evaluation of the puppies offered for sale. However, the notion of mating bulldogs, bull terriers or fighting dogs of other breeds to greyhounds to produce tough gutsy crossbreds is by no means new. Lord Orford, the Norfolk eccentric, hybridised bulldogs and greyhounds to improve the coursing ability of his hounds. In all probability the bulldog outcross did virtually nothing to improve the coursing qualities of the greyhound – the blood was much diluted before it entered the main lines of greyhound breeding anyway and Orford's eccentric breeding plans were held in little regard by the breeders of the day – for at Tattersalls some of Orford's best stock sold for 'puppy prices' shortly after the demented lord's death. It is highly likely that equally good greyhounds were being produced by selective breeding without recourse to outrageous outcrossing of the kind practised by Orford.

However, I shall return to the merits of the bull terrier greyhound, if

Hancock's Remus sire of many excellent winning lurchers.

indeed the hybrid has merits. It is a curious fact that greyhounds readily absorb bull breeds and produce even first crosses that are finely built and fleet. The tale of Sonny the bull terrier hybrid from the Isle of Man is well known, and the dog remained fast and dextrous virtually to its death. At the 1979 Whaddon Chase Lurcher Show Grant Renwick, owner of Standfast Press, expressed his amazement and doubt that such an elegant animal was in fact a bull terrier hybrid, for even finely built collies mated to greyhounds produce cloddier, heavier hybrids.

It is argued that a dash of bull terrier will fire up a greyhound, but few greyhounds will not try desperately hard to catch a hare anyway, hence extra fire seems a shade superfluous and certainly unnecessary. Yet certain coursing enthusiasts swear by the blood. Rambo, the saluki/greyhound/bull terrier/greyhound owned by Irish Bob, did in fact enjoy a great reputation of staying with its hare after terrifyingly hard courses, but whether this stamina was conferred by the bull terrier blood or by its saluki ancestor is debatable. Still, the dog became a very famous single-handed hare catcher and has certainly entered into the pedigrees of many successful longdog composites.

At one time it was considered that the most suitable bull terrier to produce light-bodied hybrids was the English bull terrier, a type of refined, elegant pit fighting dog whose evolution was inspired by James Hinks, a dog breeder and animal dealer from Birmingham. Indeed the Welshpool hybrids of the early 1960s were produced from track-bred greyhound bitches mated to a pure-bred, but pedigree unknown, English bull terrier dog. At one time these crossbreds were in vogue as lamping dogs though few had the early pace needed to catch hares. Yet this line too faded into extinction in the early 1970s or else was absorbed by the sundry agglomerations of canine sins that were sold as deerhound × greyhounds. Yet these bull terrier hybrids did enjoy a great popularity during the late 1960s and early 1970s particularly as fox-catching dogs, for bull terrier hybrids have a well deserved reputation for taking the fight to any quarry that will retaliate or engage in a display of violence. Surprisingly exponents of the hybrid are amazed at how soft-mouthed these bull terrier greyhounds usually are, but this subject will be discussed presently.

Shortly after the American pit bull terrier, (Apbt) became popular, but long before the Dangerous Dogs Act of 1991 was passed – an absurd piece of legislature that served no useful purpose other than to act as a sop to Cerberus to certain very vocal groups within the general public – Apbt greyhound hybrids were commonly advertised and quite popular. Some of the first-cross – Apbt × greyhound hybrids were wonderfully constructed pieces of canine anatomy with the stocky muscular build one associates with a middle-distance runner and strong, heavy-jawed heads. If anything they were more typey than the Staffordshire bull terrier × greyhounds that were popular a decade before. John O'Keefe, chairman of the National Lurcher Racing Club, once said of one of these dogs that he bred by mating an American pit bull terrier male to a greyhound bitch, 'I have never seen him "run out" [run to a state of exhaustion] at lamped rabbits nor have I seen him attack another dog. He is soft-mouthed, rarely unable to catch the "twistiest" rabbit and would keep on trying long after I had had enough. It was difficult to find enough work for him even when there were plenty of rabbits living near Helmsdale', [a coastal town near the Sutherland Caithness border at one time famous for its rabbit population that approached plague proportions]. O'Keefe had rented a cottage twixt Melvick and Helmsdale and had achieved a great reputation in an area that produces an abundance of albeit poor-grade mongrel lurchers.

It must be added that clauses in the Dangerous Dogs Act make it illegal to breed and sell or give these hybrids, though it is perfectly legal to breed Staffordshire bull terrier or English bull terrier-bred hybrids. Britain is a wonderful country with the best legal system in the world. What a shame such a record was spoiled by the passing of the Dangerous Dogs Act, and what a shame Parliament is so easily swayed by aggressive and vocal minority groups.

The subject of whippet lurchers as opposed to whippet longdogs is hotly debated among the lurcher fraternity. Many swear by these tiny hybrids as ferreting dogs and lurchers that are required to hunt up quarry, rabbits etc. out of rough cover. Others, and I confess I am one, believe that no useful purpose is served by breeding these hybrids as the tasks expected of these dogs can be equally well, if not better, fulfilled by pure-bred or track-bred whippets (track-bred whippets have a dash of greyhound blood in their make-up and are usually faster and more tenacious than the Kennel Club-registered pure-bred whippet – I shall deal with the subject at greater length later in the book). E. G. Walsh too is of the opinion that these tiny lurchers are seldom as effective as pure-bred whippets.

The most popular whippet lurcher is the whippet Bedlington hybrid, a crossbred that owes its popularity as much to its cute appearance as to its working ability. These are certainly very attractive dogs and can be produced as even as peas in a pod – that is, of course, if the hybrid is a first-cross Bedlington whippet hybrid and not simply the result of mating crossbred dogs with a Bedlington-like appearance. There is very little variation in a litter of puppies resulting from mating a pure-bred Bedlington terrier with a K.C.-registered whippet, though there is often some disparity in the size of the progeny if the whippet used is track-bred, for most track-bred dogs have a strong hint of greyhound in their pedigrees.

I have never favoured whippet lurchers but my views are not shared by everyone, and this type of diminutive lurcher has more than just its share of devotees. In fact a good and regular living awaits anyone who can obtain cast whippets (not nearly as easy to obtain as are cast greyhounds, one should add, for many of the best racing whippets are also fireside pets) and the services of a good, reliable Bedlington terrier stud dog – if possible a dog free from copper toxicosis for it is morally wrong to allow such disorders to enter the mongrel lurcher gene pool. Then I predict that a breeder could sell almost as many puppies as he or she could produce.

Collies seldom blend well with pure-bred whippets to produce good, typey, useful lurchers. I am reluctant to be dogmatic about this hybrid but I have seen none that I wished to own and, unlike the Bedlington whippet hybrid, collie whippets simply do not breed true to type. The whippet, unlike the greyhound, simply does not have the frame to carry a collie mating and most of the puppies bred from the union of a collie

A pair of Norfolk-type lurchers.

and a K.C.-registered whippet are too cloddy to be versatile. Twice, via the pages of *Shooting News*, I have been taken to task for making such statements and both of my critics claimed to have collie whippet hybrids that were the very best of hunting dogs. Both dogs were, however, of dubious origin and had been passed from hand to hand several times before their owners acquired them, and neither were, in my opinion, collie whippet hybrids – one in fact measured twenty-five inches at the shoulder and was rough-coated. And now perhaps it is expedient to mention collie coat and type in lurchers to explain my comments.

First-cross Border collie whippet puppies are seldom if ever feathery-coated as is a collie and are usually smooth-jacketed with rat tails that are rarely feathered. Collie greyhound hybrids bred by mating Border collies to greyhounds are also like coated. The unique feathered ears and tails sported by many collie lurchers are a result of mating two collie-bred lurchers together and roughly a quarter of the resulting litter will be feathery-coated. Two of these feathery-coated collie hybrids mated together will usually produce 100% coated puppies. Should coat and type be the only qualities a breeder wishes to fix in a strain it is then relatively easy to breed a true breeding strain of collie whippets or collie greyhounds, and the problems of collie eye anomaly and progressive retinal atrophy will be dealt with later in this book – and at the time of writing these are indeed problems!

From time to time incredible exotic hybrid lurchers are seen advertised in the sporting periodicals and why these lurchers are produced would constitute the ingredients for a separate book. Otterhounds, harriers, Dobermanns, Australian cattle dogs and even rottweilers have been mated to greyhounds in an attempt to breed a new top-rate lurcher type. Personally I should fight shy of acquiring any of these exotics to train and avoid breeding them. There simply isn't a market for these experimental crosses and frankly the sort of buyer who would approach a breeder of these exotics would not be the sort of person to whom I would willingly sell a puppy. Such experimental hybrids usually appeal only to those with a short-lived interest in lurchers and people of this nature are usually only too eager to part with a young lurcher should the whelp experience a slight hitch in training. One of my favourite tales concerning the production of exotics is told by David Hancock. A lady phoned David and stated, 'I have a borzoi collie and want to mate it to a Rhodesian ridgeback × saluki greyhound. What would I expect to pay as a stud fee?' David thought for a while and replied, 'I can't really say, but I would be fascinated to hear how you disposed of the litter. Such puppies would be virtually impossible to sell and the very devil to home.'

The subject of exotics leads us quite neatly to yet another hot potato, namely the lurchers whose make-up is composed as multiple crosses, or what is popularly known as the 'bitza' lurcher (bits of Bedlington, bits of collie, etc.), and are of variable value. One of the age-old adages of lurcher breeding – the fewer the crosses the better the running dog – has clearly been disregarded in the production of these crossbreds and the breeding of these has clearly been a very hit and miss affair with little thought to the end product. Most of the supposed pedigrees of these dogs – deerhound greyhound saluki/collie greyhound Bedlington terrier whippet – is largely guesswork and the lists of ancestors of the litter can change from week to week as the needs of the owners dictate. Often these crossbreds have been produced for convenience's sake – a bitch comes into season and a fertile male resides next door and no more thought than that has gone into the breeding of the litter. Every housing estate in Britain produces litters of bitzas which are usually sold for a song and frequently pass from hand to hand before meeting with a miserable sort of death.

Having painted such a gloomy picture I must admit that I have seen quite impressive bitza lurchers though it is fair to say that the majority of the stock offered for sale has far too much greyhound blood to make it first-rate. I have, however, seen far more unsuitable bitzas which were not fast enough to be considered good longdogs and without enough baseline to be considered lurchers. Most of these supersaturated bitzas are short on nose and shorter still on intelligence and, frankly, I should be very careful about buying such a dog from a person of whose dogs I had little knowledge. Good mongrelised lurchers do exist – my own strain are inbred bitzas – but unless the breeder has a goal in mind in breeding such a litter or has a good knowledge of the antecedents of the parents of the lurchers it is very risky to purchase a pig in a poke, particularly if one requires a lurcher that is meant to be versatile rather than simply fleet of foot.

There are few hard and fast rules about such mixtures but it can be fair to state that the more mongrelised the breeding the greater the chance of the litter throwing up undesirable characteristics as undesirable genes pair up to produce puppies with unpleasant abnormalities. However, these problems will be dealt with later in this book. It is also reasonable to state that one has less of a chance of purchasing an unsuitable puppy if one sees both the parents, notes that they are similar in type and are both what the purchaser requires of a lurcher. Still, buying a lurcher with a very mixed pedigree can be an extremely risky business – but then the purchase of any pedigree unknown type of livestock is always risky.

I have stated that a lurcher's principal quarry is the rabbit and that any hares the dog catches must be regarded as a bonus, and vice versa for a longdog. Thus it might be assumed that the very best, the most versatile dog imaginable would be a longdog/lurcher composite. Nothing, dear reader, could be further from the truth.

2

Obtaining a Lurcher

Shortly after 1974 it was possible to sell any crossbred greyhound as a lurcher and often for quite an inflated price. Dealers had waiting lists for grown dogs which had a greyhoundy shape and rough-coated lurchers, even dogs and bitches with damaged feet and a hang-dog expression that bespoke misuse from a dozen or so homes, commanded high and often ridiculous prices. Litters of puppies, most of which boasted the inevitable deerhound/greyhound pedigrees (virtually all large mongrelised lurchers are of supposedly deer-hound/greyhound breeding), were sold as soon as they appeared in the pages of *Exchange and Mart* – at that time virtually the only paper which advertised lurchers – and some of the very worst lurchers imaginable found a ready market. So popular was the lurcher that amazing sleights of hand were practised in order to sell puppies – an anecdote will suffice to explain. In 1975 I attended the Whaddon Chase show and stood next to a young couple who had a pair of smooth-coated dogs on slips. The long snake-like heads and racy bodies created some interest and so I asked after the breeding of the pair. It transpired the couple had bought them as puppies from a breeder who claimed that they were sired by a deerhound out of a track-bred greyhound bitch. Indeed the distaff side of the pedigree was correct for both the puppies were earmarked with N.G.R.C. tattoos. It seems that a bull in the market for lurchers coincided with a bear in the market for greyhound puppies and it was worth the breeders' while to see good-class greyhound puppies as lurchers. One of the brindle bitches later became the dam of one of the winners of the last ill-fated Lambourn show – but the dam was a greyhound not a lurcher.

These days it is decidedly a buyers' market. Advertisements for puppies often appear for several weeks before the litters are sold and quite good, mature dogs will remain in the dealer's kennels for many months before a potential buyer appears at the said kennels. A vast array of lurchers of all shapes and sizes are available for the buyer to select and the selection process should therefore be conducted with care and in a more leisurely manner for there is little chance that a litter will be snapped up by hosts of buyers, or that a grown dog will be rehomed quickly.

At the risk of being anything but precise there are three methods of obtaining a lurcher and I propose to discuss each of those methods at some length. A visit to one of the all too numerous lurcher rescue societies will invariably secure a lurcher, or several lurchers for that matter, for the cup of the lurcher rescue societies surely runneth over. There is often no kennel space to cater for the enormous number of slinky-bodied waifs and strays that are waiting to be rehoused. These dogs can be obtained for a song or sometimes free of charge for the rescue societies are often desperate to find homes for their wards. As to how these unwanted dogs came to be rejected and in need of rehoming should be of interest to any lurcher enthusiast, particularly one who is contemplating breeding a litter of puppies.

David Hancock, the world's most successful lurcher breeder, estimates that one in every five lurcher puppies he breeds will change hands before it is ten weeks of age, for such is the ephemeral interest manifested by many lurcher people who will seek to own a lurcher puppy one day and terriers the next, and bantams or pigeons the following week. Once a puppy finds it way on this hurry-on-down treadmill its future is unenviable and it is virtually inevitable that the animal will finish up with a rescue society, for the grasshopper-minded lurcher keeper will have associates with similar short-lived interests and the hapless whelp will be passed from hand to hand many times, becoming more and more dispirited, craving affection and a permanent home until it finally finishes up in a rescue society kennels. This is indeed a sad state of affairs, but Hancock's figures do if anything paint a somewhat rosy picture of the lurcher world. Hancock's dogs are quite expensive and hence a lurcher enthusiast with a temporary interest will attempt to keep a puppy for which he has paid dearly for far longer than he would an inexpensive puppy which he will often treat as a disposable commodity. The cheap, easily obtained puppies of doubtful lineage change hands very, very frequently I'm afraid.

It is unfashionable and perhaps unwise to criticise the New Age Traveller (a delightful euphemism) or the more established denizens of the road, but the lot experienced by many of their dogs is far from enviable. Many, many lurchers are simply abandoned when these people move to another site and hapless creatures are found wandering, baffled by the disappearance of their owners. Tiny mites, puppies scarcely weaned, adult dogs and ancient veterans who are in need of shelter rather than work are often found when their owners move on. These too are rehomed by lurcher rescue societies, though the tale of Geoffrey Battans' supposed G.S.D. × greyhound puppy has a somewhat happier ending. Many lurchers become unwanted when married couples separate and neither wife nor husband has place to keep a lurcher, and breeders should remember that a great many people who buy lurcher puppies are likely to separate, for a passion for lurcher work is scarcely conducive to a happy marriage (unless the wife too has a passion for these running dogs) and lurcher widows are all too common, I'm afraid. Hence, yet another crop of lurchers finds its way to the rescue society kennels.

There are some bizarre tales concerning how lurchers arrive at these kennels. A few weeks ago a newspaper reported on the plight of a lonely young woman who kept seventeen dogs in her council flat, some of which were lurchers. The stench was apparently disgusting and the young lady was forced to rehome her bobbery pack – some of these found their way to lurcher rescue kennels. On a more macabre note, many dogs, of all breeds, are abandoned on the edge of motorways perhaps because it is easy to jettison a dog on such roadways and remain incognito, and, more unpleasant still, perhaps because the fate of the unwanted dog is both certain and bloody. The fact that abandoning these dogs on the motorways may also cause the death of motorists seems to escape the perpetrators of such deeds. Should the reader believe I exaggerate my story I might say that twice I have attempted to capture lurchers found wandering on motorways around Glasgow and I often hear tales of friends who have attempted similar rescues. Glasgow has a huge lurcher population – some may argue too big!

On a somewhat happier note is the tale of Marge Holman's rescue of a greyhound found tied to a fence on the edge of a motorway. Marge, who died in 1991, rescued the hound and ran the bitch on unregistered tracks, entering her hound as Motorway Lil. The animal performed tolerably well despite the nature of its acquisition and on retirement was given to David Hancock who bred a number of very fine working lurchers from the animal. Such happy endings are, however, extremely rare, and if the dog abandoned on a motorway is not rescued fairly quickly its fate is inevitable and extremely unpleasant.

Dogs abandoned in the countryside are legion and a bored lurcher can create havoc when it finds itself among livestock, and here the reader is asked to have patience with me while I relate the incredible tale of The Beast of Watten – a story that is still talked of in the area in which I live. Some twenty or so years ago a spate of stock killing broke out in Caithness, the most northerly county on the mainland of Great Britain. Sheep and calves were found slain and disembowelled with copious amounts of the victims' blood scattered around the kill. Some talk of giant cats, the size and shape of panthers, was heard and one observer concluded that the attacker was a puma, a beast famed for the bloody method by which it kills. Reporters, short of sensational stories perhaps, flocked north, but as soon as they arrived the killings stopped and disgruntled editors bleated angrily at the expense incurred seeking out yet another Loch Ness monster-type creature. However, shortly before the reporters returned south the killings began again, this time with a vengeance. Crofters awoke some mornings to find carnage in bloodied fields, littered with the cadavers of sheep and half-grown cattle that had been disembowelled by some very powerful animal. Pressure from public opinion provoked one of the biggest organised searches to take place in the Highlands as keepers, crofters and interested spectators beat the heavily forested area around Watten – a village in the centre of Caithness – while a helicopter carrying a police marksman circled overhead. Eventually a huge smooth-coated saluki hybrid was flushed from the woodland and killed by the police marksman. The killing stopped forthwith, but crofters are still wary of lurchers found wandering abroad. The general opinion is that this huge dog was brought from further south, found wanting and simply cast adrift to fend for itself. No doubt the various lurcher rescue societies rehome dozens of dogs that have been subjected to similar trauma and hence prevent incidents such as those committed by The Beast of Watten.

Old dogs, animals too old to work, prematurely aged by over-hunting when the dog is unfit, or dogs that have developed maladies induced by living in damp conditions also find their way to rescue societies. Untrainable dogs, dogs driven demented by a youth lived out in tiny kennels experiencing no contact with people during the critical socialising period, also find their way to rescue kennels, and this pitiable flotsam and jetsam sits out the days waiting for someone, any-one in fact, to offer them a home. It should be made compulsory that any lurcher owner contemplating breeding a litter should visit such places to see the fate that possibly awaits the puppies he is intending to breed. Yet many lurcher owners will not only house or rehome some

of these dogs but make an excellent job of training these animals, and
it is not unusual to hear of obedience test winners and best-in-show
lurchers that were obtained from lurcher rescue kennels. I cannot but
voice my admiration for these people who not only take on the training of these unwanted dogs but compete and win against dogs with
much more salubrious backgrounds.

Should the reader feel that I have dwelt too long or too thoroughly
with the subject of obtaining a lurcher from a rescue society kennels I
suggest that he or she considers the plight of these pitiable denizens of
such places should rescue kennels cease to exist. It is indeed a commendable act to rehome some of the wretched animals that find their
ways to such places.

A would-be lurcher owner may well seek to eschew a visit to such
kennels yet seek to buy a young grown dog that can instantly be put to
work, or if the animal is untrained entered as soon as the lurcher has
settled; and there are grown dogs in abundance available for selection
at the time of writing. However, the purchase of a trained lurcher or a
dog that is ready for entry is pockmarked with caveats and the reader
would do well to consider why the vendor is wishing to part with the
lurcher he is offering for sale. A good, well trained lurcher is seldom
offered for sale. Such an animal will provide sport and in an area where
game is abundant some income – pin money perhaps, but an income
nevertheless. Thus to sell such an animal is false economy, particularly
as the price asked for such lurchers is seldom much more than a reputable breeder would ask for a puppy. It takes at least two years of work
to produce a good, sound lurcher from an eight-week-old puppy and
much of the work involved in training such an animal is both tedious
and repetitious, so having stated this let us cost out the production of a
trained lurcher and I shall let the reader work out the logic behind
a trainer selling such an animal:

Cost of purchase of puppy	=	£80+
Cost of inoculating puppy	=	£20
Cost of rearing whelp to two years at £2.00 per week (a very low cost)	=	£208
		£308

This, however, doesn't take into account the time spent training and
entering the whelp or the cost of transporting the sapling to country
where game is abundant enough to allow the lurcher to be entered. Nor
does it take into account the numerous sundry expenses attendant on

the rearing and training of the whelp, such as veterinary treatment. Few trained lurchers are sold for more than £150, however, and so the would-be buyer should consider why the vendor is prepared to accept such a financial loss, and let me assure the reader that few lurcher trainers are philanthropically inclined nor are they in any way altruistic and willing to pass on such valuable animals for a song. Something is clearly amiss with the product that is being offered for sale. Vendors are also aware of the economics involved in the sale of a trained lurcher and seek to explain the reason for the parting with the animal by affixing to their advertisement the expression 'Genuine reason for sale'. Let us now consider the sundry 'genuine reasons for sale' that are likely to be offered by vendors so that the reader might evaluate the logic behind the purchase of a trained dog.

I have already explained that phenomenon the lurcher widow, and also related how many marriages are broken up when a newcomer to lurcher work neglects his wife and family in order to spend more time with lurchers. Reader, I do not exaggerate how addictive lurcher work can be, and I have known many previously happy families torn asunder when the husband or wife has developed a passion for lurchers – and in recent years lurcher widowers have become more common than hitherto. Sometimes well trained dogs are sold to save a marriage, so to speak, and sometimes these dogs are well worth the money asked for them, for the obsessive training and entering that has been lavished on the lurcher will have paid dividends and produced a well trained animal. It can, of course, be argued that such paragons would not need to be advertised as friends of the lurcher fanatic would buy the dog and be only too glad to purchase such a well trained animal. However, many lurcher buffs deprived of their *raison d'être* would wish never to see their lurchers again and not wish to sell the dog close to home. Such a purchase may well be worth considering.

Many behaviourists believe that the behaviour of a dog reflects the behaviour of the family that owns the animals. A wild, unruly dog will indicate an undisciplined, unruly family in which the children are a shade out of control. A nervous, neurotic dog will often mirror its owners' neuroses, and frankly I would be a shade unwilling to allow a puppy I had bred to be homed with any person I suspected was neurotic or unstable. Thus when marriages go adrift and couples prepare to separate the dogs owned by such families will sometimes develop peculiar traits, almost as if they too are affected by the warring and arguments that usually precede a separation. Thus when the genuine reason for sale offered is 'breakdown of marriage' buyers or

would-be buyers should carefully examine the animals before conclud-
ing the purchase. True, not all dogs are affected by the turmoil of a
home that is about to be rent in two, but a great many dogs will behave
badly when marital problems manifest themselves in the house where
the dog resides.

Readers would be surprised to realise just how many dogs are sold
when their owners are faced with the prospect of a custodial sentence,
and while some of the capers of lurcher owners might seem hilarious
to the reader they often have a catastrophic effect on the dogs these
people own. Just recently an advertisement appeared extolling the
virtues of a strain of lurcher of great sagacity and antiquity. So intrigu-
ing was the advertisement that I investigated further and was informed
by some lady that the owner of the said animal had been incarcerated
after firing a shotgun through an adversary's letterbox – a somewhat
noisy and rather destructive practice I feel. I shall refrain from
commenting on the ethics of purchasing a dog from someone who has
criminal tendencies except to say that the dogs have seldom taken part
in the crime for which the owner has been convicted and are usually
blameless. It would be fair to say that the unwanted after-sales service
that may well follow the purchase of such an animal might be a little
distressing, however.

Sometimes a person is forced into moving house and the new
premises may not be suitable for keeping a dog. Thus the lurcher is
offered for sale, and this is one of the most common 'genuine reasons
for sale'. Some of these adult lurchers may well be mentally unscarred
and worth considering unless, that is, they have known two or three
owners before they have been advertised, and I shall deal with this
presently.

The most common reason for an owner parting with his ward is
quite simply that the owner has become disenchanted with his lurcher
and wishes to part with it. The dog may not be fast enough to suit the
trainer or perhaps not dextrous enough to catch the required number
of rabbits or hares. Other vendors will consider that there is not
sufficient game in the district to justify the keeping of a lurcher. Such a
dog reared and trained in a country that is deficient in game is hardly
likely to be a particularly dextrous hunter, however, for practice is
the only way to make perfect where lurchers are concerned. Some
advertisements stating that the owner has no opportunity to work a
lurcher may well be genuine, and the dogs such people are selling
may well be suitable for the would-be purchaser. It must be added,
however, that many of the owners who sell dogs stating the pressure

of work or that they have no work to justify keeping a lurcher will be found with another lurcher within days of selling their 'genuine reason for sale' dog. Such, alas, is the nature of far too many lurcher enthusiasts I'm afraid. Many are simply bored with seeing the same dog each day and swap and change dogs with great regularity.

A lurcher that has known several homes should be treated with some apprehension by a potential buyer. Not only has the dog known several owners, but the chances are each and every owner will have attempted to teach the dog something, and some of the training methods employed by some lurcher enthusiasts smack of witchcraft. The chances are that changes in ownership, diet and training methods will have produced a dog that is a touch less than perfect – and that is a magnificent understatement by any standards. In all probability the animal will have been worked in conjunction with other dogs and hence will be an erratic retriever. If it has run in conjunction with other dogs, and modern lurcher enthusiasts are often far too gregarious to be really efficient trainers, it may have been bruised by contact with other lurchers. It will have been pitted against other dogs to assess its ability before being passed on to yet another owner, and will gain nothing through its constantly changing ownership. It speaks highly of the mental stability of these dogs that they are not very mentally scarred by their lifestyles – though many are disturbed animals and have acquired undesirable idiosyncrasies as they have been passed from hand to hand. I have heard of one lurcher that had known thirty homes before its third birthday, and for a buyer to expect such an animal to be undamaged by such treatment is naïve.

On the subject of chopping and changing lurchers and the mental and physical damage wrought by such treatment, it would be virtually impossible not to mention the curious machinations of the lurcher dog dealer, and each large conurbation nourishes at least one of these people who ply their trade just out of reach of public health regulations and often beyond the realms of human decency. It must certainly puzzle the newcomer to the world of lurchers that while it takes two years of constant and meticulous training to produce a good, sound, reliable lurcher, many supposedly trained lurchers are offered for sale by downmarket dog dealers. So just how does a dog dealer or an unregistered downmarket dog dealer produce the spate of trained dogs he offers for sale – and many claim to sell as many as five hundred adult dogs a year! Firstly it is wise to investigate how such a dealer acquires livestock and to plot the progress of the stock through the dealer's kennels. Firstly let us debunk the notion that it is physically possible to train five hundred lurchers a year. In fact it would be very difficult to train five lurchers per annum, though it is perfectly simple to train five slip and run longdogs to a desirable standard if, that is, one has the quarry at which to slip these dogs. A dealer will usually acquire stock from lurcher owners who have failed to enter or failed to train relatively young lurchers and the saplings will usually be less than fifteen months old before they come to the kennels. Few dogs will reside at these kennels for long and many dealers claim an amazingly rapid turnover in dogs. Broken down, dispirited, wild, untrained dogs arrive at the kennel and are offered for sale as soon as they arrive as dogs that are 'ready for starting' or dogs that are 'doing a bit', a delicious sobriquet. Such dogs are usually put on trial so that the would-be purchaser is able to assess the value of the animal before paying the purchase price, and the buyer is usually required to leave a deposit with the vendor.

To understand the ins and outs of a dog dealer's lifestyle it is now expedient to describe the sort of client a dealer in grown dogs is likely to cater for. Most people wishing to buy a grown dog ready trained and entered to quarry will be young, impetuous with a furious though often short-lived interest in lurcher work. Such owners are likely to subject the animal to an equally furious testing process during which the animal, no matter how unfit or unready it is, will be given more than enough practice at rabbits, or if the animal is more of a longdog rather than a lurcher, hares – though hares are so desperately taxing a quarry that no unfit or unready lurcher will put up much of a show at coursing these creatures. It is virtually a racing certainty that any client, unless he or she (though women seldom patronise dog dealers) is exceedingly easily satisfied or has taken a fancy to the dog, will return the lurcher to the dealer stating the animal is not what is required and request some, if not all, of his deposit, and once more the animal joins the menagerie at the dealer's kennel. However, as stated, it is rare for such an animal to reside at the kennels for long, for yet another client with yet another furious interest in lurchers will arrive to take the animal on yet another trial once again the wretched animal is subjected to yet another furious testing period before being returned to the dealer's kennel. Sooner or later the animal will acquire sufficient hunting powers to satisfy some undiscerning client and the deal is concluded, though once again it is fairly certain that the new owner will offer the lurcher he has purchased only a temporary home. Within months many of these purchases will be once more on the lurcher-swapping roundabout and in all probability will finish up at the lurcher dealer's kennels yet again. The final fate of these dogs is often unpleasant, for animals of this type change hands rapidly and age at an appalling rate.

It is worth noting that the lurcher dealer specialises in lamping dogs (which are easily trained to what many would consider to be an acceptable standard) and slip and run longdogs (which require virtually no formal training). Dogs that will actively work with ferrets, as opposed to dogs which are simply not antipathetic to ferrets and refrain from killing them, are seldom, if ever, sold by dog dealers, for ferreting dogs require a great deal of careful training to make them proficient at the art of working alongside ferrets. I have, in fact, never seen a bona fide ferreting dog offered for sale by anyone, possibly because animals of this worth need to develop a bond with their owners to be efficient.

It is, of course, possible to buy a grown and entered dog from a private seller and there are many grown dogs offered for sale by lurcher enthusiasts every week in magazines such as *Shooting News* and *Exchange and Mart* but caveat emptor, for few of these trained dogs are first-rate lurchers. Many will be intermittent retrievers, some will be hard-mouthed while others will have suffered physical damage during their working lives – damage that will only manifest itself when the dog is subjected to a testing course or night's sleep. Blown dogs, dogs that have sustained damage to heart, lungs or diaphragm, are frequently offered for sale to unsuspecting buyers who will all too soon be made to realise how unwise the purchase was. Stories of newly purchased dogs collapsing and dying after a long and testing course are legion, for a hare is a formidable adversary for even the fit and sound dog, and the hound that is unwell yet endowed with great courage will certainly come to grief when matched with a strong, fit winter hare.

Lamping dogs offered for trial are often lurchers that will tire rapidly and begin to mouth rabbits they are carrying to hand. This peculiarity will usually manifest itself when a dog becomes tired or winded after which he will usually kill, and damage, the rabbits rather than carry the struggling rabbit to hand. Lampers who are keen to sell a hard-mouthed lurcher will usually show a client the dog performing on one or two rabbits, but will refrain from subjecting the dog to a particularly testing night's work. Sellers of slip and run longdogs, dogs that are required simply to run and catch a hare, will usually offer a trial on a hare that is given little or no law and afforded little chance of escaping the initial rush of the lurcher or longdog. Having said this it is only fair to mention that few dogs are capable of putting up a fair show at a hare that is afforded law of a hundred yards. Potential buyers who hope to purchase a longdog that will catch two out of three hares that have been given reasonable law will either be very disappointed or else they must be prepared to pay a very large sum indeed. In 1991 a longdog bred down from Jeff Smith's Fly and several saluki greyhound hybrids sold for £3,850, and this is not an excessively large sum to pay for a super-lative hare catcher, a dog that will compete well at the now very popular single-handed hare-catching contests. I have in fact been offered a huge sum for my own saluki greyhound hybrid Canaan, though I have declined the offer, I must add. Tales of dogs found wandering on travelling sites, covered in sores and emaciated, that have become great hare-catching dogs are legion and, frankly, lies. If a dog has had a chequered career health-wise it is most unlikely to make a proficient single-handed hare-coursing dog, particularly as it has to compete against dogs that have been reared to perfection and have led an injury-free life.

Thus are the pitfalls of acquiring a grown dog, and there are obviously pitfalls I have failed to mention. I confess my own vanity would not allow me to buy a grown dog or a dog that has started train-ing, for such a purchase would suggest I was unable to train a lurcher to a proficient standard. However, I will concede that there are people who have a use for a trained dog and there are also people who have been satisfied with their purchases.

There is one supreme advantage concerning buying a dog as a puppy and training it oneself: only one person will be responsible for the success or failure in the field – the owner. Hence, while I would avoid buying a grown, trained or partly entered lurcher, I would certainly consider purchasing a well reared, properly bred puppy of eight to twelve weeks of age. Here again, however, there are numerous caveats the would-be buyer should observe if he is to obtain a suitable puppy.

Firstly the lurcher enthusiast must ask himself what he requires of a lurcher before purchasing a puppy. If he requires a dog to course hares he should consider a longdog or a lurcher that has a large proportion of sighthound blood in its make-up. A first-cross collie greyhound or a Bedlington greyhound hybrid might well grow into the best of companions and be loyal and devoted to its death. It will seldom be fast enough to course hares, however, though it may well catch them by stealth or by accident no matter what the breeder says to the contrary. Conversely a man who requires a dog to work with the lamp, to assist on ferreting forays and to snap up the occasional gamebird would do well to consider collie greyhounds or Bedlington greyhounds and to avoid longdogs or supersaturated sighthound mixtures. From time to time one hears of longdogs that are excellent ferreting dogs – I have yet to see one I considered efficient and would not consider training a longdog composite for such a task. Some longdogs can be trained to make satisfactory, though seldom perspicacious, lampers, however, but longdogs are never top-flight lampers.

However, here is the rub: few of the pedigrees of lurchers advertised are authentic and are often invented on the spur of the moment in order to sell the litter. Hence it is wise to see the parent of the litter before parting with one's money, and if there is the slightest doubt about the authenticity of the lineage of the whelps it is wise to pass over the purchase, for at the time of writing it is a buyers' market and there are many, many litters from which to choose a puppy. If, however, one is satisfied with the parents of the litter, and one is certain these are the actual parents of the litter and not substitutes brought in in order to effect a sale, then by all means purchase a puppy, but it is well to remember that pedigrees true or false, lists of ancestors real or made up to sell the litter, do not guarantee the health of the puppy one is con- templating buying, nor do spacious, elaborate kennels for that matter, for I have seen badly reared puppies purchased from quite smart and well established kennels. Various factors can influence the rearing of puppies and I write this statement with a sad heart. A few days ago my kennels experienced an outbreak of E. Coli infection that killed almost every puppy in a litter leaving only one whelp of somewhat question- able constitution. The dam has been well fed, recently inoculated to provide a high antibody level in her colostrum, yet the litter died shortly after birth, and to sell the remaining puppy as a good potential would be somewhat dishonest for the havoc wrought by the bacterium would not be conducive to the whelp having the excellent constitution one would expect of a working lurcher that needed to endure a hard, testing career.

An unhealthy puppy is easily recognisable and should not be purchased no matter how appealing the whelp may look. An unhealthy puppy will seldom grow into a first-class adult no matter how much care, money and love is lavished on it. Lurcher and longdog puppies should be wildly excited at the appearance of strangers and should attempt to greet their owners with a great display of affection. Puppies that are unusually reserved or lacking in vigour are suspect and should be avoided. It may be that the whelps have been reared in isolation and are unused to people – and saluki hybrids are particularly prone to becoming nervy if they are not socialised. It may be that the whelps are ill and are infected with one or more of the myriad of illnesses to which puppies of all breeds are susceptible, but whatever the reason for the behaviour of these puppies it should not concern the potential buyer for it would be unwise to purchase such puppies.

Healthy, happy puppies are the only ones to contemplate buying and unwormed puppies – whelps with bulging pot bellies that are indications of worm infestations – are not good purchases even if the wormy puppies are active and happy. A wormy puppy is an indication that the breeder is not *au fait* with the rearing of puppies and may well have made other mistakes in the rearing of the whelps. A puppy should be treated to clear roundworm infestations twice before it is offered for sale – once when the whelp is three weeks of age and again when the whelp is six weeks old. The havoc a bad roundworm infestation can cause is often underestimated, but a wormy whelp will not grow into a satisfactory healthy adult. A wormy whelp is symptomatic of mismanagement and I would question whether such a puppy had been fed an adequate and complete diet.

A good breeder will frequently ensure his puppies are vaccinated against Parvo virus before they are sold and this is a sensible practice by any standards. A whelp leaving its dam for the first time will experience a shock to its system and is open to Parvo virus infection during its settling-in period, and many puppies become ill or die at this stage. Yet some breeders neglect to inoculate puppies and still rear excellent whelps. However, a buyer purchasing an uninoculated whelp would do well to remedy this omission as soon as the puppy arrives home.

Puppies reared in antiseptic kennels where they seldom encounter people are often shy and reluctant to come to hand, simply because they have not been socialised correctly. Whelps seldom recover from inadequate early socialising and rarely achieve their full potential in later life. Many breeders go to considerable effort to socialise their puppies. Hancock of Sutton Coldfield says that he finds an hour spent sitting among the whelps is time well spent and few remote, untrainable whelps are produced at the Blake Street kennels. Andy Baron, the Gisburn-based deerhound longdog breeder, allows his children access to his kennels and encourages them to play with the puppies to socialise them properly, although deerhound hybrids do not seem to suffer from lack of socialising as much as do saluki-bred longdogs, which can become extremely introverted if they are denied socialising. Puppies reared indoors, particularly puppies reared among children, are usually very bold and very ebullient, and if the children of the house are sufficiently well disciplined not to molest and hurt the puppies, whelps reared under these conditions are preferable to whelps of like breeding that have been reared in kennels. Few children can resist playing with puppies and the whelps benefit greatly from this constant contact with human beings. Rearing puppies in the same house as children has its problems, however. Puppies are seldom free of roundworms despite frequent worming and the frequent worming of the dam prior to parturition, and children are so easily infected with roundworms. Sensible breeders would do well to keep puppies away from children until the whelps have been wormed, but it is not an easy task to stop children handling small and appealing puppies.

There are certain magazines that specialise in advertising lurchers and longdogs. At one time *Exchange and Mart* was the only magazine to buy if one wished to purchase a lurcher. Indeed the magazine was once referred to as a lurcherman's bible. These days *Shooting News* carries a great many advertisements for lurchers of all breeding and all ages, and once again it should be remembered that it is a buyers' market at the time of writing and many of the advertisements will appear for many weeks before the whelps are sold. Personally I should avoid advertisements that are simply ridiculous exaggerations and simply eulogise the quality of the puppies offered for sale – for instance, 'these puppies will catch four out of five hares anywhere', which is clearly ludicrous, or, 'these puppies will catch a hundred rabbits a night', which is virtually impossible, as will be explained later. Advertisements of this type set my teeth on edge for they are simply an insult to people's intelligence. Yet the sporting papers are often filled with such advertisements, some of which are absolutely ludicrous. An intelligent person avoids buying from anyone who expects them to believe such bombast and forthwith might I indulge in a tale to illustrate my point. At the Waterloo Cup meet at Lydiate a few years ago a man standing just behind me was shouting as two of the finest greyhounds in the country chased the greatest mammalian athlete in the world and failed to catch it. 'Our Ben would have caught that hare,' mumbled the spectator quite loudly and went to his van where he sold a dozen assorted puppies all sired by the incredible Ben to equally incredulous punters who knew nothing of longdogs or the ways of the brown hare. Ben, it transpired, was a hotchpotch of canine mistakes with a rough or broken coat, flat feet and a bad physique, while the dam of the litter was a poor-grade flapping track greyhound. Yet some people believed the exaggerations uttered by the vendor.

Buying puppies at lurcher shows, or dog shows of any sort for that matter, is a dubious practice. Young babes still suckling are to a certain extent protected by the antibodies secreted via the dam's colostrum, but a dog show must be a melting pot of all the canine ills imaginable, and it is highly likely that puppies taken to such shows will become infected with some disorder. Puppies of this age may have some protection against the four major canine ills – distemper, hardpad, hepatitis and Parvo virus – if their parents were inoculated, but against the various gastric disorders than can plague young dogs the puppies will have little immunity. There are, of course, tales of satisfied customers who have bought puppies out of the backs of vans. Likewise, there are tales of very dissatisfied purchasers who have bought inferior, infected and dubious stock at lurcher shows. The appearance of a breeder touting young puppies at Kennel Club shows would cause an uproar, and in recent years the sight of young puppies being sold at lurcher shows has also become a rarity. More distasteful still was the sight of a lurcher paraded around the show with a 'for sale' notice around its neck. Nothing degrades a noble animal more and it also puts the perpetrator of the deed (the vendor) in a very poor light. Puppies are appealing and lurcher puppies particularly so. Thus the sight of lurcher puppies, tails wagging with pleasure, being hawked from the back of a van for an outrageously low price will often encourage a chance purchase and yet another hapless babe is hurled onto the lurcher roundabout to be passed from owner to owner enduring a life of misery and temporary homes. While I will concede that good puppies can be purchased at lurcher shows, the practice of selling puppies from the back of vans is not to be condoned.

Once again I cannot resist an anecdote to illustrate a caveat. I write a weekly column for *Shooting News* and receive numerous letters, some less than complimentary, concerning lurchers and allied subjects. One letter received in March 1991 clearly illustrates the perils of buying a lurcher puppy at lurcher shows, and I shall quote the letter in its entirety: 'I went to a show in the south of England and saw a litter of deer-hound/greyhound/collie/greyhound puppies for sale from the back of a Transit van. I saw a bitch I liked and bought it but it grew into a dog that looks more like an otterhound than a lurcher. The chap who was selling the puppies gave me an address in Peterborough and asked me to call whenever I wanted to. I have since found the address does not exist and I haven't seen the chap at the shows again. What can I do about this?' The answer is 'not a lot', and this illustrates my point about buying 'pig in a poke' purchases quite nicely. A buyer has little or no redress if he buys an unsatisfactory puppy from a reputable breeder. He has even less redress if he chooses to buy a puppy from a total stranger who is touting puppies around a show and furnishing the buyers of the puppies with a non-existent address. 'Yer pays yer money, yer takes yer choice' as the saying goes.

3

A New Puppy Settles In

On the night of the arrival of a new puppy the lurcher owner must expect squalls. When the mite arrives at its new home for a few hours it will usually be the centre of attraction. The puppy will be offered food, often unsuitable food, it will be encouraged to play and will almost certainly enjoy its first hours at its new home. All will be well until its new owners decide to retire for the night, after which bedlam is likely to prevail. Dogs are gregarious creatures, especially when they are very young, and puppies sorely miss their litter mates when they are separated from them. Thus when the tumult of the house has settled and the rooms are plunged into darkness, the puppy suddenly experiences a hybrid mixture of fear and blind panic. At first it will bark excitedly but finally the barking will give way to a piteous wailing that is almost certain to distress the new owner of the whelp so much that the householder wishes he had never acquired the puppy.

So traumatic is the first night after the acquisition of a puppy that it is by no means uncommon for breeders to awaken to find the owner of the whelp sold the previous day waiting on the breeder's doorstep desperately trying to return the creature. Some of these new owners are so distressed that they will depart leaving the whelp with the breeder and not request the return of the purchase price. Many of these new owners look so harassed that it is obvious that it will be a very long time before they contemplate the purchase of another puppy. Yet I have met dog owners who have lived adjacent to a steel foundry and slept through the cacophony of rolling mills and steel hammers who have not only been kept awake by the cries of a tiny puppy but who have been decidedly distressed and ill because of the pitiful howling and barking. Might I be permitted to offer an explanation for the phenomenon – though my explanation would probably not stand examination under the cold light of scientific reasoning. The cries of infant mammals and birds (also some forms of reptile, I believe) are pitched to attract the attention of adults of the same species, and the adults of that species find it impossible to ignore the distress signals of these babies. A ferret keeper has only to observe the distress of a jill ferret if the kits residing in the cage next to the jill become upset and vocal to realise how important the response to the distress cries of the young are to the survival of the species. My contention is that the dog has been domesticated for so long and has integrated into the social structure of the human family so well that human beings have become geared to the distress cries of puppies to such an extent that most people are unable to ignore the plaintive bleat of an unhappy whelp. Enough, however, of speculation. The owner of the puppy must therefore devise methods of reducing the distress cries of an unhappy puppy to a bearable level.

The presence of another dog in the household, an older dog, a more established dog perhaps, may well reduce the incidence of howling, but it is extremely wise to observe the way the older dog reacts to the youngster before leaving the pair alone for the night. Some dogs, males and females alike, are very tolerant of a new puppy and may clean and nuzzle the youngster or apparently take over the role of the infant's dam. Others may be extremely hostile and will certainly kill or maim the whelp if left alone with the puppy. An older dog that seeks to avoid the attention of the youngster, endeavouring to climb out of the reach of the babe, menacing the whelp as it attempts to ingratiate itself with the older animal, should under no circumstances be left with the puppy during the whelp's first night on the premises. A dead or crippled puppy will almost certainly result from this action.

Many trainers swear by allowing a radio to play softly during the night, so softly in fact that it may be inaudible to human ears though the puppy may have no difficulty in hearing the sounds. One of the larger Dobermann kennels of America supply piped music to litters of puppies that are about to be weaned and sold and advise new owners to play similar music until the puppy has settled into its new home. The presence of a loud ticking clock seems to have an equally soothing effect on the youngster and may well reduce the barking and howling to an acceptable level. It is argued that the sound of an old alarm clock – the sort of cheap, noisy clock that was once available in every department store – may imitate the sound of the bitch's heartbeat, but this seems a rather absurd notion. What is more likely is that the sound of the alarm clock causes such interest that the puppy neglects to howl and finally becomes tired enough to sleep in its new premises.

A hot water bottle placed in the puppy's new box or basket is also efficacious and will often reduce the trauma experienced by the puppy. Perhaps, but this again is difficult to prove or disprove, the puppy associates the warmth of the hot water bottle with the body temperature of the dam, or what is more likely finds it more comfortable to be in a warm spot and sleeps. Whatever the reason many dog owners use a hot water bottle to comfort a puppy during its first night in a new home. Frankly, so stressful is the howling of a lonely and frightened puppy that any method of quietening the whelp, short of hurting the creature seems justified and if all three methods of settling the puppy can be used in conjunction with each other, so much the better.

If the puppy is to live inside the house rather than in kennels it must be house-trained, and an untrained puppy can reduce a well managed home to a hovel in days if it is allowed to foul where it wishes. Time observing the behaviour of a puppy is time well spent. A puppy will usually defecate and urinate immediately after it wakes up or immediately after it has eaten. Now, puppies are creatures of habit and will repeatedly foul in the same spot if allowed to do so. Indeed, most adult dogs will if possible soil certain distinct areas to establish territory. Hence, if the owner watches the puppy carefully and as soon as it wakes up takes the puppy out of doors to a spot where it is convenient for the puppy to foul in a very short while the whelp will seek to visit that spot to evacuate its bowels and bladder. Very young puppies can indeed be house-trained in a very short time. I have met trainers who claim to be able to render a puppy 'house-broken' in two or three days, though my own personal best seems to be closer to two weeks.

Yet another method is to get the puppy paper-trained, to encourage the whelp to foul only on sheets of newspaper. A puppy is placed on sheets of newspaper every time it shows an inclination to foul or urinate, and in days the whelp will usually seek out the paper sheets before it evacuates. Many untrained puppies will seek to soil newspaper without the training programme, possibly because some race memory reminds it that its ancestors fouled on dead leaves or dead grass and then scratched loose earth and vegetable matter over the excrement. Dogs that have been paper-trained will in fact often try to scratch the paper to cover the faecal matter they have voided. Once a puppy deliberately seeks out the paper to defecate or urinate the sheets of fresh paper can be moved nearer to the door and finally passed under the door and outside the house. The puppy may experience some confusion when the sheets are placed outside the door, but most will be able to understand what is required of them and soon become house-trained. Some pharmaceutical firms have patented esters which have a similar scent to dog urine and these esters are sprinkled onto paper to hasten the house-training process. These esters have little discernible scent, at least as far as human beings are concerned, but are delicious, aromatic and attractive to dogs and puppies. I cannot resist mentioning that my first encounter with these liquids was when I found a particularly difficult boy I was required to teach dousing the hair of the girl in front of him with the esters – shades of Rabelais I thought at the time!

It is possible, but extremely difficult, to house-train a puppy if the owner is out at work all day and returns home only in the evening, and the mess the whelp will create before it becomes house-broken is often horrendous. Lonely puppies will often seek out articles of clothing and soil them with their excrement, possibly because they are attracted to the scent of the clothing which first acts as a bed for the whelp before taking on the role played by the forest floor for their wild ancestors. The puppy who does this is usually regarded as filthy and antisocial by the new dog owner and often beaten for its pains – an action that usually bewilders rather than educates the youngster and certainly serves no useful purpose whatsoever. It is wise to take a few days off work when acquiring a puppy and to spend those few days educating house-training and settling in the whelp. Personally I find that training a dog to use a litter tray when it is confined indoors for any length of time is worthwhile, and filling the tray with peat fibre or micaceous material absorbs and to some extent deodorises the excrement and urine. When the puppy awakens it should be placed over the litter tray and kept there until it voids its waste, and two or three days of this treatment will usually result in a litter tray-trained dog.

Dog owners who must leave puppies indoors alone for several hours should not be surprised to find the puppy has inflicted damage on furniture and clothing during the owner's absence. It is virtually impossible to prevent such damage completely, but with a little common sense the owner can reduce such damage to an acceptable minimum. Before leaving the house the owner would be wise to look around the room in which the puppy is to be confined and remove or place out of reach any articles the whelp may easily damage. Curtains should be tied up and out of reach to prevent the puppy either ragging them or, if the curtains sweep the floor, fouling on them. A large bone or an old shoe can also be given to the puppy to occupy its attentions during the hours it is awake and possibly (in the case of a heavily scented old shoe) to give the puppy some sense of security.

I make no excuses for spending so much time on the subject of settling a puppy in and house-training the whelp. Many of the lurchers that pass to and fro from dog dealer to temporary owner were denied a permanent home simply because their first owners could not understand how to train and settle a puppy.

4

Lead and Recall Training

U nless a puppy is lead-trained and will accept the restrictions imposed upon it by a leash, it is virtually impossible to continue to train or enter the dog, and to those who blandly state that they have yet to see a traveller with a dog on a leash (and this is commonly stated, I must add) I say I have yet to see a traveller with a dog that was trained to any acceptable standard.

There are various types of leashes available, ranging from soft leather slip-over leashes that will not terrify nor intimidate the most nervous puppy to hard choke chains that if jerked sharply could bring a rottweiler to its knees, and I shall refrain from commenting on the merits of any specific type of leash and engaging in an age-old debate. It is sufficient to say that most sighthounds or lurchers are rather shy animals that are easily lead-trained.

I must confess I do not enjoy lead-training a new puppy for the activity causes the puppy and myself some stress no matter how gently the training exercise is performed, and it is only my insufferable pride that prevents me from delegating the lead-training of any puppy I am contemplating running on. Some gundog trainers who are running on several puppies take a shortcut during the lead-training sessions, so that many whelps can be lead-broken at the same time. The whelps are fitted with collars and allowed to wear these collars for a few days before a length of rope is attached to the collar. The whelp then runs around with a length of line hanging from its collar, and should the line snag or be seized and held by the other whelps this is regarded as part of the training process. The method of simply tying up a dog and allowing it to bark and rear until it is accustomed to the restricting leash is one that has been used by horse wranglers since the times of the Mitanni tribe, but it has little to recommend it when it is applied to dogs. It is to say the least dangerous, and terrifying for the whelp and while it is said to be a shortcut to lead-training it is scarcely a method one might consider to be efficacious or efficient. A whelp that is about to be lead-trained should be fitted with a soft collar and allowed to resume its normal lifestyle for a few days. It must then be taken to a familiar and quiet place to be lead-trained, and the more gently this exercise is performed the better the training of the whelp.

A puppy fitted with a leash for the first time will behave in one of two ways: it will either flop or fight. A flopper is a nightmare to lead-train unless, that is, one has both patience and props. A flopper simply flattens itself on the ground, becoming limp and inert, refusing to rise and often adopting a terrified expression once the lead is put on the dog. The animal will often adopt this pose and remain down for an entire morning and afternoon unless the trainer can devise methods of encouraging the puppy to rise to its feet. Some can be coaxed into standing, others seem adamant about remaining prostrate. If I might make a confession, my own strain of lurcher without exception flop when a lead is affixed to them, hence I have learned to deal with this problem efficiently and with the very minimum of stress.

Shortly before I start lead-training a puppy – and I begin the task when the whelp is twelve weeks of age – I kennel the puppy with one of the more gentle bitches I have and allow a relationship to develop between the whelp and the school-ma'am bitch until the puppy becomes ecstatic at the sight of the older animal. I then start to lead-train the puppy. Once the leash is placed on a puppy I literally expect it to flop, and I am seldom disappointed for my strain is naturally submissive and flopping is simply an indication of submission. I allow the puppy to remain prone for two or three minutes so that it might recover from the shock of having a leash placed over its head and promptly have the older school-ma'am bitch walked past the puppy. If sufficient time has been allowed for the puppy to recover from its initial fright or trauma the chances are the whelp will rise and attempt to follow the older animal. Once this response has started I simply walk the puppy behind the older bitch until it is used to the lead. Should such an animal not be available to facilitate the training the puppy must be coaxed to its feet and encouraged to walk on the lead. There are no shortcuts to the lead-training of a puppy that decides to flop rather than fight when a leash is placed over its head, and I suspect that perhaps 80% of the whelps that change hands before they are twelve weeks of age are floppers whose behaviour has daunted an inexperienced trainer. The puppy is pronounced 'no good' and offered for sale, and thus begins the migration from incompetent trainer to incompetent trainer. This is a terrible pity for most floppers are so submissive that they take to training like ducks to water and will do virtually anything to please the trainer.

Once these whelps are lead-trained it is so easy to teach them to retrieve and come to hand, but such is the ease with which lurcher puppies can be obtained that the puppies are sold on and another whelp obtained for a song if the trainer encounters the slightest training problem.

Other puppies will fight the lead and these are usually simplicity itself to train. A fighter will usually buck and rear like a rodeo horse with an inexperienced rider in the saddle, and this might disturb the new handler somewhat, particularly as some of the very worst fighters will savage their leashes in an attempt to escape. The fighter will merely choke itself in its efforts to wrap the leash around its owner's legs, but if the owner turns with the puppy and prevents the lead tangling around the trainer's legs and feet the puppy can fairly well be lead-broken within the hour or so. True, the puppy will tug and jerk the leash for a few days after the initial training session, but compared with the problems of training the persistent flopper – I have trained many of these, all of which became excellent workers – the lead-breaking of a very active 'fighter' is simplicity itself. Care must be taken to ensure that the fighter does not injure itself in the initial training sessions, however, for some will finish a ten-minute training lesson in a state of exhaustion during which they will have often attempted to bite the initial portions of the lead and injured their teeth and gums. However, I would rather lead-train ten fighters than one flopper.

Lead-training should continue, giving the mite ten minutes of lead work every day until it ceases to pull and jerk the lead and accepts the restraint imposed on it. Lengthy training sessions are seldom effective and may well deter the puppy from enjoying the training period. A dog that has been properly lead-trained by a thinking, caring trainer will become ecstatic with delight once it is shown its lead.

I meet a great many young men who claim to have the fastest of lurchers, dogs almost as fast as greyhounds and capable of coming to terms with most hares. My own lurchers are not as fast – not by any means – and I own not a single working lurcher that is capable of outrunning a strong hare that is afforded fair law. However, my lurchers will back off hunting and come to hand as fast as any dogs I have ever seen and this I believe is due entirely to the methods I have used in training them. I can bring in my lurchers with a snap of my fingers and cause them to stop hunting and return to hand with a command that is little more than a whisper.

Nothing looks worse than a man standing in the middle of a field shouting commands to a recalcitrant lurcher that is paying not the slightest attention to its owner's bellowing. Might I correct that statement somewhat. What does look even worse is the self-same incompetent trainer whose dog is vanishing over the hill uttering the comment, 'He'll be back when he's ready'. The fact that while the dog readies itself to return it might indulge in a spot of sheep-chasing or may become a liability by wandering up and down the country roads, or may be chasing hares into the next county, obviously escapes this trainer who is seeking to disguise his incompetence by his acceptance of the dog's outrageous disobedience.

A lurcher is virtually useless if it cannot be called to hand swiftly and quietly, and frankly I have no patience with the coursers who will accept a very low standard of obedience from their saluki-bred longdogs providing the dog will catch a hare. I have, in fact, seen many trainers racing around the fields attempting to outrun or trap longdogs that have not the slightest intention of coming to hand. Yet if the longdog is obtained as a puppy even saluki hybrids can be taught to come to hand instantly and respond to commands swiftly.

I am a heretic so far as dog training is concerned and have little faith in the modern 'enter into the social structure of wild canids' method of training where the handler is expected to become one of the alpha members of the pack. However, when it comes to training a whelp to come to hand I must admit that it is often wise to observe the way wild (and even domesticated) dogs behave and utilise one's knowledge of canine behaviour during the training session.

A bitch will often return to a litter with a stomach full of food which she is prepared to vomit to feed her whelps – a nauseating sight to those who are not *au fait* with canine behaviour perhaps, but the bitch's stomach is a suitable carrier bag in which to carry food for her offspring. I urge the trainer to watch the behaviour of the bitch as she approaches her litter. She will usually drop her head to achieve facial contact with her puppies who will nuzzle and nose her muzzle to induce her to evacuate her food. This facial contact will make the bitch vomit the contents of her stomach and her litter will then feed on the warm, partly digested food.

So, just how does observation of this type help the trainer? I ask the reader to perform a simple experiment. The very next time a family of visitors arrives at the reader's home the reader may wish to note how his dogs behave towards various members of the family. Adults may be greeted with a friendly wag of the tail, but small children will be welcomed more enthusiastically and, wonder of wonders, the dog will nose the face of the smallest child. I do not believe that this gesture is simply due to the fact that most dogs love children, for most dogs are very badly treated by small children. My contention is that the infant's face is at the same level as the dog's and the sight of two eyes and a nose placed at the same level as that of the dog awakens racial memories of the bitch fetching home food for her whelp.

I ask the reader to perform yet another test. Encourage the puppy to play while the trainer remains standing. Then lie upon the floor near ground level and observe the ecstasy the puppy experiences as it prods and probes the face of the handler yet ignores the back of the handler's head and shoulders. The handler must utilise the whelp's interest in the handler's facial features to good advantage during a training session.

Let us set the scene for the most basic of training sessions, a training game that can be played shortly after the puppy arrives at its permanent home, but before the handler begins the game I suggest that he indulges in a spot of common sense – sadly not a commonly encountered quality among lurcher owners. A puppy must have a name before training begins and he must experience pleasure when the handler utters that name. Furthermore, the handler must be constant in his use of the puppy's name and must refrain from calling it Spot on the Monday, Mac on the Wednesday and Gyp on the Friday. If he decides that the puppy is to be called Mac (or Gyp or Spot) he must not change the dog's name ever again. (I cannot resist the anecdote concerning one of the most successful lurcher breeders, Lana Gadzer, who calls her dog Oi, a name that rolls so easily off the tongue when a lurcher starts to misbehave.) Let us assume that the handler has chosen to call the puppy Mac, for lurcher owners are seldom inventive people, at least as far as the names of their dogs are concerned. The handler should now make sure the room is clear of interfering people and other animals. He should crouch at the far side of the room and utter the word 'Mac' as excitedly and appeasingly as he can manage. Furthermore, he should avoid using the sharp, harsh command during the infancy of the whelp except, that is, when the dog shows an unwanted interest in livestock, such as sheep, cattle or poultry. The puppy must always experience pleasure at the sound of its name. Should the puppy come to hand it should be rewarded with effusive praise and much physical contact, for dogs enjoy being stroked and patted. The owner may also wish to reward the puppy with food, though feeding titbits is a frowned-upon training method at the time of writing. I feed tiny pieces of minced meat, pieces so tiny that they have little feeding value, but by feeding such slivers I can prolong a pleasurable training session for several minutes.

However, should the puppy choose not to come to hand the trainer should drop his head so that his face is level with that of the puppy's and utter the whelp's name softly and cajolingly, and it is a racing certainty that the whelp will come to nuzzle the handler's face with its head. Reward in the form of food or effusive praise will then reinforce the recall and minutes later the handler should repeat the exercise and repeat the praise and reward. I have seen many six-week-old puppies, puppies still with their dams, that would come to hand on command and answer to their names. Yet the reader would be astonished to find how many lurchers do not answer to their names and completely ignore the pleas and entreaties of their handlers.

Once the puppy is coming to hand quickly and with some enthusiasm in the house or in the garden and is over its inoculation (no puppy should be taken off the premises until it is inoculated), it is time to begin training away from familiar territory – or at least far from familiar territory as far as the whelp is concerned. At this point in the recall training the handler must be prepared to accept squalls, or at least a slight setback. An apparently lifeless stretch of country, a playing field or a bare patch of tarmacadam will harbour scents that are exciting to a dog, particularly to a puppy that is unaccustomed to such smells. A cat might have walked across the field or a mole ambled from hole to hole on the land, birds might have fed on stale scraps of food or other dogs played on the area. All will have left their highly individualistic scents on the land, scents the puppy will certainly find irresistible. Thus, when the handler calls the whelp to hand he might find the puppy has suddenly become deaf to his commands as it explores and almost drinks in the exciting odours it has just encountered. It is therefore good policy to allow the puppy time to explore and to accustom itself to its surroundings.

It is wise to take great care not to start to train a puppy in a place where other dogs are likely to exercise. Some of these dogs will display great hostility to a puppy – though this is uncommon and I would suspect any dog that attacked a puppy without provocation to be a shade disturbed. Even my most ferocious terriers have been very tolerant with puppies and have seldom even menaced them. However, the appearance of another dog during a training session with a very young puppy is likely to cause chaos and I would strongly advise any tyro lurcher enthusiast to leash up his puppy as soon as a dog of any sort appears on the training area. Training simply cannot be continued when another dog is present for it is a very strange puppy that will not cut and run when another dog appears. The chances are, if the puppy is running free when another dog or bitch suddenly appears, the puppy will totally disregard the commands of the trainer and race off to play with the strange dog, leaving the trainer to rant and rave, but there is virtually nothing one can do to bring back the puppy into the training session until it has finished its romp. Chastising the whelp will be counter-productive, and chasing after the puppy howling oaths will serve only to make the handler look foolish, or at the least a shade undignified.

Frankly, the best a trainer can do is to wait until the puppy has tired of its romp with the strange dog and is prepared to break off the game, to return to the trainer and, if possible, the trainer should adopt a nonchalant attitude as if he had expected the whelp to behave in such a way. It can be very humiliating and infuriating for the trainer to watch his puppy 'cut and run', but the trainer must disguise his anger and greet the returning puppy with pleasure, albeit feigned pleasure, and I cannot help but feel that the finest actors who ever trod the boards are dog trainers. After the puppy has engaged in a romp that has made the handler look an absolute buffoon and perhaps caused onlookers to roar with laughter, he must greet the returning puppy cordially. I confess that I have twice punished puppies which have made a fool of me but my chastisement did nothing but harm to my relationship with the animals. Competent dog handlers must expect to be humiliated when their puppies appear in public.

Clearly, it is best to start training in spots where the trainer is unlikely to encounter other dogs or to select a time of day when other dogs are unlikely to be present. Small children, also apt to behave noisily (and sometimes hysterically), will attract puppies like magnets and furthermore the trainer must realise that non-dog owners who are not *au fait* with canine behaviour will often make a trainer's life rather difficult. When a puppy approaches these people many will bend down in an attempt to fend off the attentions of the whelp, but the proximity of the human face to the puppy has the reverse effect, as I have explained. It is foolish to expect these people to behave as a handler would wish for this is far from being an ideal world.

5

Teaching a Puppy to Sit, Lie and Stay

I simply could not believe it when in 1990 a lurcher enthusiast wrote a series of articles proclaiming it was totally unnecessary to teach a lurcher any obedience work and promptly relegated obedience training to the status of 'teach a dog tricks'. What was even more bewildering was the fact that many readers agreed with this notion. These ideas are fairly easily explained once one considers the type of person who frequently owns lurchers. Many lurcher keepers are among the worst dog trainers and should such people ever consider transferring their allegiances from lurchers to gundogs they would be regarded as objects of fun or pity by the gundog fraternity. It has, in fact, been said that all most lurchermen require is a dog that can be taken on a slip and released at a rabbit or hare. If the dog chases and catches the animal the owner is satisfied and if the dog carries the catch to hand most lurcher enthusiasts are delighted. However, in recent years a new band of enthusiasts is entering the world of lurcher training and it appears likely that the lurcher trainer will no longer be regarded as the ridiculous Cinderella, the figure of fun, of dog training.

Of course the lurcher trainer is entitled to decline training his ward to sit, lie, stay or perform any of the tasks I shall discuss later, and many lurcher owners are totally unable to train dogs to perform these tasks, so what exactly is to be gained from training a lurcher to a high standard of obedience?

At the time of writing it is extremely difficult for a lurcher enthusiast to obtain permission to hunt on land throughout the country and this is entirely due to the reputation the lurcher owner has built up over the years. Lurcher owners were always regarded as dishonest, untrustworthy folk since the early 1800s and recently the lurcher as much as the lurcher owner has acquired an unsavoury reputation. Landowners virtually expect lurchers to run riot, damage livestock and behave in a wild, untamed manner – and sadly the majority of lurchers are wild, wilful and destructive simply because they are not trained or stock-broken. A landowner is more likely to allow lurchers to hunt land if he sees the dogs that are likely to be working his land are well behaved and totally under control, and this fact alone should be an incentive to the lurcher enthusiast to train his or her dog.

Frankly, I have every sympathy with landowners who are reluctant to allow lurchers to hunt their land for the majority of lurchers I see are damnably badly trained and wilful with livestock, and I am always reluctant to allow visiting lurchers out of the cars until I am convinced they are totally biddable. Ironically the very worst-trained lurchers are the property of some of that band who claim to be proficient hunters – 'I want a dog to catch rabbits not do tricks' – and the very best are trained by women handlers. Might I also add that some of the very best hunting dogs are trained by women and some of the least efficient I have seen working in the field are the property of those who claim they are hunters rather than trainers of dogs that do tricks. A trained animal is a pleasure to own: an untrained, wilful brute is a liability.

Enough, however, of why one should train a lurcher to a high

Sitting a dog prior to a bolt – a questionable practice.

66

standard of obedience and on to the teaching of rudimentary obedience, and the first of these skills a puppy should learn is to be able to
sit on command. Now, while I confess I have seen many tiny five-
week-old puppies sitting on command I would never consider teaching
any dog to sit until the dog had not only been lead-trained but become
well accustomed to the lead around its neck. Few puppies enjoy being
made to sit and when being trained to perform this task are liable to run
off and play unless restricted by a lead. Hence, it is bad policy to start
sit, lie and stay training until the puppy can be restricted by a leash
during the training session.

So the puppy restrained by its leash is taken for a walk either around
the house or garden, or to a quiet place where the puppy is at ease with
its surroundings. The trainer should walk his dog a short distance, stop
and press down the rump of the puppy at the same time uttering the
command 'Sit', very gently and very quietly. The rough, sharp, staccato
commands used in some dog training classes have no place in the training of a lurcher puppy, which is usually the most nervous of animals.
A few sessions of training lasting perhaps a minute each will usually be
enough to convince a tyro trainer how easy it is to teach a lurcher to sit
on command, and because success is so easily achieved during sit training I always advise young trainers to teach a dog to sit before
proceeding with further lessons, but should the puppy still fail to sit on
command after a few brief lessons the trainer should persist. One of the
most obedient lurchers I have ever seen – a pleasure to own and a great
hunting dog – was the very devil to teach to sit on command and on
the first sign of pressure being put on the rump would roll on its back
and adopt a placatory pose. The animal took nearly a month to teach to
sit, but its owner persisted and produced a wonderful hunting dog out
of a very effete puppy.

If it is at all possible the trainer should punctuate sit and lie training
with another training module and, once again, I shall attempt to illustrate the point with a tale. Many years ago I owned the ancestor of my
present strain of lurcher, the most wonderful hunting dog I have ever
owned. He had only one tiny fault. If I placed him at the sit position
and then requested him to adopt the 'down' posture he would anti-
cipate my command and adopt the down position as soon as I placed
him at the sit. The reason for this peculiarity was that I placed him at
the sit position and then pressured him into the 'down' and henceforth
I simply could not break him out of going down within seconds of
being made to sit. A small fault for a lurcher one might argue, but a
training mistake I vowed never to repeat.

So how should the trainer induce or compel the puppy to assume the down position? Firstly it is virtually impossible to teach the puppy the down position unless the puppy is lead-trained – and now I hope the reader will realise why I have spent so long on the subject of lead-training. Let us assume the trainer is walking his puppy on the training area. At a chosen place he must stop and press down the puppy's shoulders, uttering the command, 'Down' as he does so but deliberately avoiding the puppy's rump lest he induces the puppy to sit, thereby confusing the training programme somewhat. If this training session is pursued for five minutes a day, a week or so should produce a puppy that will assume the down position without the owner touching its back or shoulders. If it does not respond to training this quickly the handler should persist, but he must always assume that the failure of a training module is the fault of the handler, not the whelp. I frequently make mistakes training a puppy but I have yet to handle a puppy that is to blame for my mistakes.

Puppies do not enjoy sit or down training sessions and may develop a forlorn expression when such activities begin. No training session should finish on a sour note and I always end any training module with a wild game so that the puppy returns home exhilarated by the activity. The game should be fun for both the trainer and whelp and both should look forward to the next training session. If a tyro lurcherman is rather embarrassed at the prospect of engaging in a play session with his puppy he must mask this feeling or else find another hobby, for dog training is scarcely the hobby for him. I confess I often look foolish playing with a puppy that has just finished its training session, but I accept this and hence I succeed at training my puppies.

Once the whelp is prepared to prostrate itself on the command of 'Down', it is time for the trainer to consider teaching the dog to stay at the down position until the trainer wishes it to come to hand. Stay training must be conducted with care and common sense at all times, for a puppy that sickens of the training session will cut and run and ignore the cries and pleas of the trainer, and once a puppy has learned that it can bring an end to training exercises whenever it wishes it is the very devil to educate. To overdo the training, to persist with the training session once the puppy has lost some of its zest is decidedly counter-productive and frankly a minute or so of sit/stay, down/stay training terminated by a wild romp is enough for the young whelp to endure. The session must never continue to the point where the youngster sours of the game – and if the activity can be made to resemble a game so much the better.

The youngster should now be placed at the down position and the trainer must run back, away from the whelp, fixing the puppy with his eyes and uttering the word 'Down' as he retreats. If the puppy stays at the down position while the trainer moves ten yards away the handler may congratulate himself for his training session has proceeded well. The trainer must now return to the puppy and lavish effusive praise on the whelp, and perhaps offer the youngster a titbit. I am very much against calling a youngster to hand and rewarding the puppy after it has performed a satisfactory stay, for the youngster may consider it has been rewarded for coming to hand and not for completing a satis-factory stay. Hence I always return to the puppy to reward it and never call the youngster to me after it has completed a satisfactory stay. I con-tinue to teach the stay fixing the puppy with my eyes for some time before I proceed further with its education, and will walk backwards for perhaps fifty yards while the youngster stays down, repeating the command 'Down' if it attempts to follow me, and I don't proceed with further training unless the whelp stays fixed at the down position. At this point in the training programme I engage the youngster in a game as soon as it has completed its stay and do not return to training for five or so minutes after the youngster has completed its exercise. However, once the puppy shows it is ready for further training it is time to progress to the next stage of the down/stay training session.

Once again I choose a quiet, out of the way spot for this training module, partly because there is absolutely nothing to distract the puppy and partly because at this stage of the training I expect the puppy to make me look a fool. I drop the puppy to the down position and walk backwards from the whelp (fixing the youngster with my eyes) and then turn my back on it. It is almost certain the youngster will attempt to rise and follow me once I have failed to fix the animal with my stare, so as I turn I utter the command, 'Down', which usually stops the puppy rising to follow me, and I take four or five paces before return-ing to praise the puppy, should it still be in the down position. I literally expect failures or setbacks at this point in the training and I am prepared to repeat this part of the training module many times until the puppy stays at the down position, even though I am walking away from it and not fixing the puppy with my stare. Eye contact is one of those seldom mentioned training aids, and if I might digress a little, one I constantly use when my own lurchers are working with ferrets and I can stop with a glance a puppy that is about to behave badly. Once eye contact is removed during sit/stay/down training session puppies will usually attempt to rise and follow me, and the trainer must expect similar responses unless he or she is able to have sufficient 'presence' (I can think of no better word than that to describe the strange charisma some trainers have) to keep the whelp at the down position after turning his or her back.

Once the trainer is able to keep the puppy at the down position with his back turned, further training can proceed, and the trainer can increase the distance he can walk from the whelp until he is perhaps a hundred yards or so from the puppy. A useful training aid that can be used during the training module is a small handbag mirror. Several years ago I watched a woman handler keep a young puppy at the down position with uncanny success as she walked away from the puppy. She seemed to be able to predict when the puppy was wanting to rise and follow her and she was able to stop the puppy with a sharp word at exactly the right time. Her mental control of the whelp seemed to be phenomenal until I realised she carried a tiny fragment of a mirror in which she could observe the movements of the whelp as she walked away from it. I have used this training aid ever since that time and after a while a puppy comes to believe that it is under observation at all times.

Puppies detest being left at the down position while the owner/handler walks away from them, and so do grown dogs for that matter, so this is one of the more distasteful aspects of training as far as the dog is concerned. I have observed many dogs about to be given down/stay training sessions display a forlorn hangdog expression once they know that this training module is about to begin, and it is the trainer's duty to ensure the puppy does not sour of the activity before and after this training module. I cannot overstate the importance of a game to put the dog in the right frame of mind before this training programme is about to start and after the training programme is concluded. A dog is a forgiving type of creature but is not tolerant of being bored and a trainer must go to some trouble to devise methods to alleviate the more boring aspects of training – and above all the trainer must never display anger if a training session goes awry, and it sometimes will. Nothing is more counter-productive than a trainer venting his anger on a young dog after the whelp has failed to perform some task or other. I have been totally exasperated with the behaviour of a puppy on many occasions and to be perfectly honest I have acted irrationally and displayed my anger to the puppy, but the training session has always taken two or three backward steps when I have shown the animal my displeasure.

Once the puppy will stay at the down position while the owner walks a hundred or so yards from the dog it is time to progress to the next stage of the training module, often referred to rather ungrammatically as the 'out of sight stay'. If the trainer has progressed this far and not encountered a single setback in his training programme, at this stage it is almost certain that he will. Once the handler walks away from the dog and 'vanishes' behind a wall or some object the dog is almost certain to attempt to rise and follow the handler. I have always found that the best way of fixing a dog at the down position when I am out of sight is to utter the word 'Down' as I disappear from view and to station myself on the other side of the object behind which I have vanished from sight so that the dog comes to believe when I vanish from view I am waiting round the corner, so to speak. This portion of the training programme can take several days before the puppy masters the 'blind stay'.

If it is wise to train a puppy to sit, lie and stay in total privacy it is doubly so to teach the blind stay far from prying eyes. The public generally regard any dog trainer as something of an oddball I'm afraid, and regard anyone who walks away from a dog fixed at a stay position and then hides behind a wall as little short of a lunatic. Hence the dog trainer must accustom himself to the comments of neighbours and strangers alike and ignore such comments, or abandon dog training as a hobby.

These days the lurcher tests organised at country shows invariably include blind stays in their agenda and the handler is required to walk away from the dog and hide behind bales of straw for a minute or so while the dog remains at the down position. This is often quite a test for the animal, particularly as the dog is in a strange place surrounded by strange dogs (and even stranger people) who are invariably trying to entice the dog to break the down position – for while the majority of lurcher buffs are totally incapable of training a dog to perform any task they are often singularly adept at creating an annoyance and disturbance. However, such training has a practical application in the field. There will certainly be times when a lurcher trainer will need to leave the whelp behind while he performs some task or other, releasing a sheep from a fence into which the sheep has lodged its head, for example, a situation where the presence of a dog will exacerbate rather than help the problem.

A few weeks prior to writing this chapter I had ample opportunity to be able to test the value of such 'blind stay' training. I was out hunting with lurcher and ferrets when I observed a small flock of runner ducks had found their way through the hedgerow of a field where I had been refused permission to ferret and work lurchers, simply because the owner was a duck breeder and ducks, particularly runner ducks, are terrified of dogs; if harassed or frightened the ducks simply go off laying and begin to moult. So I respected the landowner's ruling and though his dry, sandy fields were infested with rabbits I stayed well clear of the field. The sight of thirty soldier-like ducks wandering down the road had caused the traffic to grind to a halt and a carload of noisy children was clearly distressing the terrified ducks further. So I placed Merab at the down position on the roadside and hastily shepherded the platoon of terrified ducks through the gap in the hedgerow and patched up the exit with dead sticks and loose wire. My good turn coupled with the good behaviour of my lurcher did not come amiss, for I have now added several acres of rabbit-infested land to my hunting country and I spend much time ferreting fields in which tall stately ducks are the only witnesses to my inevitable mistakes. To those who believe that it is not necessary to train a dog to such a high standard of obedience, such as I have just described, might I say that these people have absolutely no right to complain when landowners forbid such owners and their lurchers permission to hunt the properties owned by these landowners. Nothing gives a farmer more confidence that his stock will remain unharmed than the sight of a well trained dog. Conversely, nothing is more certain to distress a farmer than the sight of a wild, untrained brute that refuses to heed the commands of its handler.

6

Teaching a Puppy to Retrieve

I hate lead-training and get no pleasure from lead-breaking a puppy. However, I really enjoy teaching a puppy to retrieve and confess to experiencing an almost childlike pleasure when throwing a dummy and getting a puppy to return the object to hand. Retrieving should be fun for the puppy to learn and fun for the handler to teach if this training module is to be successful. In fact, any training session that looks like

A soft-mouthed lurcher in action.

becoming a bore is counter-productive, and the very best training sessions are those that are conducted as a game.

The hallmark of the incompetent lurcher owner is the dog that simply refuses to retrieve and the explanation offered by the owner of the dog: 'If a dog catches it's all I want – I can fetch the rabbit myself.' Once more I cannot resist relating an anecdote to explain a point. Caithness is well known for producing some of the worst lurchers in the country despite the availability of game to train dogs. One seldom sees a trained dog in the county and many dogs are swapped and sold until a host of very confused lurchers is passed from pillar to post. Lurchers trained to any standard are, in fact, very rare in the county and the lurcher owner is regarded with very low esteem by the sheep-dog handlers and the gundog trainers, for some the world's best sheepdogs and gundogs are bred and trained in Caithness. So the scene is set and now I shall relate my tale. An elderly Midland P.E. organiser came north to holiday near John O'Groats and brought with him his lurcher – a dog that had performed well at every event at which he had been entered. Within hours of the organiser's arrival in Caithness he was accosted by a local lurcher owner who engaged him in the customary tales one expects of Caithnessian lurcher buffs. 'See this bitch, I send her down the beam, catches rabbit. Harry' – he turns to a burly half-witted friend – 'fetch it. Harry down beam, fetches rabbit. Beam on, down the beam goes Nell [the lurcher], Harry fetch it. A hundred a night we catches. Don't we Harry?' The half-wit nodded in agreement and, turning to the P.E. organiser, the raconteur added, 'I bet you'd like to buy Nell.' The organiser shook his head. 'No, I wouldn't, but I'd take on Harry to train for the marathon!' This tale illustrates how a lurcherman with a lurcher that will not retrieve is regarded by competent trainers.

Yet not only is retrieving easy to teach a puppy, it is also fun for both the handler and the puppy to engage in, and I must confess I experience a childlike pleasure when I succeed in teaching a puppy to retrieve. I am always eager to start a puppy retrieving as soon as it settles in its new home and I have had six-week-old puppies eagerly retrieving a large variety of objects. I hasten to add that such is the pleasure I experience that I have taught pigs and goats to fetch objects I have wanted them to return to hand.

So let us assume that after a fairly quiet night the puppy has settled in to its new home and is playing fairly happily with its new owner. I always start a puppy retrieving a ball of rolled-up newspaper, for not only is the ball pleasant for the puppy to mouth and completely disposable if it becomes a soggy mess, but it makes a rustling sound when the ball is rolled and this is irresistible to a young puppy. I begin by crouching down until my face is near to the puppy and start batting the ball from hand to hand until the puppy becomes interested in the activity. When the puppy comes to investigate the cause of the sound I pick up the ball as though I am jealous of its ownership, but resume my game when the puppy starts to find some other activity interesting. After a while I attract the puppy's attention to the ball and will roll the object along the floor. The puppy will be fascinated by the rustling sound and attempt to pick up the ball in its mouth. I then put my face near to the floor so that is is level with the face of the whelp and speak to the puppy cajolingly. The puppy attracted by the eyes and mouth that are presented to it (I have explained why earlier in the book) rushes to the handler and with luck will carry the ball with it. Effusive praise follows and once again I play at batting the object from hand to hand before throwing the ball and repeating the face to face contact with the whelp. Sometimes the puppy will drop the ball and then come to be petted or fed. If this happens I never despair but fetch the ball and guard it jealousy. This action will soon rekindle the puppy's interest in the paper ball.

Some puppies, particularly saluki hybrids, will show a reluctance to chase a paper ball that is simply rolled in front of them and will some-times show no interest in the object. I find that the very best method of encouraging such whelps to retrieve is to harness their desire to chase – and most saluki hybrids will show an interest in chasing. A fold of paper attached to a string jerked in front of the puppy, and drawn across the floor in front of the whelp will almost always excite the puppy's interest in chasing the object. Once the puppy shows an interest in the folded paper the 'mouse' should be drawn in front of the puppy and the whelp allowed to catch the fold. As soon as the puppy has seized the object the handler should lower his face to the level of the puppy's and cajole the whelp to come to hand. A good trainer is a flexible trainer, one who will adapt his training methods to the needs and nature of the whelp he is training.

Each training session should be a pleasure to both the puppy and the trainer and should stop before the whelp tires or sours of retrieving. Just as the excitement of a puppy when its collar and lead is taken out is a clear indication of the efficacy of the lead-training method, so the excited face of a whelp when retrieving aids appear is an excellent indication of just how well the retrieving training is progressing. If a puppy becomes wild with delight when its ball or dummy is taken from the shelf, all is well. If it pays not the slightest interest to these objects the trainer has either soured the puppy of the training or else not engendered sufficient interest during the initial training sessions. A trainer who adopts a reserved attitude during a retrieving training session, one who is afraid to make himself look foolish or one who will not let his hair down is unlikely to make a success out of dog training and certainly not out of training a puppy to retrieve. I have observed that the very best lurcher trainers will make absolute fools of themselves in order to teach a lurcher a certain skill, and while I have read of dour, taciturn lurcher owners with wonderfully trained dogs I have yet to encounter one.

Puppies will sometimes sour or grow tired of retrieving the same dummy time and time again, particularly if the dummy starts to taste or

A Border collie lurcher returns to hand.

smell unpleasantly, and as soon as the puppy seems a little less than enthusiastic about the dummy it is time to change the object used for retrieving training. Some dogs have a favourite toy. One of my own lurchers has an old moth-eaten teddy bear to which she has become deeply attached. When she tired of retrieving a particular dummy, I had only to fetch out her favourite toy for her to go wild with delight. Another of my dogs becomes ecstatic at the sight of plastic milk bottles and will retrieve them long after she has tired of fetching other dummies.

I try to make a game out of all aspects of lurcher training, particularly the teaching of retrieving, and spend some time devising games to reinforce retrieving. I start most of my training in a corridor that is not cluttered with furniture under which a puppy can take the dummy and play with it – a quite serious setback in retrieving training, actually, particularly if this habit is allowed to continue unchecked. In such a corridor I have described there is no way the puppy can hide with the dummy and must come to the trainer with the object it is carrying. Later I use the same corridor to engage the puppy in retrieving games, hiding the dummy on window ledges or jamming the object in the handles of doors and requesting the puppy to search for the dummy. The more fun the puppy gets from its training session the better its retrieving will be in later life. I believe my own lurchers get tremendous pleasure retrieving their rabbits to hand and are only too willing to give up their catches.

As time progresses it is expedient to train the puppy to retrieve a fur dummy, and such a dummy can easily be made by skinning a rabbit and drying the skin until it loses both the moisture and much of its offensive smell – though puppies and adult dogs will find the smell of fresh rabbit captivating. I seldom bother to fill such a skin or to stitch the pelts to make a life-size dummy, but simply roll the skin fur side out and tie it in such a way that the dog is able to carry a neat bundle rather than a large, heavy dummy. Puppies will usually retrieve furry dummies eagerly once they have been allowed to sniff and play with them a while, and seldom will they sicken of dummies made from these objects. I have used the same dummy for an entire season and continued to use it until it became threadbare, but such rolled-up skins are so easy to obtain that using a rank, evil-smelling skin for retrieving sessions is false economy and frankly rather pointless. If fresh rabbits cannot be caught, if the puppy is the trainer's only lurcher, then road casualty rabbits should be collected, skinned and a dummy made from these skins.

When the puppy becomes sufficiently well trained to take into the field it should be encouraged to retrieve the cadaver of a rabbit to complete its training. Some puppies, even very bold puppies, become very frightened when confronted with their first cadaver and will often be very chary of approaching the carcass. I urge readers not to give up at this point and sell the puppy. This apprehension concerning the carcass will soon give way to interest, and in no time the puppy will be eager to mouth the cadaver. Puppies will sometimes tire of fetching a dummy and sometimes even a rolled-up rabbit skin, but the majority of unentered whelps will retrieve the cadaver of a rabbit eagerly – and no untrained whelp should ever be allowed to see, let alone chase, live game. If a dog is not trained in the yard, so to speak, it won't be trained in the field.

At this point it seems wise to mention again that no other dog should be present while a puppy is being trained to retrieve. Virtually every ruined lurcher, every dog that circles rabbit in mouth or stands over its catch but refuses to bring its catch to hand has been ruined by training alongside another dog or having dogs near the puppy when it retrieves its catches. My own lurchers are naturally enthusiastic retrievers and will carry a catch from some distance – a mile or so in some cases – yet they are very unreliable if I have another dog alongside me when my lurchers are carrying to hand. The huge band of lurcher owners who indulge in lamping forays with a dozen or more dogs are virtually encouraging their dogs to be intermittent and unreliable retrievers, dogs that will circle their owners, rabbits in mouth, but are reluctant to part with their catches. The lurcher is a solitary type of dog, an animal that should enjoy a one man – one dog relationship if it is to give of its best in the field. To train the animal, or worse still, to work the animal, alongside another dog is decidedly counter-productive to the development of a lurcher.

There are many points for and against force-training a dog to carry to hand and it is perhaps wise to mention them before proceeding to describe the force-training of a lurcher. Most continental police search dogs are force-trained to retrieve, for it is argued that 'activities that are acquired naturally are also lost naturally'. To explain a little more simply, a dog that enjoys carrying to hand may one day decide that it does not wish to carry to hand and refrain from doing so. A force-trained dog will always carry to hand because it has been conditioned to believe it must.

I detest force-training, though I must confess I force-train all my saluki-bred longdogs. I write a lurcher column for a sporting magazine and by doing so I set myself up as an Aunt Sally I'm afraid. If any of my dogs make the slightest mistake when they are performing in public I am held up to ridicule. Should any of my longdogs fail to retrieve, and few saluki hybrids enjoy retrieving, then I would be regarded as a laughing stock by the lurcher fraternity. Thus I force-train my longdogs before allowing them to perform in public. But I dislike it and experience some distress when I watch the puzzled face of the dog that is being subjected to this training, and I would not recommend force-training to anyone whose lurcher displays a natural propensity to carry to hand or who has developed a fine working relationship with the owner after experiencing what I choose to call force-training. I endeavour to make every aspect of training a game, and if I return home after a training session with an excited, happy dog in tow then I too am satisfied. No dog enjoys being force-trained and a wise trainer must attempt to punctuate a force-training session with a game. So now it behoves me to describe force-training.

Force-training consists of persuading (what a delightful euphemism when one considers the fearsome torture described by Konrad Most) a dog to open its mouth to take and carry any object that is presented to it. Some dogs – once again, saluki hybrids are the worst – will simply catch their quarry and stand over it refusing to bring the catch to hand,

A whippet greyhound hybrid returns its catch to hand.

and it is these dogs that will benefit from force-training, though once again I should advise any tyro lurcherman attempting to force-train an animal to watch a competent trainer attempt it before embarking on the training project. Firstly the trainer should ensure that the dog he is about to force-train is reasonably obedient for the animal is unlikely to enjoy the first stages and will attempt to resist. I always advise engaging the animal in a game before and after each training session. So, we arrive at the point where force-training proper begins and the dog is leashed ready for training. I place the dog in the sit position to make the training session less traumatic for me, if not the dog, and begin. Firstly I place my hand over the muzzle of the dog and gently squeeze, the dog's lips against the gums. It is most likely that the dog will respond to such pressure by opening its mouth, and once the animal has obliged a dumbbell should be placed between the animal's jaws and the command 'Fetch' or 'Hold' uttered. Most lurchers and longdogs will attempt to spit out the dumbbell as if it has an unpleasant taste. Some, baffled by what the devil the owner is attempting to do, will hold the dumbbell between their jaws with a quizzical look appearing on their faces. However, the dog must be gently persuaded to hold the dumbbell, and must always be praised if it manages to keep the object in its jaws. If the trainer is adept and gentle the time will certainly come when the hound will open its mouth to take the dumbbell once the object is presented to it.

The time now arrives when the dumbbell will be cast on the ground before the dog and the animal told to fetch the object, and now once again the handler must expect squalls. It is extremely likely that the dog will gaze blankly at the dumbbell the trainer has cast before it. The trainer must now gently press the dog's head towards the dumbbell and utter the word 'Fetch' or 'Hold', and once the trainer has persuaded the dog to perform in such a way force-training is virtually completed. I have dealt with the subject at some length in my book *Lurcher Training*, I should add, and it is expedient to be more brief in a book of this nature.

Force-training should be avoided by a tyro lurcher trainer unless it is absolutely necessary to have a rock-steady animal that has been virtually brainwashed into retrieving. It is not fun to teach force-training and most lurchers do not enjoy being force-trained no matter how the trainer punctuates the training programme with games. I force-train longdogs simply because I am expected to produce animals that will perform superbly on the day, every day, but I experience a deep gloom when I embark on this training project and feel as though a great weight has been lifted from my shoulders once I have completed it. Newcomers to lurcher training should persist at fun training retrieving methods and not attempt to force-train a lurcher unless it is absolutely necessary to do so. Mistakes made during such training will often result in bitterly upset owners and desperately maladjusted dogs.

7

Teaching a Lurcher to Jump

Lurchers are naturally terrific athletes and they really enjoy jumping if, that is, they are encouraged to jump as youngsters and perfect the technique early in their lives. However, even hoary oldsters, lurchers that would seem more in place sitting out the rest of their lives in fireside seats, can still be taught to jump. In Caithness it is generally believed that a lurcher that will not jump naturally when coursing cannot be taught to do so. This is absolute rubbish and such logic could only be proposed in a county where dogs are constantly swapped and changed and never subjected to a proper training programme. Any dog can be taught to jump and the curious agility tests where tiny toy dogs run the circuit joyously and competently demonstrate this fact clearly. A lurcher that will not jump is the hallmark of a substandard lurcher trainer; it is worth only a fraction of the value of a properly trained dog, and a longdog that refrains from jumping is worth virtually nothing.

However, perhaps it should be explained why it is so important to teach a lurcher or longdog to jump and why a lurcher handler should go to considerable pains to ensure his dog is able to jump on the run or command. Improvements in British agriculture have only been wrought by enclosure and hence the British countryside has been divided into quite small fields which are separated by ancient hedges or fences. A dog that will not jump these hedges and fences and which insists on running up and down them to seek a gap is a less than efficient hunter and an unsatisfactory courser – unless, that is, the dog is only required to perform on the wide open plains of Norfolk or engage in an illicit tilt at hares on the Salisbury Plains. In the Peak District, where dry-stone walls separate the fields, a non-jumping dog will look ridiculous and make its handler look even more ridiculous, one should add. In the broken country of the Midlands, country that changes from plough to pasture to 'set aside', a non-jumping dog will need to catch in the field in which it is released if it is to be of any use whatsoever. I cannot but wonder why

All lurchers should jump.

people will tolerate a non-jumper when it is so simple to teach a dog to hurdle or long jump, yet many lurchers refrain from jumping simply because their handlers haven't the slightest idea of how to teach these animals.

The teaching of the jumping action is simplicity itself and with certain reservations the smallest puppies can be taught to scramble over obstacles and even hop over low boards. I rear lurcher puppies in an old stable, a large, fairly spacious, though somewhat down at heel building that adjoins my yard. I place a board some six inches high across the entrance to the stable and at feeding time call the puppies to be fed in the yard. The whelps soon learn to scramble over the board to be fed and develop the technique of jumping while doing so. As the puppies approach eight weeks of age I place a board some twelve inches high across the entrance, and long before puppies leave for their new homes I have seen excited youngsters clamber over boards two feet or so to be fed. I seldom allow a puppy with soft, pliable bones a chance to jump higher than this lest it damage bone and cartilage, but I have seen very young puppies scale great heights with considerable ease. I'm not certain that allowing puppies to do this isn't very damaging indeed, but it is very tempting for a trainer to exploit any quality a whelp seems to manifest even though the dog becomes damaged by the activity.

Once puppies develop the technique of placing and lifting their limbs to leap these boards their jumping education regarding field work at least is virtually complete, and many successful coursing longdogs are taught by these calling-on methods. At four months, a particularly gangly age for deerhound hybrids – at all ages the most agile and elegant of these hounds is a clumsy beast – I should expect such a hound to be able to hop over an obstacle some two feet in height when I called it. Saluki hybrids, which mature more quickly, should be able to manage to clamber over boards some two feet six in height, but it is unwise to encourage large longdog babes to jump any higher than this. Some of the very best competitive high-jumping dogs are deerhound hybrids. Indeed the hound that scaled twelve feet six inches in 1992 was a deer-hound-bred longdog, but if such hounds are bruised, lamed or frightened during their puppy training they will not fulfil their potential in later life.

The handler will experience his first problems in the teaching of jumping when he encounters the first sheep wire fences the puppy is expected to jump. A fence through which a whelp can see will often prove to be a problem, for the puppy will endeavour to squeeze through such a hurdle rather than leap it. If the handler simply walks off and allows the puppy to take its time to explore the structure of the fence the youngster will normally leap the obstacle and attempt to follow the handler. It is, however, wise to keep a weather eye open for problems that puppies might encounter scaling such fences, for whelps panicked by the sight of their handlers walking into the distance will sometimes leap awkwardly and tangle in the meshes of the sheep wire. Should that happen the handler must rush back to the tangled puppy to prevent further damage. Puppies and adults often panic badly when they find themselves tangled in sheep wire.

One of the most placid lurchers I have ever owned, my stud dog Ilan, tangled in sheep wire on his first trip into the country (I am reluctant to take a dog off the premises until it is well trained and stock-broken so no whelp of less than seven months of age is ever taken off country). I saw him hanging by his hind leg and howling piteously and rushed to free him. In his panic he bit wildly and only my waxed jacket prevented serious damage to my arms for Ilan is a powerful male with a tremen-dous bite. I urge the reader to take care when untangling a lurcher from sheep wire. Barbed wire is a curse and is said to be an invention dreamed up by a woman, but it is commonly encountered in the British country-side and dogs should be taught to avoid it if at all possible. My current longdog bitch Canaan is extremely perspicacious where barbed wire is concerned and should she encounter sheep wire that is not topped with a barbed wire strand she will simply hop over the obstacle. If she notices that there is a strand of barbed wire atop the fence she will leap high to avoid contact with the wire. Wherever possible I avoid allowing my dogs a chance to injure themselves on barbed wire and I usually place my arm across the wire and allow my puppies to jump over my arm rather than over the naked wire. It can be argued that dogs are going to encounter barbed wire anyway and thus such protection is a shade superfluous. However, whenever possible I prevent my dogs experiencing hurt from the tines of such wire.

If the lurcher handler wishes to compete at competitive events or the handler ever wishes to jump a dog over a fence without clambering over the fence himself and calling on the dog, the lurcher should be taught to jump by a training process known in the lurcher fraternity as 'running up'. This method of training can be enjoyable for both the trainer and the lurcher he is training, and can be taught by the use of the most inexpensive props.

Before running-up training can proceed the whelp must not only be lead-trained but very much at ease with the leash around its neck. Those wishing to train by the methods about to be advised would do well to spend a few days lead-training and to be certain the dog will perform happily on the lead and will not fight the restricting leash. One of the most unhappy sights I have ever seen was a very nervous saluki hybrid (pedigree unknown, but obviously saluki-bred) desperately fighting the leash while its owner attempted to drag it over some low jumps.

Let us now assume that the puppy has not only been lead-trained but is happy about having a leash placed around its neck. A board one foot high is now placed across a doorway and the dog walked to the hurdle. When the board has been reached the handler steps over the board, utters the word 'Up' (or 'Over') and jerks the lead slightly to encourage the dog over the hurdle. If the puppy seems slightly perplexed by the action of leading it over this low hurdle it must be given effusive praise or titbits and the activity ceased for the day. To continue jumping training once the dog becomes upset is decidely counter-productive, for to become a really competent competitive jumping dog the lurcher must adore the activity. My best competitive jumper – he retired unbeaten after five years of hard competition – went wild with delight when he saw jumping

A typical spring jump.

frames being erected on the showground and needed to be restrained if he saw another dog jumping hurdles. He literally lived to jump and came to grief leaping a hedge and breaking his neck as he landed on some obsolete farm equipment. Curiously, not one of his children manifested this outrageous desire to jump and I can only believe that some curious quirk in his early training produced this obsession for jumping.

A competitive jumping dog needs to be taught to run at the frames and scramble over them and so the handler must lead the dog into a canter as he approaches the frame, and as the handler steps over the frame he must jerk the lead and utter the words 'Up' or 'Over', but there comes a time when unless the handler is both an acrobat and a high jumper he will be unable to step over the frame. My own practical tip regarding the training of a dog to jump at competitive events is that before the frame becomes too high for the handler to step over the dog should be run several times at the frame and occasionally the handler should decline to step over the hurdle, but by dint of exciting the animal on the run-up to the frame encourage the dog to leap the obstacle. At this stage I spend a full week simply jumping the dog at this height, and only proceed further when the dog will bound over the low hurdle on command.

So the time arrives when yet another plank is fixed to the frame and the handler finds it impossible to step over the hurdle with the dog. The handler must now run to the hurdle, jerk the leash and step to the side of the hurdle as the dog jumps the frame. One tip I can offer concerning this stage in the training is not to allow the dog to leap the hurdle while a long lead dangles from its collar, and I usually manufacture a short binder twine plait to attach to the collar specifically for this part of the training. A dog that is required to jump with a lengthy lead fixed to its collar is likely to hurt itself sooner or later, and usually sooner, I must add. If a dog sustains serious hurt during jumping it is extremely difficult to engender the same enthusiasm for jumping for some time to come.

Might I digress slightly and discuss the problems wrought by jumping a youngster over a shaky jumping frame or a jump that is liable to collapse as the dog makes an attempt. I can think of no more certain way of ruining a competition dog than to jump it over such a construction. If I jump a dog over any object that falls or clatters badly as the lurcher attempts to jump it I race forward and praise the dog effusively and engage it in a wild outrageous game lest it be soured by its experience, but it is more sensible to inspect the frame over which the dog is required to leap and to refrain from jumping the dog if the frame is at all suspect.

If the training of the lurcher has proceeded well and the dog has not been injured by the training process the sky seems virtually the limit where high jumping a lurcher is concerned. The spectacular twelve feet six clambered by the deerhound hybrid in the south-west of England in 1992 can, I believe, be bettered, though not without considerable effort on the part of the handler and the dog. However, to attempt such feats with a puppy or with an animal whose bones have not hardened enough to withstand the shock of both jumping and landing after a jump would be bad practice indeed. If a youngster will leap (and leap happily, one should add) over a four-foot obstacle the handler must consider himself a happy man and jumping a puppy higher than this is not advisable. Once the dog is fully grown then by all means attempt record high-jumps, particularly if the handler feels the dog enjoys the activity, but a lurcher seldom attains the peak of its athletic prowess before it is four years old.

A dog scaling six or more feet lands on the far side of the hurdle with considerable force and the ground needs to be buffered if the dog is not going to hurt its feet or damage its wrists. At one time I saw rubber gym mats used as shock absorbers, but bales of straw seem to be commonly used at most events. If the ground is not buffered with some suitable shock absorber it is extremely dangerous to jump a dog over a very high hurdle or scaling platform. In the mid 1970s when jumping events were very popular it was common to see competition lurchers with damaged feet and wrists as a result of their activities. These days shows and jumping events are far better organised and the sight of dogs limping away after they have scaled some very high frame is fortunately rare.

I always train a dog to long-jump as a matter of course, but there are those who would say such training is superfluous. Yet there are times when a lurcher or a coursing longdog will need to be able to leap across ditches or even canals, hence it is expedient to teach a dog to leap across obstacles. I have twice won single-handed hare coursing matches with longdogs that achieved their successes simply because they were able to jump across drainage ditches. On numerous occasions I have observed hares swim these ditches while baffled longdogs ran up and down the banks of these waterways only to watch their hare escape. Yet teaching a dog to long jump is so simple that it is bewildering to find that few longdog keepers teach this exercise.

To teach long jumping a handler will need three or four hurdles and providing these hurdles are stable they can be Heath Robinson in design and construction. At one time I constructed low hurdles out of old and damaged Latin textbooks and many times have I used tomato crates in the place of more conventional, professionally built trestle hurdles that were used at the local dog training clubs. Thus, while one should be prepared to spend money constructing very stable high-jumping frames, one should be very chary of spending the same amount on trestle hurdles.

However, costings aside, on to the teaching of long jumping. A single hurdle is placed on the training space and the dog walked to the hurdle and commanded 'Up' or 'Over', a feat the young dog will accomplish with considerable ease. This game (and game the exercise must be to get the best results) is repeated a few times until the lurcher is excited, whereupon a second hurdle is placed behind the first. The dog is then hopped over the two hurdles two or three times before being engaged in a wild game and the training session terminated for the day. The following day the hurdles are moved perhaps two or three inches apart and once more the puppy is encouraged to jump over these obstacles a few times before being encouraged to join in yet another game with its owner. If the puppy shows an enthusiasm for jumping then the trainer may decide to attempt two training sessions during the course of a day, but the lurcher sapling must never be allowed to sour of jumping training.

The trainer should now gradually increase the distance between the two hurdles until a distance of two or three feet separates the trestles. At this point the dog may well consider hopping each of the hurdles in turn, so a third hurdle should be placed between the two trestles and the dog instructed to jump these objects. Few dogs will need to be able to spring more than perhaps eight feet in their coursing careers but I have seen many lurchers and longdogs leap great distances during a course. Some dogs greatly enjoy jumping huge and apparently impossible chasms. In 1984 I watched Eddie Jones's great collie greyhound Celt spring across a twenty-four-foot chasm in Cambridge, and simply because the group which observed the feat showed their approval by clapping and cheering (it was difficult not to cheer, so great was the leap) the dog jumped the chasm on its return to Eddie. This particular family, Dai Fish's Merle to a Linden Eland × Minisotta greyhound bitch, produced obsessional jumpers. A brother from the same litter, Alan Hooten's Blue, jumped goalposts simply 'for the hell of it'. This was a remarkably good breeding and for a while at least it was believed that the virtue of the breeding lay in the sire, a blue merle half-bred collie greyhound. Later, however, the bitch was to produce both Taffy and Wendell when mated to a half-bred beardie/Border collie, two of the most influential sires in lurcher breeding history. I watched a son of Taffy working some blue hare near Cambridge in 1993 and observed the self-same bounding, leaping style I saw when Celt made that phenomenal leap in Cambridge.

8

Stock-breaking

L et us make no bones about it, lurchers can be the biggest nuisances imaginable if they are not stock-broken, and sadly many lurchers are so badly trained that they run riot when they encounter stock of any kind. An uncontrollable lurcher is indeed a problem among problems. The dog's natural inclination is to chase; an inclination inherited from its sighthound ancestors is often coupled with the herding instinct inherited from the collie, hence stock worrying is often set about systematically and with the maximum amount of damage inflicted on the livestock.

Furthermore, the very nature of the work conducted by a lurcher brings it into contact with a great variety of livestock, so the high incidence of stock worrying for which the lurcher is justly notorious can easily be explained. Sheep favour dry pasture, and so do rabbits, so a lurcher out hunting is likely to encounter sheep and, if not stock steady, is likely to do them awesome damage. Even if a dog does not actually attack sheep a wild, unruly, free-running lurcher can induce such panic that a flock can damage itself running into fences, over steep banks and sometimes into the paths of passing cars, as happened in Sutherland some five years ago.

Chickens and ducks seem to drive some lurchers to frenzy. Most believe that dogs are by nature cowards (though it is illogical to credit animals with human emotions) and are more likely to attack animals and birds that show fear of them – and poultry (ducks in particular) are decidedly paranoid, though frankly they have every reason to be paranoid where lurchers are concerned. At the time of writing I am attempting to create a high-egg-yielding white-bodied duck and so I have many ducks feeding on the moors near my croft. During summertime I am plagued by uninvited visitors, the majority of whom have lurchers in their cars and vans, and for some reason these people believe they have a God-given right to allow their lurchers to run free and foul when they arrive at my croft. I have every reason to believe the majority of lurchers are not stock-broken and when I observe a car approaching my home I race out to prevent the driver allowing his vehicle to disgorge a host of wild, very untrained lurchers.

Yet it is relatively easy to stock-break a lurcher puppy, though a lot more difficult to retrain a puppy that has worried stock of any kind. I do not believe stock-breaking can be taught too young – in other words the younger the puppy the easier it is to break to stock. A young puppy is usually overawed by the presence of livestock and will usually avoid conflict with creatures that not only appear alien but tower over the whelp. Hence it is expedient to walk a youngster through sheep and introduce it to chickens and ducks shortly after it has been inoculated and is safe to take out of doors. If the puppy shows the slightest inclination to chase or attempt to play with livestock (and most stock worriers begin their careers by playing with livestock after which the game becomes an extremely bloody one) a sharp tug at the leash accompanied by an ever sharper 'No!' will usually steady the whelp and prevent further interest. However, such instant stock-breaking needs to be reinforced by frequent encounters with the said livestock if the training is to be effective. A week's training consisting of a ten-minute walk per day among sheep or poultry will usually steady even the most boisterous puppy. However, it is unwise to allow the puppy off its leash until it shows either apprehension or no interest in the livestock among which it is being walked.

I find the very best animals to sheep-break a puppy are orphan, bottle-reared lambs which will seek out the puppy and quizzically examine the whelp, nosing it, butting it and attempting to play with the youngster, and it is good policy for anyone considering training a saluki-bred longdog (which has an unenviable reputation for stock worrying) to purchase an orphan lamb and rear it in the company of the young longdog. Longdogs and lurchers alike must totally disregard the sheep among which they may be required to hunt and course and they must come to accept the presence of these animals with indifference, even if the terrified flock is fleeing at the very sight of a dog. When I trained my current longdog Canaan I reared her with a pair of twin goat kids who played with the saluki hybrid, ate with her and slept in the same pen as the whelp, and I have never regretted obtaining the kids because Canaan is totally indifferent to the sheep through which she often courses. On two occasions she sprang over the backs of sheep to chase the rabbits on which she was entered and was oblivious to the presence of the flock. It is curious that sheep will often instantly recognise a dog that is hostile to them long before the dog begins its pursuit. Conversely I have observed that while sheep will move away from any dog that appears among them they display an indifference to a dog that is totally stock-broken. It is almost as if both sheep and dogs retain race memories of the time when there was a predator–prey relationship between the species, for prey animals will often ignore the presence of a predator that is not actively engaged in hunting them. A totally stock-steady lurcher will seldom panic even the wildest and most nervy of sheep. Time spent stock-breaking is time well spent.

I would never allow a free-running, unbroken puppy to encounter ducks, even ducks that are protected by a wire enclosure. A wild, unruly puppy racing up and down the fence will terrify ducks and once ducks are distressed they cease to lay and often pass into moult thereby causing great financial loss to their owners. It is a little known fact that ducks kept under optimum conditions will lay considerably more eggs than chickens, but are so easily upset that they can be decidedly unprofitable if a dog is allowed to terrorise them. It is also ridiculous to suggest that lurchers that are completely stock-steady to ducks will not hunt or catch mallard or teal. My own lurchers are fine hunters of feather yet were reared alongside ducklings and totally ignore my flock. I constantly take young dogs among ducklings and ensure that they are steady with water-fowl, and give refresher courses to any puppies that sometimes show an interest in ducks.

Once a dog of any breed has worried livestock it is a devil's own job to break the dog of the habit, and a dog that worries sheep is a terrible liability to own. It is fairly easy to understand the measures the British legal system has taken to prevent sheep worrying, particularly as the British economy was once virtually dependent on sheep farming – the Lord Chancellor still sits on the Woolsack. The majority of sheep worriers can still be broken of the habit (though with some difficulty) but there are, of course, dogs which cannot be retrained and the fate of these creatures is unenviable.

The most commonly used method of breaking a confirmed sheep worrier of the habit is based on Most's notion that a dog is most likely to attack an animal that displays fear in the presence of the said dog. Conversely the dog is unlikely to attack any creature that displays hostility towards the dog. Thus a confirmed sheep worrier is introduced to a tame, hand-reared ram, the sort of sheep that will stand its ground against the most fearsome attacker, and should the dog show the slightest animosity towards the sheep the ram will soundly trounce the dog for its fool-hardiness. Some of the best dog-breakers I have ever encountered were Shetland rams, small horned sheep that survived an inclement climate for centuries and if sufficiently tame will face down a furious dog. Once again I must resort to a tale to illustrate a point. Some of the very worst sheep worriers I have encountered have been Irish setters and Dalmatians – unlikely candidates for the sheep worrier of the year award but nevertheless awesome pests if allowed to run riot in the countryside. In 1979 a breeder of both setters and, for a while, Dalmatians phoned me and mentioned the interest her dogs showed in sheep. The lady was obviously perplexed by the frenzy the local sheep had aroused in her dogs and asked how I would remedy the problem and I recommended a Shetland orphan male lamb. While hunting near the kennels where this lady kept her setters and Dalmatians I called in to see her and found her dogs so terrified that they refused to leave the kennels until the ram was penned. I found this quite amusing until I saw that my two lurchers, Merab and Fathom, had climbed a wall to escape the attentions of the ram.

The legality of allowing a ram to batter a sheep-worrying dog to submission is one of those curious grey areas of the law, and sooner or later a private prosecution is likely to be brought against someone who allows such a conflict to take place. Is such cruelty justifiable or does it contravene the all-embracing 1911 Protection of Animals Act Section 1 (1) (a) that states that it is an offence to cause an animal unnecessary suffering, and the excessive use of such a ram (or a ewe guarding a new lamb) may well amount to the unreasonable abuse of the dog? I must confess I have seen some sheep-worrying dogs reduced to cowering, bloodied brutes by the attentions of a ram, and I must also confess that I saw the same dog chasing sheep a few weeks later.

There is, in fact, some evidence to suggest that some dogs will learn to differentiate between a ram that will hurt them and ewes that will flee with terror once they are approached by a dog. Sheep worriers of this nature are devils to break to sheep even though subjected to a spell of what is called aversion therapy. The dog is leashed to a lengthy check line and as it endeavours to charge forward to chase the sheep a starting pistol is fired. The loud noise terrifies the dog, but once it has recovered from the shock of hearing the explosion it once again attempts to chase the sheep. Again the pistol is fired and once again the dog is terrified. The theory is that the dog will associate its urge to chase sheep with pain or terror rather than the ecstatic enjoyment a sheep worrier experiences as it chases and seizes the sheep – shades of Anthony Burgess's *A Clockwork Orange* perhaps – and like the treatment meted out to the luckless Alex, is far from an effective method of stock-breaking a dog. If a lurcher is obtained as a puppy such terrible aversion therapy is superfluous as the whelp is easily stock-broken.

In my book *Lurcher Training* I have dealt at some length with Barbara Woodhouse's notions concerning the breaking of confirmed chicken worriers and will mention it but briefly in this book simply because her notions are quite interesting — ludicrous and bizarre perhaps, but certainly interesting! Mrs Woodhouse, in her book *Training Dogs My Way* suggested that a dyed-in-the-wool fowl worrier should be taken to a chicken pen, one of the fowl lifted out and promptly beheaded! The dog is then allowed to attempt to attack the decapitated fowl but is chastised for its efforts. I will allow the reader to form his or her own opinions about such a method and pass on to another subject.

So let us assume the handler now has an obedient, all-jumping, all-retrieving, stock-broken lurcher. It is now time to enter the dog to quarry, but before the trainer ventures into the field the lurcher needs to be virtually fully trained. It is wise to remember the adage that if a lurcher isn't trained before it is entered it won't be trained afterwards. Time spent on training a puppy to be biddable is time well spent, and while such training may not be particularly exciting for the tyro lurcherman it is absolutely essential if one is to produce an efficient, well mannered hunting dog.

9

Entering the Lurcher and the Longdog

A t the time of writing there is some debate as to whether the longdog needs to be entered in the same manner as a lurcher. Thus it is perhaps expedient once again to define the role of the longdog and the working lurcher before proceeding further. A longdog, if the reader remembers, is primarily a hare chaser and catcher and rabbits caught by such a dog should be regarded as a bonus. A lurcher, on the other hand, is an all-round hunting dog whose principal quarry is rabbit, and hares taken by stealth, coupled with speed perhaps, should be regarded as a bonus.

E. G. Walsh, writing in his masterly *Lurchers and Longdogs*, suggested that a longdog or hare-coursing lurcher should not be entered to rabbits but allowed to mature until it is eighteen months of age before being slipped at a hare that has been run by another hound. This is indeed a commendable practice but it does involve the longdog spending a good proportion of its youth simply being trained and never seeing quarry. Walsh argues that a rabbit which seldom offers a longdog a course of more than twenty-five yards before disappearing into a hole is apt to daunt a longdog and perhaps take the edge off its enthusiasm to chase. There is some truth in what Walsh says and frankly I have always regarded a lurcher, or at least my strain of lurcher, as a twenty-five-yard dog – a dog that is able to catch a rabbit before it disappears down its hole some twenty-five yards away.

Many, single-handed hare-coursing dogs, the so-called match dogs, are kept well clear of rabbits by their owners. The dogs seldom see a rabbit during the daylight hours and their owners are often shy of lamping their dogs. It has been suggested that longdogs that are worked on the lamp are shy of following a hare into a thicket and will often pull up when a hare approaches a fence or hedge, but personally I find such beliefs illogical and I encourage all my longdogs to run any legal quarry.

Rabbits seem to be the logical starting point for any lurcher or longdog about to embark on a hunting career for rabbits are once again plentiful and decidedly unpopular with landowners on whose land they are feeding and burrowing. However, while it is true that rabbits do not have the terrific speed of the brown hare, it is quite a difficult creature to catch. Few feed more than twenty-five yards from home during daylight hours and when frightened can run that distance at a great speed. It is often said that rabbits are quick rather than fast, but they are more than a match for most whippets if they are sprung during the daylight hours.

Before proceeding further perhaps it is well to mention that while it is perfectly legal to 'drop' live wild rabbits before a lurcher or longdog in order to encourage the hounds to chase (providing, that is, the rabbits have a chance of escaping and are not encumbered or damaged in any way to prevent their escape), it is an ill-advised practice. Rabbits released near to home can usually reach the sanctuary of the burrow in which they have been living. Rabbits released off country will make a feeble attempt to escape before squatting in the faint hope that their immobility will cause them to pass unnoticed. More important still, however, is the fact that releasing bagged quarry before a dog of any breed is distasteful to any sane and sensible person and such a practice is likely to attract criticism from the general public, many of whom are already antipathetic to fieldsports. Any activity that shows hunting in a poor light must be avoided at all costs.

It is often suggested that the best way to start a lurcher puppy is to take the whelp to a spot where the rabbits are infected with myxomatosis and to allow the animal an opportunity to chase and perhaps catch an infected rabbit. On the surface of it this might seem an unsporting activity that borders on the inhuman – the rabbit is crippled, it is blinded and hence unable to escape and is highly likely to die in the next few days. The morality of hunting such a creature is perhaps debatable, but there is little doubt that an infected rabbit is easier to catch than a healthy one and would therefore seem the ideal quarry to start a lurcher or longdog on its hunting career. However, there are those who disagree with such notions. It is argued that a rabbit infected with myxomatosis will run in a manner which is quite unlike that of a healthy rabbit and there is little doubt that many lurchers, particularly lurchers that have had great experience at catching healthy rabbits, pursue an infected rabbit gingerly, for the rabbit is not behaving in the manner the dog expects it to behave. Some puppies will, in fact, run alongside an infected rabbit as if mystified as to why the rabbit is behaving as it is. Others will readily mouth and catch an infected rabbit.

The simplest way of entering a puppy is to allow it to chase a lamped rabbit – and the subject of lamping will be dealt with presently. It is sufficient to say that a rabbit will often afford a lengthy course at night for it is then the rabbit will be feeding a considerable distance away from its burrow. A rabbit disturbed during daylight hours will seldom feed more than twenty-five yards from the safety afforded it by its burrow, but a rabbit becomes more adventurous as darkness falls and may well seek out provender half a mile from home. There is an instance where pinks and carnations were destroyed by the nocturnal raids of rabbits that were living nearly eleven hundred yards from the plant nursery.

There is no mystique about lamping. It is, in fact, the simplest, most easily learned of sports. Admittedly there are useful tips a beginner can pick up from an old hand, but a dark night, a large number of rabbits and a good lamping kit will produce a competent lamper in a matter of hours. Some dogs learn to lamp quite quickly, others less so. Phaedra, my youngest lurcher, caught the first rabbit she saw illuminated by the beam. Ilan, her great grandsire, was much slower to learn what the beam of light was meant to reveal yet he became a competent lamper and an extremely dextrous catch dog before an accident eased him into premature retirement and ensured his worth as a stud dog. I still have yet to encounter a lurcher puppy that could not be 'started' by two or three lamping trips.

Might I urge the tyro lurcher keeper to shut his ears to the twaddle he will hear at the beer tents at country shows. Tales of ten-week-old puppies catching lamped rabbits are commonly heard at such places but while I am absolutely confident that I could produce a six-month-old puppy that would catch the occasional lamped rabbit, I have yet to produce a capable mite of that age. The childhood or infancy of a lurcher is best occupied with obedience training rather than entering of the dog. It is interesting to note that should the listener to such tales of five-month-old puppies working well in the lamps enquire as to the fate of these dogs he will find that these puppies have been sold on before they are a year old and have joined the lurcher merry-go-round – that band of dispirited dogs that are permanently in transit between dealer and temporary client. A yearling lurcher is sometimes ready to be introduced to lamped rabbits but only if that lurcher is well trained and obedient. Once a lurcher is used to chasing and catching rabbits further training is difficult, though not totally impossible perhaps.

Many lurchers are started on ferreted rabbits, but not as many as the pre-war lurchers, for lamping is a relatively new method of starting young lurchers to hunt rabbits. A ferreted rabbit is no mean opponent, however. When disturbed by a ferret a rabbit will often explode from its burrow at great speed and reach the sanctuary of another burrow in seconds. Young lurchers are often bewildered by this burst of speed and take some time to come to terms with ferreted rabbits. I have always found that a few minutes spent reconnoitring the fields and the 'stopping' of nearby sanctuaries affords the young lurcher a better chance of catching a ferreted rabbit and also helps to reduce the souring a lurcher experiences when it watches its rabbit escape down a nearby burrow. It is worth mentioning how many rabbits a young lurcher nearly catches only to see the rabbit flash to ground. The fact is a rabbit will slow down slightly as it prepares to dive down a burrow to escape its pursuer. An experienced dog will sense when this is about to happen and will do its utmost to catch its rabbit as it prepares to run to ground. Phaedra, my youngest lurcher, will frequently attempt a flying tackle to prevent ferreted rabbits escaping – a somewhat dangerous technique, I must add, but a method that has proved more than satisfactory at preventing rabbits escaping. Young lurchers need time to perfect such techniques and may miss many rabbits before they learn to catch. Merab, my best lurcher, the best lurcher I have ever owned, missed over three hundred rabbits before she perfected the technique of catching them, yet she became amazingly dextrous in her later life and I have yet to see a better ferreter's dog.

A word of warning before proceeding further. The best lurchers are always trained on a one to one basis for a lurcher should have a one man–one dog relationship with its owner. The presence of another dog when a lurcher makes its first catch is decidedly counter-productive to retrieving. A lurcher or longdog is usually so excited at its first catch that no matter how well it has been taught to retrieve it will wander around its owner with the rabbit in its mouth. At this point the owner must drop to his knees and coax the lurcher to bring its catch to hand. The presence of another dog tugging at its leash to snatch the rabbit is scarcely conducive to retrieving and the majority of bad retrievers are ruined at this juncture in the training programme. There is nothing to be gained by working two lurchers together and a lot to be lost by the practice.

10

Lamping

Virtually anyone can teach a dog to lamp for it is the most easily learnt of skills which involves little practice and little knowledge of dogs to perfect. Yet the practice of lamping invites more discussion and more debate than any other facet of lurcher keeping. This is simply because lamping is such a simple technique to learn that most lurchermen are lampers.

Firstly let us discuss the best type of lurcher for lamping, and in order to decide which breeding constitutes the ideal amalgam it is perhaps expedient to evaluate the qualities a top-rate lamping dog should possess. However, before discussing the qualities an ideal lamping dog should have it is wise to mention that virtually any dog with the merest dash of sighthound blood can be taught to work with a lamp. In fact I have seen pure-bred German shepherd dogs catch tolerably well 'on the lamp' and at one time I was almost convinced that a pure-bred leggy collie made a better lamping dog than a lurcher for I observed many collies that were amazingly dextrous at walking up lamped rabbits and catching them by guile rather than just with a blinding dash of speed.

Many rabbits, particularly in country that is heavily lamped, will sit tight as the dog approaches them and remain immobile despite the fact that they are illuminated by a beam of light and are clearly visible. These squatters or sitters will form the bulk of a lurcherman's catches in the early part of the season, though by the end of a season few rabbits will use this technique to escape capture. One in perhaps three or one in five rabbits will adopt this technique to escape capture and many squatters can be taken by elderly lurchers that have lost their speed. Pure-bred collies can be trained to catch such rabbits with ease and I own one such dog, a Muirhead-bred bearded collie, that will stalk squatters illuminated by the beam, seize them and return them live to hand. This collie finds some difficulty in catching a lamped rabbit that is running for home and is hopelessly outrun by a rabbit surprised during the daylight hours, but is easily as good as a fast lurcher at the art of picking up 'sitters'.

Few lampers favour huge lurchers, giants with deerhound blood close up in their immediate pedigrees, for such dogs while they are often very fast are seldom agile enough to work rabbits that are feeding close to fences or among tangles of farm machinery, which can prove to be a death trap for even a whippet-sized lurcher. Yet in some conditions a large dog will give an excellent account of itself. One of my best lamp dogs was Burke, the sire of my antique bitch Fathom, and Burke was a full twenty-eight inches tall. He had an excellent turn of speed and an agility that belied his great frame. At one time I became a fearful exhibitionist because of his ability to lift rabbits at the very moment they disappeared through the middle of a fence. Another extremely good lamp dog was Hancock's Timmy, a large dog and a very powerfully built lurcher, but an acrobat of the first order when he pursued lamped rabbits into hedges. He could turn on a sixpence, change gear when he needed to and was extremely soft-mouthed. His brother Romulus mated a great many bitches and produced a large number of competition dogs. Yet because Timmy was a gay pied (more white than colour) he was seldom used which is a great pity for I believe he was a better dog than his brother.

Thus most lamping dogs are quite small when compared to lurchers and longdogs that are used for daytime coursing. Most lampers seem to favour a small twenty-two- or twenty-three-inch dog with a medium turn of speed but with great agility. Rough or smooth coats make no difference to the efficiency of a lamp dog for such a lurcher is not expected to follow its game into cover but to return to hand immediately the game runs to ground or into thickets. Many lampers do in fact favour a smooth-coated lurcher as such a jacket is easier to stitch and will not conceal punctures and tears the way rough coats do.

A lamping dog needs stamina to complete a night's work, though tales of lamping dogs catching a hundred or so rabbits a night should be treated with some suspicion or regarded as harmless fibs. Few places host such a huge rabbit population anyway, and to perform such feats a dog might be required to run for perhaps thirteen miles a night. I ask the reader to visit a greyhound track and watch hounds that have run 800-yard races (a mere half a mile). Most are exhausted by their efforts and will be required to run this type of race perhaps only once a week or three times a fortnight. Tales of dogs catching a hundred rabbits every night of the week should be treated with some care. Young lurcher enthusiasts on hearing these absurd lies are apt to despair of the progress of their own puppies when they compare them to the wonder dogs owned by these beer-tent braggarts. It is sufficient to say that very few lurchermen catch a hundred rabbits a season, and never a hundred rabbits a night. Frankly, I despair of the fools who fill the heads of youngsters with such nonsense. If the lurcher enthusiast catches six or seven rabbits a night he is exceeding the average haul a lurcher makes and should shut his ears to nonsense. I confess that while I hear tales of phenomenal dogs that catch eight hares in eight runs or catch a huge number of rabbits a night, I have yet to see such animals.

However, I should expect any lurcher to retrieve the catches it makes 'on the lamp' and during the daylight hours, and here the tyro lurcher buff may be surprised to realise how many of these legendary hundred-a-night dogs refuse to retrieve or carry to hand. If the training described earlier in the book has been practised to the letter and if the lamper has been careful not to have a dog present while his lurcher carries and attempts to retrieve the rabbit, the chances are that his dog will be a competent retriever and thus will ensure that his nights are not spent chasing a difficult dog around a field or exhausting himself retrieving every catch his lurcher makes.

I prize a lurcher with a good nose like fine gold and would never breed from a lurcher that would not hunt like a spaniel. Yet a good nose can be a disadvantage where a lamp dog is concerned, particularly if the said lurcher has not been thoroughly trained. A lamp dog should, in theory, come straight back to hand should he fail to catch the rabbit he is chasing. A dog that continues to hunt up other rabbits, running head down on the scent oblivious to the calls of the handler, is not desirable. For this reason many handlers prefer to lamp dogs that have a poor or underde-veloped olfactory sense and decline to work the same dog with ferrets or allow the dog to hunt up rabbits during the daylight hours. This limits the lurcher's versatility somewhat and frankly reduces the dog's value considerably, for many strictly lamping dogs are sold for a song once their speed diminishes somewhat. However, if the trainer has spent some time over the initial training of the dog and has declined to take it into the hunting field until it has been thoroughly trained a lurcher need not be hunted to simply lamping, but I shall deal with this subject more fully later.

When I lived in Lichfield, Staffordshire my cottage overlooked some fields that were frequently lamped by poachers and I had ample opportunity to observe the performance of several types of dog. Some nights I would spend many hours simply watching youngsters with lurchers and lamp attempting to catch some of the rabbits that lived in the far hedgerow, and many of the antics I witnessed were highly entertaining but seldom indicative of good training. Most of these lampers owned dogs which were very poor retrievers and seldom were these dogs able to jump the gate that led out of the field. Many times I saw lampers shine their lamps on the gate and then lift their dogs over the gates or fence. The sight looked incongruous and smacked of amateurism. Yet some lampers claim it is bad practice to teach a dog to jump. It is argued, somewhat illogically I must say, that a dog that shows an inclination to jump while lamping will attempt to jump fences in the pitch darkness of a lamping night and thus come to grief when it leaps into the darkness and crashes into some chasm, deep ditch or onto ancient farm machinery of the type one finds on the edges of fields. Personally I have never been able to follow this line of reasoning and I have come to the conclusion this theory has grown out of the fact that many lurchers are so badly trained that they will not jump on command, hence the presence of a non-jumping lurcher is explained by an incompetent trainer who has been unable to train his dog to jump.

Some of my best lampers have been good all-round dogs though I freely admit that few of my lurchers are fast enough to put up even a reasonable show against a hare raised during daylight hours, though indifferent dogs will catch hares if the lurcher is aided by a lamp. All of my lurchers and longdogs have been taught to jump and the only lurcher I have owned that came to grief jumping was killed during the daylight hours when he leapt a hedge and landed on some abandoned farm machinery.

Virtually any cross-bred lurcher or longdog can be taught to lamp, after a fashion, though some crossbreds are more suitable than others. Some of the best lamping dogs I have seen had a strong baseline with only 50% greyhound in their pedigrees. I have seen half-bred German shepherd dogs, Bedlington hybrids and collie crosses perform dextrously on the lamp, and providing that the quarry that appears in the beam is not hostile, or likely to cause them harm, my own lurchers, which are essentially warreners' dogs, will also perform well on the lamp. Longdogs are not specifically tailored to work the lamp but can be trained to give a tolerably good performance as lampers.

Hancock of Sutton Coldfield, the world's most prolific breeder of collie/greyhound hybrids, states that most lampers prefer a half-bred collie greyhound hybrid to the more versatile three-quarter-bred hybrids, and the advantages of the half-bred are many. Most are easily trained and because of their strong trace of collie blood will respond to discipline readily. Furthermore, the sturdy, aesthetically unpleasing shape of first-cross collie hybrids usually means the dog will be durable and able to cope with collisions with fences and with tumbles that are likely to be sustained when running on wet grass. The life of a lamping dog that is worked regularly can in fact be very taxing and the turnover of lamping lurchers is often staggeringly high. Hancock records that one lamper who works a particularly thickly populated area of rabbits has purchased five half-bred collie lurchers over a period of ten years. Two were killed by what can only be described as freak accidents, one broke a shoulder blade after a collision with a fence and another damaged its feet by pursuing a hare out of the beam and running it along a tarmac road and the damage such a course can cause a dog is often horrific. If I might digress just a little to explain this point and perhaps deter lampers from working dogs on aeroplane runways, Merab, my best ferreting dog, ran two rabbits along a tarmac-covered road in 1990. The courses lasted only perhaps ten seconds apiece but her feet and stops were terribly skinned and she was lame for a fortnight. I hasten to add she has survived many seasons hunting rabbits on scree and very rough country indeed. Hancock, who breeds a variety of collie hybrids, states that the feet and frames of some of the bearded collie hybrids are far superior to their Border collie counterparts, and he has tales aplenty of beardie lurchers that have survived frightful accidents and lived to lamp another day. Beardie hybrids are, however, slower to mature and will remain quite infantile until they are two years of age. Chris Gilchrist of Cumbria tells the tale of giving one of these hybrids away when the youngster was eighteen months old only to watch it blossom into a useful working dog two months or so later – and such tales are legion.

The less common G.S.D. greyhound hybrids often make quite exceptional lamping dogs, if, that is, these hybrids are allowed a chance to mature, for G.S.D.s often take a lengthy period of time to grow up and take training seriously. These hybrids too are extremely durable and learn to retrieve readily. Few are aesthetically pleasing and many are too heavy to appeal to the less than discerning eye of the average lurcher enthusiast. Still, I have seen many of these hybrids that were incredibly versatile lamping dogs and I have yet to see one that was deficient in courage or stamina. I have often thought that for anyone wishing for a lamping dog that had size, courage and tractability it would be policy to breed such a dog. As I have mentioned, Steve Barton of Abergavenny has achieved an excellent reputation using a G.S.D. greyhound hybrid as a lamping dog.

Almost as popular as the collie greyhound as a lamping dog is the Bedlington greyhound lurcher. These dogs really look the part and this hybrid is apparently everyone's idea of what a lurcher should be, type-wise if not performance-wise. Though scarcely as versatile as the collie hybrid the Bedlington greyhound is fairly easily trained and quite tenacious despite the somewhat fragile appearance of the Bedlington terrier. There is certainly a terrific market for genuine Bedlington grey-hound hybrids as lamping dogs and anyone starting a lurcher-breeding kennels would be wise to consider the production of a Bedlington grey-hound project.

Some of the best lamping lurchers are some of the very mongrelised twenty-two-inch lurchers advertised in papers such as *Shooting News* and *Exchange and Mart*. Many of these dogs, though sporting dubious and entirely spurious pedigrees, have several generations of successful lamping dogs in their pedigrees, and this fact coupled with their extremely low price (many are sold for far less than they cost to rear to weaning) make them extremely good buys. I have seen some very good mongrelised lamping dogs, dogs of very questionable pedigrees perhaps, that resembled very large, heavily built whippets and some of these lurchers are prepared to give their all to catch rabbits and even the occasional hare that appears in the beam. Some of these dogs were purchased as puppies for as little as ten pounds and as lamp dogs pure and simple they were truly excellent value though admittedly I have seen better all-round workers.

I have yet to see true-bred longdogs that were satisfactory lamping dogs for dogs bred for lamping need at least some base blood to give them durability and tractability. Deerhound hybrids, splendid as they are, are too big to give of their best at lamping, while the cut and thrust experts, the whippet greyhounds, are not durable enough to endure the knocks and bumps of regular lamping. Saluki hybrids are rarely biddable and are quite unsuitable lampers' dogs. It is in fact absolutely bewildering as to why anyone would wish to breed saluki lurchers with an eye to the production of lamp dogs. Most are slow off the mark, seldom possessing the early pace that is needed in a lamping dog, and the stamina for which the saluki is renowned is a result, in part at least, of the strange loping style of running adopted by this desert hound. A lamping dog needs to be quick thinking, quick to act and must have good early pace. Saluki blood will nullify rather than enhance these qualities and I have yet to see a saluki-bred longdog I considered to be an efficient and suitable lamping dog. As single-handed coursing dogs saluki composites are ideal, particularly when the courses are long and arduous, but saluki blood should never be used in the creation of a lamping dog.

Now to the equipment that needs to be carried by this hunter. Some of the lamping kits that are available are truly amazing and so technical that they are quite difficult for the layman to repair. Having said that these pieces of equipment are virtually foolproof and are often quite robust and indestructible. Most are quite expensive and are quite attractive pieces of equipment. Cheap but useful lamping kits can be made if one visits a breaker's yard and obtains a motorbike battery and a quartz halide lamp. It is relatively easy to wire up the battery to the lamp and if one attaches a switch to make or break a current a cheap yet efficient lamping kit can easily be constructed. Frankly, I am anything but technical but I have constructed some hideous Heath Robinson devices that have worked reasonably, though not particularly, well. One of the advantages, indeed perhaps the only advantage, of using these home-made lamping kits is the fact that the parts are so easily and cheaply replaced by yet another visit to a breaker's yard. Lamping forays are not only strenuous affairs but often destructive to the lamping equipment. I have broken many batteries and quite a few spotlights on lamping trips, and once lost an entire home-made kit when I stumbled into a peat hole, but I was always able to rebuild or repair such kits at the minimum of expense. My kits were always carried in knapsacks on my back and the fabric of the knapsack (and also my jeans) was corroded by the acid that spilled from the battery. After one trip the spillage was so bad that my legs and abdomen were a mass of sores that took some explaining to the school doctor who examined me one day. Later I was to resolve the problem, and the tale of how I did so is perhaps worth the telling.

At the time I was hunting an estate near to my cottage in Lichfield and the estate was greatly troubled by poachers. After one party was disturbed by the police and a gamekeeper one of the lampers abandoned his kit and I observed that his battery was carried in a cut-down gallon-sized plastic container which contained the inevitable acid spillage. Henceforth I adopted this method of protecting my knapsack and clothes. It's an ill wind, so to speak.

The art or technique of lamping is simplicity itself but the stories concerned with lamping techniques are legion. Many lampers function outside the law so to speak – a delicious euphemism for poaching – hence lampers take stringent measures to avoid capture or apprehension. It can be argued that a broad beam sweeping around the estate is likely to attract attention so poachers take certain measures to make the beam less conspicuous, if, that is, any beam of light can ever be considered inconspicuous on the darkest nights that are favoured by lampers. There are many ways such a beam of light can be restricted – a cowl made from a large tin can will direct the beam somewhat but others favour painting in the perimeter of the lamp with a black bitumastic paint to produce a very narrow beam, but I believe these devices are nothing but superfluous and little short of being simple affectations. A broad brilliant beam of light will not only illuminate the quarry but will also illuminate the dangers and pitfalls into which a lamping lurcher may run. It is generally believed that the larger or broader the beam of light, the more land is illuminated and the less likely the lurcher is to come to grief during a lamping session.

At the risk of being accused of glorifying the poacher by discussing his techniques, it can be argued that a pencil-thin beam of light sweeping the fields is more likely to attract attention than a broad beam which may be mistaken for the light of a motorbike. Lampers have the notion that they can become invisible when they lamp, and so fascinating is the pursuit of a rabbit by a lurcher that many lampers are oblivious to the dangers of poaching after dark. Certainly the poacher can shine the beam on anyone approaching him and then switch off the beam and vanish into the darkness, leaving his pursuer baffled and blinded. Few lampers are caught red-handed in the act of poaching. At one time tales of police officers and gamekeepers alike engaging in pursuits of lampers across grass and plough were legion, though it takes a very determined keeper to venture out after dark to apprehend a lamper. It is virtually impossible for the keeper to determine whether a band of poachers is accompanying the lamper and few poachers will accept a 'fair cop' and come quietly when apprehended by a single gamekeeper. Furthermore, a lamper chooses an inclement night to practise his hobby, a night when wind and sometimes rain will conspire to make the blackness of a moonless night even more forbidding, and it requires a very tenacious keeper to venture abroad on such a night, particularly as at one time the courts treated lampers as jokes or curious eccentrics.

During the late 1960s and early 1970s, when lamping became very popular, there were tales of some sickening schemes used by thwarted keepers to deter poachers who lamped game and disturbed pheasants. One tale that is still repeated around Leicestershire is the story of a particularly persistent lamper who continued to plague a certain estate even after he was apprehended and fined. In revenge the keeper strung piano wire twenty-three inches above ground level between two gateposts and by dint of a key tightened the wire until it literally 'sang' on windy nights. Game, rabbits and hares passed under the wire unharmed but a pursuing lurcher was virtually decapitated by it. Yet another grisly tale is that of the embittered keeper who stuck pointed sticks into the ground – in a manner similar to Welsh archers to prevent a cavalry attack – and the keeper found lurchers impaled on these devices the following morning. Whether or not these tales are apocryphal or simply meant to deter poachers is questionable, but the rising popularity of lurcher keeping in the early 1970s produced a spate of embittered and thwarted gamekeepers who seemed helpless against the hordes of lampers who plagued certain estates. It was said that the land around Wolverhampton was so fearfully over-poached that as soon as a rabbit came out to feed nine or ten beams of light illuminated it.

Keepers are now more efficient at apprehending lamp-carrying poachers and seldom venture into the fields to arrest them. They now simply wait near the poacher's car for the lamper to return and arrest him as he tries to load the swag. Many lampers will park a car two or three miles away to avoid detection or simply cache the game and return for it the next day when they are unlikely to be detected. Whether or not poaching by dint of lamps is decreasing is questionable. Certainly one hears of few poachers who are apprehended these days, though in the early 1970s arrests and convictions were commonly reported.

Before leaving the subject of poaching and returning to legal lamping (and it is not an offence to lamp rabbits if one has permission to do so) it is perhaps of interest to analyse a poacher's motives for practising his vocation. Romantic fiction would have the reader believe that the poacher was simply an honest man driven to lawlessness to support a wife and family or a Robin Hood figure out to avenge the wrongs committed by some landowner. In point of fact a number of studies concerning poachers and poaching have revealed that if a person is convicted of poaching there is a strong possibility that the poacher will have already committed several petty thefts. Most convicted poachers have previous convictions in fact and are seldom in such desperate plight that they need to poach to support a family. Poaching has simply been regarded as fun and arrest and conviction regarded as an occupational hazard. True the odd law-abiding person out to seek work for his lurchers will occasionally be arrested and convicted of poaching, but the majority of dyed-in-the-wool poachers were criminally inclined long before they discovered the pleasures of owning a lurcher.

Let us now turn to the subject of legitimate lamping and the conditions that make for a profitable night's hunting. A moonlit night is scarcely conducive to a good night's lamping. The rabbits are often able to watch the lamper and his dog approaching and, as rabbits are unsporting creatures, will race to the security of their burrows long before the lamper has a chance to slip his dog, or, if the dog is well trained, to urge the dog to chase the rabbit. It would be false to say that a moonlit night will result in a totally fruitless venture, but there are better nights for lamping. A pitch-black moonless night with a high wind and perhaps a slight drizzle presents the most productive of conditions for lamping. Such a night would give encouragement to the rabbits to feed far from the burrow and thus afford the dog the chance of a lengthy run and possibly a catch or so. Rabbits are unlikely to wish to feed in heavy rain but light drizzle and a high wind will deaden the sound of the footsteps of the approaching lamper and his dog. Ideally a rabbit should feel confident enough to sit tight until the hunter is close enough to slip his lurcher. The further a rabbit is feeding from its burrow the more likely the lurcher is to catch the rabbit. Rabbits sitting close to hedgerows or near to the mouths of burrows will seldom be caught and are often ignored by an experienced lurcher. In March 1992 I buried my elderly lurcher Fathom. One of her gifts was to be able to gauge just how far from its burrow a rabbit was feeding. If it was too close to a burrow or hedge she ignored it but pursued it with great enthusiasm if she gauged it was far enough from home for her to catch. Her ability to shortcut a rabbit, to get between the rabbit and its burrow, was little short of incredible and as she grew older she became even more dextrous at catching lamped rabbits. She would espy squatters and attempt to walk around them in order to cut off their escape routes should they decide to run, and frankly I could not ask for a better lamping dog. Her daughter is not as fast nor as adept as a lamper but has other qualities I value as highly.

A tilt at rabbits on a moonlit night is not only likely to be unproductive but counter-productive. Rabbits are not particularly intelligent creatures but they do learn what exactly constitutes danger. If rabbits are lamped regularly and manage to escape from the lurcher the chances are that they will associate a beam of light with danger and run for home as soon as they observe it. Thus a stroll out with a lurcher on a moonlit night is likely to educate rabbits rather than capture them. In some district rabbits are lamped so regularly that they are virtually impossible to approach, racing back to their burrows as soon as a lamper steps into the field where they are feeding. It is worth noting that in September a lamper may catch quite a haul of unsophisticated rabbits, but as the season progresses his haul will get smaller. Not only will there be fewer rabbits out feeding at night but those which have survived the autumnal onslaught will be aware of the dangers a beam of light may bring. It is so desperately frustrating for a dog to fail to catch every rabbit it chases that the lamper would do well to find other interests during that period of the month lit by a full moon.

A dog just starting out on a career as a lamper needs all the help it can get to start it catching lamped rabbits. Some lurchers may take some little time to follow the course of the beam and may sniff the ground near their feet to savour the scent of rabbits, but ignore the rabbits moving within the beam of light. However, once the dog begins to associate the beam of light with rabbits it is virtually entered, or at least as far as catching lamped rabbits is concerned. The first rabbit the dog is allowed to run should provide an easy chase, for nothing succeeds like success and young dogs soon sour of the game if rabbit after rabbit escapes them. If possible the young dog should be started at a rabbit feeding some way from its burrow and the rabbit should be sitting tight as the lamper and his dog approaches. Some rabbits will sit so tight that a lamper needs to touch them with his foot to make them move. These are the sort of quarry one needs to start a puppy, and as soon as the rabbit begins to move the dog should be slipped.

Yet I have seen some intelligent lurchers that were reluctant to follow the beam and insisted on scenting the ground near their feet. These can be encouraged to watch the beam, so to speak, by running an old-school master lurcher on the lamp and allowing the puppy to watch the lamping session – the puppy of course should be kept on the leash, for two dogs running a lamped rabbit is a formula for disaster and I have seen dogs die after collisions at thirty miles an hour. Once more I must beg the indulgence of the reader, but I feel the following tale is too good to omit.

Just as the Irish seem to be the butt of British humour and the supposed gaucherie of the Pole the American, so the ineptitude of the Caithnessian lurcher keeper occupies the same position in the lurcher world. Hence many ridiculous tales are told of Caithnessian lurcher keepers. The following tale is, however, absolutely true. I have mentioned the dangers of running dogs over tarmac surfaces and the damage wrought to the dog's feet when they encounter the mixture of tar and gravel. I have also mentioned the dangers of running two dogs together after dark. Thus when I was approached by a tale-telling, yarn-spinning Caithnessian lurcher owner who announced, 'See this dog [a lame animal with a decidedly pained expression], of the nine lurchers we lamped at hare on the airport runway this was the fastest,' I groaned aloud.

This digression brings me quite neatly to the subject of lamping hares, and the morality of such a practice is a hotly debated subject among lurcher keepers. A brown hare (I shall deal with the creature more fully in a later chapter) is a miracle of athleticism and during the daylight hours more than a match for the fastest, fittest, most tenacious longdog. However, when lamped the brown hare can fall victim to a second-rate lurcher, the sort of dog that would not be able to come to terms with let alone catch a hare during the daytime. It is argued by longdog keepers that it is morally wrong to lamp a creature that provides the greatest sporting challenge to any sighthound, longdog or lurcher. However, it can be argued that if the lurcher is kept for the purpose of filling the pot rather than as a coursing dog pure and simple, any means the hunter employs to bag the hare is fair, and lamping is certainly one of the very best ways of catching a hare. During the daylight hours a hare runs a well known, well marked circuitous route and when pursued will run only over the track it knows well. After dark a hare will often be driven from the familiar runs and in panic will fall prey to even a moderately dextrous sort of lurcher. Such is the panic experienced by the hare when it is hard pressed by a lamping dog that there are few lampers who cannot tell tales of having to sidestep to avoid the hare running into them. Many hares are in fact taken if a lamper keeps his head and sticks out his foot to intercept the panic-stricken hare.

Thus the morality of lamping hares, and I shall close the subject with yet another anecdote. One of the less speedy lurchers is my own lurcher Merab, though her perspicacity makes up for any shortfalls in speed. When she is hunting free a hare that springs up in front of her is viewed with interest and then ignored. She is only too aware that she cannot catch them, for in the past she has tried and failed. When a hare appears in the beam, however, she pursues it eagerly for she is also aware that she is able to catch a hare when it is lamped.

However, there are a few other reasons why many serious lampers will switch off the lamp when a hare appears in the beam. Despite the fact that a hare can be taken by quite an indifferent lurcher when it appears in the spotlight, the dog needs to expend considerable energy if it is to catch the hare. The reader must ignore the tales of lurchers catching fifty hares a night without raising a sweat (I am aware that dogs don't sweat). Such stories are untrue. The pursuit of a lamped hare will certainly tax a fit lurcher and deplete its energy reserves sorely. In short, the energy a dog uses up to catch a hare could be more profitably expended in the pursuit and capture of rabbits. If a hare is put up early in the evening and chased by the lamping lurcher the dog will seldom be fit enough to put up a good show at rabbits as the night progresses, and the pursuit of two or more hares will usually leave a dog looking decidedly jaded. A lamped hare run by a tired dog at the end of a hard night's lamping can easily ruin the fittest lamping dogs and I suspect that many of the myriad lamping dogs that are offered for sale have been subjected to a few too many runs at strong hares. A lamping dog, no matter what its breeding, will give many years' honest service if not overrun or overtaxed during its nights' activity. Thus when experienced lampers are working an area that is thickly populated with rabbits they are inclined to ignore hares that appear in the beam. Hares are not only taxing to the dog and heavy for the lamper to carry, but are also difficult to sell.

If I might once more refer to the contents of David Hancock's diary, the toll that frequent lamping forays takes on lurchers is little short of terrifying. Tales of dogs that have been killed by running into gates and tree stumps abound. Casualties, lamping dogs that have run over the edges of disused quarries or into craters in fields, are equally common. When a lurcher or longdog springs a hare or rabbit during daylight hours and pursues the quarry the pursuer is often in great danger for hares and rabbits alike will seek refuge in curious places where rubbish and wire sometimes combine to produce death traps for a lurcher. After dark these hazards obviously become doubly dangerous, and so frequent are the injuries sustained by lamping lurchers that one is tempted to believe that rabbits, and particularly hares, actually plan the destruction of the dog pursuing them. Some injuries lurchers receive are horrific. At one time I knew a Midlands-based lurcherman whose sole claim to fame (if fame is the correct word) was that he swapped or sold his lurchers with great regularity during the winter months and even increased his turnover during spring and summer. I have known ten or twelve dogs pass through his hands in the course of a month. All were tried, tested and found wanting before being sent back to the Birmingham-based dealer whence they came. In short, while he found the dogs he bought were deficient he never once managed to train a dog of his own.

However, one night in mid-winter I was awakened by a furious banging on my front door and I arose to find this lurcher buff bathed in blood with a very damaged lurcher in his arms. Blood poured from a wound in the dog's head and the animal moaned softly as it was moved. On examination it was found that a sharp metal prong had been driven into the dog's eye, crushing the eyeball and embedding in the skull behind the eye. I phoned my veterinary surgeon who came out and by dint of a surgical operation removed the tine, a chunk of rusted metal that was probably part of a bedstead. It speaks highly of the tenacity and constitution of a lurcher that the dog recovered, though the remains of the right eye needed to be removed. It speaks less highly of the morality of the lurcher fraternity that the dog was sold on, and some five years later the animal was still being passed around the lurcher circuit and once more appeared in Lichfield under a new name, with a different pedigree and a ficticious history. The lot of the typical lamping lurcher is indeed far from envious and I could relate a dozen more heartrending tales.

At one time I spent a great many winter nights lamping and seldom did any of my dogs acquire any serious injury as a result of the nocturnal activities. I honestly believe that the reason for my good luck was the fact that I never lamped unfamiliar ground so I knew the hazards and pitfalls the lurcher might encounter and deliberately avoided them. If I might quote the curious wisdom of Moses Aaron Smith; 'A good jockey will always walk the course before racing it', and in my case it paid off for I seldom had a lurcher *hors de combat* after a night's lamping. Certainly a recipe for disaster seems to be a hop over the fence on familiar land with an unfit dog that has been fed immediately prior to the lamping foray. Any breeders of lamping lurchers or lurchers that are used primarily as lampers could tell similar tales of the awful death rate of lamping dogs.

Pitfalls and hazards abound in the British countryside, but the greatest danger must surely be barbed wire. These unholy lengths of wire criss-cross the British countryside and it is a fortunate lamping dog that does not encounter wire during its lamping career. I have seen some ghastly rips that have been infected when a dog has brushed against the tines of the wire as it chased a rabbit or hare, and I have watched hares run to and fro under wire as if inviting the dog to chance its luck and life pursuing them. In 1979 I saw the most awful damage wrought when a coursing hound brushed against the wire when chasing a rabbit near Burton-on-Trent. I was visiting a vet who was inoculating a batch of terrier puppies I had bred and sharing the waiting room with a gentle, effete-looking lady and an enormous, aggressive-looking man who had the sort of facial bruising that bespoke the lifestyle he sought to enjoy. I was settling in for a very long wait when the door opened and a young man appeared carrying a bundle of blankets from the top of which the head of what appeared to be a very large whippet protruded. Blood oozed from the blanket and formed large spots on the surgery waiting room floor. The panic the young man was experiencing was obvious from the expression on his face, so I tapped on the receptionist window and requested that the vet attend to the young man who almost fell onto the waiting room chair and released his hold on the blanket. The bundle opened to reveal a smooth-coated bitch which was torn from neck to flank, and a huge flap of skin had folded back to reveal the muscles of the chest, neck and flanks. The effete lady stepped forward to reassemble the bundle but the tough-looking man in the corner went a strange pasty white and fainted with a crash on the waiting room floor. I have never seen such a frightful wound and the dog resembled an animal that had been partly skinned. To cut a very long story short the vet took the dog into the surgery and performed some sort of veterinary wizardry, for a month later I saw the lurcher walking near Stowe Pool in Lichfield. It speaks highly of the constitution of this particular longdog that it survived the shock of such frightful lacerations.

However, a puncture from a single tine of barbed wire can cause quite serious problems for a dog of any breed. A puncture often passes unnoticed where as a large tear cries out to be treated. I have learned from experience to check a lurcher after I have observed a collision with a barbed wire strand, and once more I ask the reader to tolerate yet another anecdote. One of the gamest lurchers I have ever owned was Penguin, one of the matriarchs of the strain of lurcher I keep, though her descendants were anything but game. Penguin, however, had the sort of reckless courage that is admired by some but not by me, I'm afraid. One day in 1970 she chanced on a fox feeding on a rubbish tip near Tamworth and chased the creature into a barbed wire tangle where without further ado she dispatched her quarry in the adept manner that had made her quite famous. Apart from a single puncture on the muzzle she appeared unharmed and I forgot the incident. A week later she looked decidedly ill and began to develop the loose skin of a dog that was obviously dehydrated. A small hole in a hind leg muscle was still open and exuding an unhealthy-looking fluid. I cleaned her wound, placed her under a heat lamp and for a while she appeared to recover, and even condescended to eat, but a week later she looked desperately ill. I took her to the surgery in Lichfield where Richard Jones, my veterinary surgeon, put her on a drip and injected her with an antibiotic, but the wound on her hind leg continued to seep something nasty and necrotic. I applied gentle pressure to the sides of the puncture and out shot the tine of barbed wire, after which Penguin returned to good health, sufficiently well to be able to breed Paul Jackson's Pip, a grand old lady who died in 1993. Whether or not Penguin would have recovered if I had not removed this badly rusted tine is a moot point, but since then I have always checked lamping dogs as soon as I have returned from a lamping session.

The working life of a lamping dog is reputed to be short and few dogs are worked until their dotage. However, with care and attention a lamping dog's working life can be increased dramatically. The lives of some of these dogs can be extremely strenuous during the winter months when this pursuit is practised. In rabbit-infested conditions a lamping dog may run great distances during its night's work and endure great hardships. Many of these dogs will run distances of up to four miles or more to secure their catches, and the toll such strenuous exercise takes on a dog is frightful. In the early 1970s when I began collecting scientific data on running dogs of all types I frequently weighed lurchers before and after a lamping trip and found that after a hard night's lamping a lurcher would have lost as much as four pounds in weight. Thus a lurcher should never be worked if it is in an emaciated condition, for no dog that is not carrying some reserves can endure a hard night's work without suffering greatly.

Tales of dogs collapsing after a furious night's work are alas not only legion but true, and discretion should be exercised at all times during a lamping session. If a dog returns to the handler winded by the exercise it has undergone it should not be run again until it has recovered no matter how many rabbits appear in the beam and no matter how tempting it is to run the dog just one more time, for lurchers, particularly lurchers with a strong trace of sighthound in their ancestry, will continue to try to catch long after they are physically exhausted. One of the common criticisms of dogs with a strong baseline is that they will not try as hard as a sighthound-saturated lurcher. This is scarcely a criticism, for a dog that knows when it has depleted its energy reserves will live to run another day; a dog that will run until it is dead (prized by some, one supposes) will see a very short working life. Indeed the production of lurchers involves, quite simply, the tempering of the sighthound disposition with base blood to give the composite more sense than its sighthound parent. Frankly I have never valued the crazy sort of do or die disposition. When my lurchers have had enough I know it. I also expect them to know it and the evening's lamping is terminated forthwith. Yet I have seen many who continue to run desperately winded, jaded dogs at rabbits long after it is patently obvious the dog is far from well. I would suggest that anyone who wants a dog that will try until it is dead (a common appraisal of the qualities of some lurchers) would do well to buy a greyhound rather than a lurcher, for some greyhounds will give their all in an attempt to capture rabbits and hares.

Far too many 'blown' dogs are doing the rounds of the dog dealers at the time of writing. These dogs have been run to a state of exhaustion and then a shade further by less than caring owners. Subsequently these dogs damage heart, lungs or diaphragm and are henceforth virtually worthless as lamping dogs or working lurchers. These are the trained lamping dogs sold by the majority of dog dealers, and only when the animal has been run hard will its problems manifest themselves. Sadly such dogs change hands rapidly, passing like ping pong balls from unsuspecting buyer to unsuspecting buyer until one night the dog's constitution can take no more and it collapses and dies, or, if it is a shade more lucky, in some kennel the day after it has collapsed. The reader would be horrified to realise how many dogs finish their lives in such a manner, and frankly such stories should deter anyone from breeding surplus lurchers. Once my lurchers begin to look jaded I head for home and ignore even sitters that appear in the beam as I walk homeward. I live in an area with an abundant rabbit population and many rabbits rise and run, thus tempting my lurcher to run yet again, but I ignore them. I prize my lurcher far higher than the price of a rabbit so when rabbits appear I simply grip their leashes tighter and turn for home. I am perhaps fortunate that my own strain of lurcher is so strong in baseline (collie bred) that they have sense to know when they have had enough, and furthermore I also have the sense to know when to stop.

Mob-handed lamping is decidedly injurious to the lurcher, for not only does the presence of another dog damage the lurcher's retrieving (lurchers will circle and stay away from the handler if another dog is waiting behind to snatch up the rabbit the lurcher is carrying) but the presence of human competitors – and every mob-handed lurcher lamping venture will end up as some sort of competition – will encourage the lurcher handler to run his dog one more time which brings about the dog's destruction. I detest meeting other lurcher owners who have dogs with them, for not only do I seldom see lurchers that can vaguely be referred to as 'trained' but I consider the state of rivalry that springs up when two or more lurcher owners come together out of keeping with a lamping trip. I will not venture out of doors if the hunting trip is likely to develop into a mob-handed caper.

Mob-handed lamping trips are often dangerous. It is a racing certainty that once a dog is running a rabbit another lurcher will escape to join it, and collisions are inevitable. When I have embarked on lamping trips and found a fellow enthusiast, lurcher on leash and an assurance he will keep the dog under control if he is allowed to come along, I return my dogs to the car and if my companion is a friend merely request he runs his dogs and I give mine a rest for the evening. However, more often that not I will go to some pains to ensure I have no company when I embark on a lamping trip. I am perhaps fortunate in as much as I am a solitary sort of person who enjoys his own company, but the reader would do well to avoid 'lamping parties'.

Lamping accidents are more common at the start of the season than at the end, or to be more accurate, a lot more frequent in September than in March. Few lampers seem to have the wit or wisdom to understand that a dog cannot be taken from its kennel unfit and be expected to give a good performance in the field. My own lurchers seldom venture onto the moor during the summer months and in August are decidedly unfit and are certainly ill-prepared for work. Thus I am aware that if I fielded them in this condition a single hard night's lamping would kill them, or at least sorely hurt them. So before they are taken on a hunting trip they are given some gentle exercise daily and the exercise increases as the hunting season approaches. By September they are moderately fit and are lightly worked for a week until they are fit enough to endure a hard night's work. Only then are they allowed to work hard and regularly.

Yet another reason for the high casualty rate at the start of the season is the incredible number of rabbits that are found out feeding in the first weeks of September. All fears that myxomatosis will ever again prevent the rabbit from becoming numerous can now be ignored, and while it is true that myxomatosis will always wipe out roughly a quarter of the rabbits infected with this disease September finds a superabundance of rabbits. A large rabbit population will always tempt the unwise lamper to try his luck and continue to lamp long after the dog has had enough. Thus a desperate situation exists in September for an unfit dog is faced with a glut of rabbits and most lampers are so shortsighted that they are unable to see the dangers of running an unfit dog too hard at the start of the season. Veterinary surgeons must surely rub their hands with glee once the summer starts to draw to a close – and the cup of the unscrupulous dog dealer must surely runneth over.

A dog may display many indications of distress at the end of a hard night's lamping. A fit dog, one not unduly winded or injured by a hard night's lamping, will have a voracious appetite when it returns home. No lamping dog (or daytime worker for that matter) should be fed immediately prior to a lamping session for no lurcher will perform well on a full stomach. Hence a lamping dog will probably be fasted for perhaps twenty hours before it is required to work. A further four hours of hard work will ensure the dog has a hearty appetite. A healthy lurcher will on returning from a lamping session set about its food with gusto before it falls on its bed and goes into a deep coma-like sleep. A lurcher that returns from a lamping session and seeks its bed without attempting to feed or actively rejects its food should be of some concern to the lurcher owner, for something is clearly amiss. It is in fact little short of lunacy to take such a dog lamping again the night following such behaviour, for the dog is clearly unwell. If the dog still rejects his food the following day it is perhaps time to seek expert advice, and the only expert advice one should seek is from a qualified veterinary surgeon. To run an unfit and unhappy lurcher is a recipe for disaster.

A dog that climbs onto its bed and is obviously in pain should be treated with some care, particularly if the dog refuses to feed. Strains and bruises are almost inevitable even if a very fit dog is worked hard, but serious strains need time to repair. A dog that is in obvious discomfort should be left at home rather than taken out again the night following a hard lamping, for the finest cure for muscle strain is rest, and complete rest I must add, and only when the dog is 'chipper' and eager to go again should it be taken out of its kennel. A heat lamp placed above the dog's bed or a warm place near the fireside is wonderfully therapeutic and it is amazing to see how quickly a dog will recover if it is kept warm. At one time I placed every dog I lamped under a heat lamp for a full hour or so after the night's lamping session and I must confess I had few lay-offs that season. Many lurcher keepers massage their wards before and after a lamping session and this treatment is said to be very efficacious, though I have neither skill nor time enough to learn to indulge in this practice. Greyhound trainers swear by massage before and after a race, and trainers of professional boxers are usually quite skilled in manipulating weary muscles.

A dog should be quite keen to drink once it has returned from a lamping session, though it is very bad policy to allow a dog to take water in between runs. I avoid letting my lurchers drink from streams, not because I am wary of the toxic wastes such waterways may carry, but because a dog with a stomach full of water will not give of its best in the field. On its return to kennels, however, a lamping lurcher should be allowed to drink its fill. When I lamped my lurcher bitch Penguin, one of the greatest triers I have ever encountered I should add, I weighed her before and after her lamping sessions. At the start of the season Penguin weighed fifty-three or so pounds and exactly fifty pounds when fit, for in her prime Penguin was a solid, heavily built, though exceedingly fast, dog. After one five-hour session of lamping near Bakewell I was alarmed to see her weight fall to forty-five pounds and she looked decidedly dehydrated. She drank a copious amount of liquid and fell into such a deep sleep that I left her on the seat of my van and travelled to school with her. She slept until late evening despite the pestering my class inflicted on her. Penguin left the van when I returned home and I weighed her immediately. She was three ounces short of exactly fifty pounds.

Some lurcher owners have a great ability to gauge weight and to ascertain the optimum running weight for a particular lurcher or longdog – and there is no doubt that lamping dogs, like running hounds, run best if fielded at exactly the right weight. Long before the reign of the huge heavyweights – the dreadnoughts of boxing – it was revealed that boxers fought best at a specific weight; Marciano was best at a particular weight which fluctuated only a little during his reign as heavyweight champion. Above that weight his performance was sluggish, below that weight his devastating hitting power was found wanting. The very best gauge of a lurcher's weight is a weighing machine but I feel that the ability of the late Hughie Levenson was as good. Hughie was a weight fanatic and dieted his own weight until the day of his death, I believe. He had boxed in the booths, fought in the legitimate rings and trained young fighters to a nicety. He was able to look at a whippet, handle it and then state its weight to the pound. I have no such gifts, I'm afraid, and I resort to a weighing machine to gauge a lurcher's optimum weight.

Still on the subject of allowing a lurcher to drink its fill, one of the most important advancements in veterinary science in the last few years is the use of the electrolyte solution. Electrolyte solutions were originally designed to replace water lost through diarrhoea and other illnesses but are priceless aids for animals that have undergone terrific physical exertion and have had the components of their body fluids altered by this exertion. These solutions should be made up according to the maker's instructions and given to lurchers immediately they have returned from lamping trips. Dogs that have undergone terrific physical exertion certainly recover more quickly if fed correctly compounded electrolyte solutions, and some lampers estimate that they can work dogs more regularly if electrolyte solutions are used to revive jaded dogs. Personally, while I use electrolyte solutions quite regularly I believe that once a dog becomes jaded or is obviously physically exhausted after a hard night's work only rest will solve the problem, though rest alone is sometimes not enough. Lurchers are tough, durable dogs but their lifestyles are sometimes extremely harsh and testing, and if these dogs are to give of their best they need a great deal of care.

I am very much a creature of habit and I attempt to lead a fairly orderly lifestyle, even though I seldom seem to succeed in doing so. At one time lamping was almost an obsession and I believe that I lost teaching posts, and certainly never advanced myself, because of my interests. For nearly two years I lamped four nights a week during winter and ratted throughout the summer. Sometimes so compulsive was my obsession that I would lamp my lurchers after my terriers retired to kennels after a ratting session and then turn up for work the following morning. I knew the moon phases by heart and could recite the lighting up times like a parrot – and I am aware that I became a crashing bore because of my passions. Such is the magnetism of lamping, I suppose.

At that time I ran Penguin and Fathom on alternate nights and often ran them to a state of exhaustion, though I became very fit in the process of doing so. My haul of rabbits varied considerably from night to night, but my routine was always the same. If the moon phase was correct (and

I actually experienced some form of withdrawal symptoms during the nights of the full moon) I would start to load up my dogs and equipment some twenty minutes before lighting up time. I would then journey to the spot I intended to lamp and continue to work the dogs until they began to show some signs of exhaustion or, as happened later, I began to feel tired. I would then load all the equipment, dogs and catch into my van and carry the rabbits in the front seat – my lurchers are decidedly untrustworthy where rabbits are concerned, unless they are very tired. Indeed I could evaluate the physical condition of Fathom by the way she behaved to the rabbits I brought home. If she attempted to set about them voraciously I knew she was well, if she ignored them I knew she was under the weather and needed rest and treatment.

On arriving home I engaged in what must have appeared an absurd ritual. I plugged in the electric kettle after filling it with three cupfuls of water and while the kettle boiled I raced through the process of checking my lamp and battery and plugging the battery into the battery charger. I then poured the water into the teapot and raced outside to bring in my dogs and my catch before drinking the tea. I then checked the dogs' feet and eyes (eyes are sometimes injured or inflamed by a night's lamping) and gave them a drink of electrolyte solution; while I watched them drink it I finished my second cup of tea. I then spent ten minutes or so checking over the lurcher for tears and rips before feeding and bedding her down, and then returned to bed for what remained of the rest of the night.

I arose at six a.m., filled the kettle and while the kettle boiled I checked the battery and battery charger. I then poured the tea and drank it as I checked the lurcher that had lamped the night before and the lurcher I was about to use that night, while I let my terriers out to exercise. I then put the terriers away in their kennels and fed the ferrets before bathing and going to school. Small wonder my job suffered, and I cannot blame any headmaster for wishing that I moved on to pastures that, if not greener, were at least newer. I looked decidedly dishevelled, but my dogs were always magnificent.

I honestly believe I would have continued my very orderly, if very eccentric, lifestyle until today had it not been for a back injury that placed me in hospital for two weeks or so and, thankfully, this period of time brought about a break in my habit pattern. Lamping is so addictive that I have known apparently happy families split asunder when the husband or wife has been bitten by the bug, and I am inclined to believe that the pursuit of rabbits during the hours of darkness awakens ancient race memories that once awakened are hard to suppress. I enjoyed many happy hours lamping and though I confess it wrecked my career and rendered me permanently weary and sleep-shotten, I don't believe I would alter a single minute if I had my life to live again. During this period I became as much part of the night as the darkness and knew every police officer by name, for I was stopped several times until the force came to accept my eccentricities and simply ignored me. It was in fact a glorious happy time in my life, one I knew only too well could not last!

11

The Lurcher by Day

These days the majority of lurcher owners are lampers, but it was not always so. The lightweight motorcycle battery is a relatively recent innovation and prior to its perfection only the extremely strong and often extremely eccentric went lamping with heavy-duty car batteries strapped to their backs. Gerald Jones, who once wrote so skilfully under the pseudonym Dan Russell, once told me of some of his college friends who took turns carrying an old jeep battery while a track-bred greyhound caught rabbits illuminated by the beam, but prior to the 1950s the lurcher was used as a daytime hunter rather than a lamping dog.

It would be ridiculous to state that without the use of artificial lights the lurcher is unable to catch rabbits feeding after dark. When I lived in Lichfield it was my custom to turn loose Fathom and Penguin in the fields behind my house immediately I returned from ratting expeditions with my terriers and to call these bitches in once I had finished watering my terriers and bedding down the team. Not infrequently one of the bitches returned with a rabbit in her mouth, and from time to time they caught hares during their forays. I was forced to stop this practice when Fathom started fetching bantam hens that were obviously sitting eggs somewhere near my home. If I was with her Fathom ignored fowl and would walk among them. If she was running loose it was a different matter and she regarded any fowl as fair game she could catch and carry to hand. I lived at peace with all my neighbours in the district so I restricted Fathom's night-time jaunts, but though I reported that I had found these silkie × light Sussex hens to the police – I neglected to say how I had acquired them – no one ever claimed them and I have no idea who bred these quaint little brooding fowl.

However, let us discuss the work of a lurcher during daylight hours. It is often said that a good lamping lurcher should have virtually no nose, or to be more exact, the lurcher should be dissuaded from using

Saluki longdogs in the field.

its nose when it works on the lamp. However, a lurcher that is required to work by day should have a fairly developed sense of smell and the ability to put that sense to good use. Frankly, I enjoy watching a lurcher hunting up game almost as much as I enjoy the sight of the chase.

Some of the most spectacular nose dogs I have ever seen were sired by Dai Fish's Merle, though Merle did not have an outstanding nose by any means. Eddie Jones's Celt had the scenting ability of a beagle, and once in the Isle of Man hunted up and caught nineteen blue hares in a single day. His half brother Romulus, who appears in many of the pedigrees of the obedience-winning lurchers of today, had an equally fine nose and could detect the presence of a fox a field or so away. He would raise his head, cause his nostrils to twitch and raise his ears if he scented a fox, and several times we were aware of the presence of foxes in earths long before we arrived at the woods where the terriers would be put to ground. Mated to my bitch Fathom, Merle bred Emma, who was the grandmother of my present crop of lurchers, and Emma was not only gifted with a great nose but was possibly one of the gamest lurchers the family has ever produced since Penguin. She marked inhabited fox earths as accurately as would a veteran foxhound and caught foxes with great enthusiasm, and her premature death from some form of hepatitis was a great loss.

A dog that not only had an excellent nose but transmitted keen olfactory senses to his progeny was Terry Ahern's Rusty, a dog that also appears in the tails of many obedience winners' pedigrees. In fact, the very successful Wright/Tay bloodline – excellent workers and wonderful competition dogs – was based on Ahern's quite ugly dog. Rusty too died prematurely of meningitis, but not before he had bred a number of excellent working lurchers. Much of the intelligence and nose of my own strain of lurcher I attribute to Ahern's Rusty, for I mated the then ageing Penguin to him and bred Duke, a dog with a fine nose and a great retrieving instinct which when mated to Emma produced my present strain of lurcher, the very soft silver-fawn coloured dogs I favour. I also attribute at least some of the natural retrieving instinct of my strain – my puppies will carry from infancy onwards – to this dog.

Once a dog has been properly trained – and I repeat the adage that a dog that is not trained in the yard won't be trained in the field – it is time to take the youngster into the field to allow it to encounter and chase game. However, while it is relatively easy to start a dog catching lamped rabbits, it is not so easy for a dog to chase and catch a rabbit it

A rabbit squatting and hoping to be overlooked.

has sprung during the daylight hours. Rabbits are extremely wary if they choose to feed by day and will seldom be far from their burrows. When surprised they will race for home at great speed and it is a very unusual young lurcher that is able to catch the first rabbit it encounters during daylight hours. Once more I must resort to a tale to illustrate a point. The best lurcher I have ever owned in my life is the one that sits beneath my table as I write. Merab has been a wonderful animal that has never let me down or failed to live up to expectations when she has performed in public. I could not wish to a more perspicacious animal nor for an animal with better catching ability, yet she must have missed over three hundred rabbits before she learned how to catch one. When she was a youngster I saw her run alongside rabbits I was almost certain she would catch, only to watch them disappear into burrows an inch or so from Merab's nose. I saw her miss rabbits I'm sure a leggy terrier would have caught, and while I confess I have a great deal of experience in training lurchers in general and of this family of lurchers in particular, I must admit that I experienced despair where Merab was concerned. One day I saw her chase a rabbit that had risen some distance from where I was walking, and so lengthy was the distance between Merab and rabbit that I didn't bother to watch the chase but limped my way back to my van. I felt Merab nosing the back of my legs and bent down to stroke her only to find she had a rabbit in her mouth – her first rabbit I must add. She was fifteen months of age and had had more opportunity to catch a rabbit than possibly any lurcher in Britain, but she never looked back after her first catch and became the best lurcher I have ever owned. Her granddaughter Phaedra (who is also her half sister as I linebreed my lurchers) caught much sooner and is much faster than Merab, but something in the alloy is missing – I can't explain what for it may well be that I have achieved some strange reciprocity with Merab that I have never achieved with Phaedra, but I am digressing somewhat.

When I start a lurcher on its career as a daytime hunter I am careful to choose the rabbits it first encounters, for I believe that too many failures can sour a lurcher puppy. I am, in fact, fairly certain that Merab had become as disenchanted with her performance as I was before she caught her first rabbit, and another month of failures would have made her a very inefficient catch dog. Thus I attempt to present a young dog with rabbits it has at least a sporting chance of catching. When I lived in Lichfield rabbits were scarce and not nearly as easy to obtain as they are here in the Highlands, and I kept one patch of hunting country specifically for entering a puppy. I took care never to disturb this patch of land and never allowed my adult terriers or lurchers to disturb the patch. The area in question was, or so I thought at the time, tailor-made for starting a young lurcher. Burrows undermined bramble bushes and gorse, and a breadth of clear ground separated the feeding grounds from the bramble patch. I entered six generations of lurchers on this patch and used the same method of entering. I stopped the van on the main road and walked the hundred or so yards to the bramble patch. I then placed a length of binder twine (in place of a more conventional but expensive slip leash) around the neck of the lurcher and carefully stalked the rabbits feeding on the fields beyond the brambles. When my lurcher saw a rabbit rise, and if I considered the slip suitable, I released the lurcher. It is, however, very difficult for a lurcher to run and catch a rabbit that is speeding towards it, so my success rate was quite low, but sooner or later (usually later) I managed to secure a catch with a young lurcher. I entered Penguin's dam on this patch when I first came to the district and shortly before I left Ilan, Penguin's great grandson, by the same method. Ilan entered so easily, and if he had not sustained the terrifying injury that relegated him to stud I feel he would have been a remarkable dog. Still, he bred me both Merab and Phaedra so perhaps the accident that crippled him was in a way fortuitous.

A lurcher springs a fox.

If I might dwell on the subject of catching an oncoming rabbit or hare a moment. It must seem puzzling to the beginner that a rabbit that is coming towards a lurcher is often more difficult to catch than one that has to be pursued. In point of fact it is fairly easy to understand why this is so if one stands back and examines the situation more carefully. A dog chasing a rabbit will have achieved roughly the same speed as the rabbit it is pursuing at the moment it attempts to catch a rabbit, but the combined velocity of the dog running towards a rabbit that is running towards the dog makes the catch very difficult. Burke, Fathom's father, developed the technique of catching such rabbits to a nicety though Fathom, although an excellent catch dog, never perfected this technique. Phaedra, Burke's very inbred descendant seven generations on, has, however, inherited this unusual technique of catching speeding rabbits that are coming towards her.

As I write these notes two rabbits are playing in the fields outside my house. It is midday and the presence of rabbits feeding at this time of the day is probably a good indication that there is a very large population in the gorse patch at the end of the field. Ordinarily rabbits feed during the night-time hours or shortly before dawn or shortly after dark, and only when an infestation reduces the amount of edible herbage will rabbits feed during daylight hours. So the would-be hunter and his lurcher must venture abroad either shortly after dawn or as dark falls if he is to encounter rabbits his dog has a sporting chance of catching, and even if the dog is successful it is highly unlikely a lurcher will take a huge haul of rabbits during the daylight hours. Tales of rabbit catchers with neither ferrets (I shall deal with the use of ferrets presently) nor lamp returning with huge hauls of rabbits are ridiculous. Rabbits feeding during daylight hours are seldom spaced over a large area and the appearance of a dog that seizes a rabbit will put the rest of the group of rabbits to ground in seconds. Likewise the squeal of a captured rabbit will startle any rabbit in the surrounding fields to flight. Curiously, after dark a squeal of a stricken rabbit will usually cause its fellows to crouch rather than flee. I have many times flicked on my lamp when I have heard a rabbit squealing only to find a fox, rabbit in mouth, walking away to feed through small groups of rabbits that have crouched as the fox approached and thus escaped detection. It is possible, but only just possible, that rabbits can distinguish between a predator that is actively hunting and one that has satiated its hunger. It is also worth recording that while foxes indulge in orgies of frenzied, unnecessary killing, it is seldom seen in the wild – once a fox has killed a rabbit it will simply feed on the kill rather than slaughtering, or attempting to slaughter, the rest of the group of

126

rabbits. Curiously, although lurchers are masters of surplus killing and will, if opportunities present themselves, wipe out entire colonies of rabbits in an evening without feeding on a single kill, foxes are classed as bloodthirsty killers by the ill-informed public – but once more I digress.

It is quite fascinating to watch the style and technique a lurcher will adopt to catch rabbits that are sitting tight in patches of bramble, and if the haul of rabbits one can obtain from such bushing expeditions is small then the excitement such a hunt can engender makes the sport more than worthwhile. Rabbits will sit tight in deep cover and the antics of young dogs as they attempt to flush and catch these rabbits is little short of fascinating. Many will out of sheer exasperation crash into cover to catch the rabbit, but such a method is seldom satisfactory and seldom succeeds in catching the prey. Penguin regularly used this method and rarely caught bushed rabbits. Fathom adopted a more successful method of catching a seated rabbit and ran around the bushes making feints but never venturing into cover. When the rabbit was panicked into bolting only then did Fathom attempt to catch it. It was my custom at one time to walk to the post box at the end of the lane and to allow Fathom to work rabbits in the bramble patches that lined the road to the village. The hauls of rabbits obtained by such hunts were pitifully small but the style manifested by Fathom was spectacular. Her speciality was to sneak belly down towards feeding rabbits in the manner of a cat and her striking speed was spectacular. David Hancock spent many hours photographing this unusual creeping stalk and I cannot but wonder whether Fathom could have been an even better hunter had she been trained on the rabbit-infested land on which I now live. She was well over twenty when I came north to live and still managed to stalk the odd rabbit or so. Shortly before she died she was wont to spend her time asleep on the heather behind my croft and one day returned with a young hare I presumed had either been crippled by some injury or had somehow run into her, for Fathom moved stiffly and slowly and was unable to catch an active leveret. She was a great age when she died – I have never owned an older dog. Her mother Penguin was twenty-one when she crossed the road in front of a car and was killed instantly.

I have caught good hauls of rabbits in thick rushy cover near the sand dunes, and rabbits seem to enjoy feeding in rush patches during the daylight hours. Whether these rabbits are eating young rushes to bulk out their diet to prevent bloat, or even feeding on the young plants that grow among the rushes, is debatable, but a great many rabbits feed in these beds and are ideal if somewhat difficult quarry for a daytime

Bad country to work.

lurcher. Rabbits sprung in these conditions will seldom make a dash for home until they are hard pressed, but simply run into deeper cover and sometimes squat. Lurchers that are frequently hunted in these conditions develop a curious style of hunting and soon learn to bound and leap above the rushes to observe the bolting rabbits. I have hunted both lurchers and longdogs in these conditions and they all gravitate towards this style of hunting rush beds. I have been privileged to watch one of the best rush-bed hunters in Britain, one whose performance far exceeded that of my best lurchers in these conditions.

In 1980 Bruce Warburton was discharged from the army and purchased a pedigree unknown lurcher which was sold as a collie/grey-hound/deerhound/greyhound, the usual title for virtually any lurcher that is of dubious breeding but above twenty-five inches at the shoulder. The dog had an underdeveloped nose but became a wizard at 'pounding the rushes'. He developed an unusual technique of point-ing sitting rabbits and even waiting for Bruce to approach him and push the rabbit out of its rush 'seat' before Sabre sprang on the rabbit and invariably caught it. I fetched several observers to watch this peculiar technique that improved and became even more precise as the dog grew older.

Not the best way to mark a burrow.

The author's Merab marks a hole by pointing.

On the subject of unusual techniques used in rabbiting I feel I must mention the technique I called poking-out that was practised by Moses Aaron Smith, and I have never met anyone else who used this method of hunting rabbits. When I first knew Moses he owned a pale blue, smooth-coated lurcher with just the merest hint of collie in its whippet greyhound make-up, but with enough baseline to blend with the strange lifestyle Moses was wont to live. In the district around the estate where Moses resided were miles of dry-stone walls that had been constructed a century or so ago when labour was both skilled and cheap. Most of these dry-stone walls were in poor repair and this decay offered ample refuge for rabbits, which infested the walls. It was possible to ferret these walls – I did so on many occasions – but one lived in dread of the ferret tying up in the wall and having to be extracted by removing large boulders from the centre of the dry-stone construction. It was virtually impossible to rebuild these walls after such a probe and the owners of the land discouraged ferreting. Moses was, however, a master of innovation and would take an old hacksaw blade – he hoarded tons of apparently valueless equipment in his garden sheds and probed the walls where his lurcher marked, sliding the blade between the cracks in the stonework to encourage the rabbit to bolt. I have seldom been successful with this method of bolting rabbits, but Moses was incredibly dextrous at this technique and his bitch would leap to the top of the wall to watch while Moses slid his hacksaw blade under the flat stones. I saw Moses catch five rabbits in a morning using this technique, and his lurcher seemed totally in tune with her owner's curious practices.

It is perhaps time to leave the subject of hunting rabbits and mention the hunting of the hare with lurchers, and now it becomes essential to remind the reader yet again that a lurcher is essentially a rabbit hunter and any hares taken by a lurcher must be regarded as a bonus. Few lurchers are capable of catching hares that have a chance to put a good distance between themselves and their pursuers. My own lurchers are extremely well trained and very efficient yet they are hopelessly outmatched by strong hares that have a hundred yards or so start on their pursuers. I have often wondered just how many youngsters have sold promising young dogs after they have listened to silly talk about hare-catching dogs from older people who should know better. A hare is a terrific athlete and while it can be taken by the opportunist lurcher or by a lurcher that somehow catches a hare off guard, in fair flight it is more than a match for any lurcher, or longdog for that matter.

Norfolk poachers, or mouchers, as small-time dog-touting poachers

It is not uncommon to catch rabbits which have been badly scratched by ferrets.

are known in such districts, often believe that the best time to seek out a hare is shortly after dawn, when the hare is full-bellied and cat-napping as hares are wont to do while the dew is drying. A full-bellied hare, like any full-bellied athlete, is unlikely to give of its best when chased and is a little easier to catch perhaps. Should the reader believe that this is an unsporting practice let us remember that if a dog is to chase and catch its hare it will need every chance it can get to tilt the odds in its favour, and I have watched many of my lurchers flush a cat-napping, full-bellied hare close on it like lightning only to be hopelessly outrun once the hare has achieved its top speed.

Fathom developed a technique of catching hares that made up for her lack of great speed and the absence of greater stamina. When she entered a field that might hold a hare she would stand watching the creature in its form and approach it carefully. If it lifted its ears as she approached or attempted to run she froze and stayed frozen until the hare resumed feeding once more, and only then would she continue to stalk the creature. When she came within fifteen yards of the creature she would freeze and remain absolutely motionless until the hare moved, and then make a lightning lunge at the creature. She caught many hares this way and missed far more than she caught, and the majority of truthful lurcher owners would tell the same tale.

I really enjoy watching a lurcher hunt up a hare though I know the

131

Myxomatosis-stricken
rabbit.

dog has little chance of catching it. Merab's daughter Little Fathom
would enter a field where a hare was feeding and forthwith start hunting head to the ground, tail feathered and oblivious to all but the
scent of the hare she was hunting. Using this method she succeeded in
catching some hares, but like her grandmother missed far more than
she managed to catch. Whatever the method a lurcher uses the hare is
never easy meat, and few lurchers catch a great many hares during the
course of a winter's hunting.

I have deliberately terminated the last paragraph with the phrase 'a
winter's hunting'. Hares should never be hunted during their breeding
season, for not only is it unsporting to hunt hares that are either pregnant or nursing young leverets, or both (for hares are frequently
pregnant and nursing young leverets during clement years), but it is
also bordering on the illegal. It is a little known fact, but hares are
afforded a closed season by law. The Hare Preservation Act of 1892
Section 2 and 3 includes provisions for the protection of hares during
the breeding season. It is illegal to sell or offer for sale any British hare
between the months of March and July, and this Act applies to England,
Wales and Scotland. The legality of the practice aside, however, it is an
extremely wasteful practice to hunt pregnant does and leverets for a
hunter must always adopt the attitude of a conservationist rather than
a man who simply slaughters wild game.

Some lurchers show a unique propensity to hunt feather, some will in
fact hunt pheasants and partridges with greater enthusiasm than they will
fur – particularly if they achieve an early success catching pheasants and

experience a series of failures at catching the rabbits that are put up in front of them. Such flukes in training will often produce animals that are wed to a particular type of quarry. A tale will illustrate this point more easily. When I embarked on the training of Fathom's great grandsire I associated with Ernie Phillips, who later became quite an esteemed lurcher judge with a penchant for supersaturated greyhound lurchers. In those days, however, Ernie's lurchers were anything but typey and he owned a curious hybrid one of the parents of which was a mongrel terrier, the Tamworth canine Casanova. Somehow the mongrel not only found its way into a kennel of flapping track greyhounds but managed to couple with one Crazy Parachute bred bitch which gives some notion of the date of the union. The puppy from the union was given to Ernie's son who tired of the whelp after the youth discovered girls. Ernie took over the training of the animal. It was never a good rabbit dog though once, and only once, it took a hare that was caught napping near the local beagle kennels, but early in its life Ernie paid quite dearly for the interests of his puppy when it broke into a pheasant-rearing pen and caused

A winning combination much used by many winners, the greyhound Shooting News *and the longdog Canaan.*

considerable havoc. It wed to pheasants of all sorts from that time on and later the brute broke into a private bird zoo, ignored the panic-stricken parrot-like birds and caught and retrieved alive a rare type of Swinhoes pheasant, a colour variation of the more commonly seen Swinhoes. Ernie swore nothing else in the zoo had been touched by the dog though the newspapers spoke of the havoc caused when a fox broke into the enclosure. I am inclined to believe Ernie's tale, and either the papers had been short of a good tale that day or some of the birds were heavily insured! Belle came to grief when she raced across the Tamworth-Whittington road and encountered a truck carrying electrical appliances – irony of irony, the driver's name was Partridge.

Some lurchers will catch feather but refuse to return the catch to hand, simply dropping it rather than retrieving it. This, however, is usually a

The author's famous Fathom foundation of his present strain.

Hancock's Romulus and Timmy, two three-quarter bred lurchers feature in the pedigree of most obedient champions.

result of defective early training. If the dog is required to return feather to hand it is good sense to use some form of feathered carcass during the whelp's early training. I seldom turn down the cadavers that result from a rook or crow shoot, and if lurchers are taught to retrieve these carcasses there is little doubt that they will retrieve game. I found few lurchers enjoyed retrieving pigeons – the fine dust casings of the filoplume are apparently distasteful to dogs but over the years I have used a variety of avian cadavers to train my dogs. At one time I worked sea nets in shallow water a mile or so off the coast and the nets trapped a variety of seabirds ranging from guillemots to cormorants, and I used all these cadavers to train young lurchers to retrieve feathered game, and some of these birds were so distasteful even ferrets refused to eat them. Curiously one of Phaedra's first catches was a crippled shelduck which she retrieved gently to hand. Phaedra is a boisterous animal who attacks her quarry with gusto but who will, in fact, carry a newly hatched pheasant chick to hand without harming it.

It may take some time for a lurcher to become a proficient catcher of feather and the average lurcher will miss much feathered game before developing a technique for catching game birds. Mallard are particularly

Saluki.

heavily scented yet very difficult for a dog to catch simply because ducks, both domesticated and wild, are very wary. Partridge will often whirr into flight thereby startling the dog that may at first decline to strike at these birds, while grouse rocket into flight so quickly that young dogs are often startled by the explosion from the heather. Pheasants are certainly the easiest game bird for a lurcher to catch and the majority of feather-hunting lurchers start their careers by catching them. The majority of young lurchers will run the scent of larks as eagerly as they will run game and I have often thought the scent of larks must be very similar to that of partridge to a dog. Indeed I have seen gundogs display the same enthusiasm for hunting larks, though lurchers grow out of the practice as soon as they realise the futility of their actions. Yet from time to time I have noticed Merab stop and flush the occasional lark, but she never follows the flight of this bird as she will a pheasant's.

Yet unless a dog shows a natural inclination to hunt and catch feathered game there is little a handler can do to encourage it. I have tried many methods of attempting to train lurchers with no natural desire to hunt feather including using feathered lines dragged in front of the dog and attractive feathered dummies (usually road casualty pheasant

Deerhound head studies.

carcasses), but I have yet to be able to generate interest in a lurcher that has no natural inclination to catch feather. Neither have I been able to discover a common denominator for what constitutes a bird-catching dog. I have seen many good bird-catching collie lurchers, but I have also observed just as many longdogs that showed this propensity. One of the best pheasant-catching dogs I have ever seen was in fact a K.C.-bred whippet bred from the Shalfleet bloodlines. This whippet had been kept purely as a pet yet indulged in a reign of terror when it escaped on the nearby shoot.

Yet despite the fact that I have observed no common denominator among feather-catching lurchers I am fairly convinced that the inclination to hunt feather is inherited. Several breeders do in fact claim to breed lurchers which are innately interested in hunting feather. Andrew 'Stat' Stainton, who has the distinction of breeding a strain of lurcher that is free of saluki blood but is still able to compete with the best longdogs in Britain, has one such strain that shows an equal propensity to hunt fur and feather. Alan Hargreaves of Gedney Dyke once described this strain as being the nearest type to that mythical chimera, an all-round lurcher, after I had written that the expression 'all-round lurcher' usually referred to a type which couldn't perform any task satisfactorily – a sort of jack of all trades but certainly master of none. Stainton's strain certainly tends to prove my theory could be a shade incorrect, but I shall deal with this family of lurchers more thoroughly in a later chapter.

12

The Ferreter's Lurcher

I have seldom owned a lurcher that I could class as a top-rate hare-catching dog, and never owned an all-round lurcher of the type that was as at home on the coursing field as in the lamp. In fact if I have any claim to fame it is that I have some of the best ferreter's lurchers I have ever seen, and that while I have competed numerous times against others who have excellent ferreting dogs I have yet to be beaten at my chosen sport. Thus the reader must forgive the length of this chapter and the almost crazed enthusiasm I display when I write about ferreter's lurchers.

Let us start with the qualities one expects from a lurcher that is to work

A pair of the author's lurchers freeze-pointing an inhabited burrow.

with or in conjunction with ferrets, and forthwith might I mention that while lamping dogs are commonly offered for sale I have yet to see a top-class ferreter's dog change hands at any price. Neither have I ever seen what I consider to be a truly competent ferreter's dog that had not seen at least three seasons of ferreting. Thus it is seldom possible to buy an off-the-peg ferreter's dog as one might purchase a trained lamping dog or a single-handed hare-coursing dog.

So what are the qualities one might expect from a top-class ferreter's dog and how might such qualities be bred in, or how might a dog be

A droving-type collie.

A ferreting dog marks the progress of a hunt.

trained to perform the functions a warrener might expect from his dog? Firstly a warrener's dog must be able to work in conjunction with ferrets, and this does not simply mean that the dog is not actively hostile to ferrets, but that the dog must regard the ferret as an ally, that once it disappears into a hole it will produce rabbits for the dog to chase. A good ferreter's dog will follow the progress of a battle below ground and estimate where a rabbit is likely to bolt. A first-rate ferreter's dog will stop above the spot where a ferret has killed its prey and give some indication of the presence of a lie up. I have owned many dogs that would if left to their own devices dig to such a kill, take the rabbit from the ferret and return the rabbit to hand. I own such a dog at the time of writing and she has taken a full three years to become proficient. She is slightly wary of ferrets and is a little less than courageous, but as a ferreter's dog she is truly excellent. I would not be without her and I will find her almost impossible to replace.

A ferreter's dog should have no fear of cover, but should not be so foolish as to leap into deep bramble and attempt to seize any rabbit that appears. Such practice will almost certainly result in a rabbit that simply escapes and a tangled, bewildered, frustrated dog watching the fleeing rabbit. Yet a good ferreter's dog should not be shy of cover. Rabbits will often burrow beneath bramble patches or construct dens in deep tunnels among gorse roots, and an efficient ferreter's dog should be able to mark inhabited burrows even in such cover and a dog that is an inefficient marker even in deep cover is of little use to the ferreter. Rabbiters may be surprised to realise what a reservoir for rabbits a patch of thick gorse can be. Not only do gorse roots facilitate the digging of burrows, but the cover the gorse affords will deter almost any medium-sized predator.

On the subject of marking, no ferreter's dog that does not have a first-class nose can claim to be first-rate at its work. A lurcher that is used for ferreting should be able to determine whether a warren is inhabited or not. A dog may indicate the presence of an inhabited burrow in many ways. Fathom pointed at inhabited burrows and stood paw raised like a pointer above the burrow that held a rabbit or so. Merab, her daughter, is ten times the worker her mother was and is so incredibly accurate that I have yet to prove her wrong. She will find an inhabited burrow, sniff delicately at one entrance, move gingerly over the top of the warren and sniff the other entrances before returning to the first entrance and deliberately scratching at the mouth of the hole. Phaedra, Merab's granddaughter and half sister (I have explained the complex line breeding project I tend to follow) is a lot more crude in her marking techniques but quite accurate, and frankly once a dog developed an efficient style I should be only too keen to take the animal's advice about the inhabitants of certain burrows, and if the marking technique is not too bizarre or not too likely to disturb the residents of the burrows prior to ferreting, I should be reluctant to modify the dog's behaviour. Dogs that develop a natural technique of marking and are rewarded for their efforts (I shall explain this statement presently) are much more efficient than are dogs that have had their marking techniques altered by handlers. A dog that will mark accurately is an absolute treasure and can lessen a ferreter's labours greatly. No uninhabited burrows need to be netted and a ferreter can go straight to a set of holes and ignore them, or else set fewer nets.

Temperament is all-important in a lurcher that is to be used for working alongside ferrets and I have yet to see a lurcher with a strong trace of saluki in its ancestry that proved to be a satisfactory ferreter's dog. A ferreter's lurcher needs to be alert but never skittish, and saluki-bred dogs are invariably perusing the horizon when there is a lull in the ferreting – when a ferret lies up or perhaps loses its rabbit in a deep warren. A ferreter's lurcher must always stay to hand and never allow its attention to wander. I find it almost incredible when ferreters boast that they have dogs that during a day's ferreting disappear for an hour or so and return with a hare. The dog should have stayed tight to hand during the entire day's ferreting and should never be allowed to wander in pursuit of other quarry. A nervous, edgy dog, a dog that fidgets or tends to cast about rather than concentrate, is of little use to the ferreter and certainly not a pleasant companion with which to spend a day.

I insist on any lurcher carrying to hand without question and would require a ferreting lurcher to retrieve efficiently with the minimum of commands from me. A rabbit that throws the nets and bolts only to be caught by a lurcher which simply wanders around, rabbit in mouth, refusing to bring its catch to hand is a great nuisance to any ferreter if the time spent taking the rabbit from the lurcher is time spent away from the nets, and time spent away from the netted burrows is invariably rewarded by the sight of yet another rabbit throwing the nets or escaping from a bolt hole overlooked by the ferreter. I ferret a great deal, so much that it contributed to my failure to achieve promotion in the teaching

A dog kept 'steady to' a netted rabbit.

143

profession, and I have been on many ferreting trips ruined by dogs that have failed to retrieve. I can all too vividly recall the time I spent ferreting near Melton with a particularly bad dog trainer who, because he had the ferreting rights to the land I was working, insisted on bringing his dog. My sloppy netting is usually compensated for by the fact that I have well trained lurchers, but after a moment's observation of my host's dog I decided to leave my dog in the van and I was faced with the sight of a very forlorn Penguin watching me walk into the distance without her. I thank heaven that I left the bitch behind for the dog was chaotic and irritating. My host's dog was an attractive deerhound hybrid, twenty-five inches tall and very typey, but it was so badly trained that it was a joke – at least until one had to tolerate a day with the brute after which the animal was something less than amusing. The beast strayed and needed to be called back in a very loud voice, but refused to stay in tight. When a rabbit threw one of my nets the dog ploughed after the animal and caught the coney as it flashed back to ground and was back-netted, and forthwith lifted both the net and the rabbit enclosed by the meshes and raced around the field, rabbit in mouth. Despite the pleas

Dog kept steady while nets are set.

and entreaties of my associate the dog stubbornly refused to come to hand, but succeeded in startling other rabbits into remaining in the burrows and facing the ferret rather than bolting. This chaotic day occurred long before locators were commonly used, and I needed to dig for several hours to recover my ferret, and I finally decided that, much as I need country to ferret, I could not tolerate this lurcher and its handler and willingly gave up my ferreting permission near Melton Mowbray. I detest chaos and could not tolerate working with such a dog.

So exactly what sort of dog constitutes the ideal ferreter's lurcher, or what should be the breeding for a ferreter's dog? Frankly my ideal ferreter's dogs are the lurchers I own today, the best of which is under the table as I write and lest the reader should consider that I praise this strain too much let me add that I have competed many times with this bitch and she has yet to be bested. My strain may be best described as mongrelised but with a strong dash of collie in its make-up, and this mixture gives my dogs great nose, not a lot of speed admittedly, fine constitution and a good thick coat to face cover without too much discomfort. What actually gave this strain its fine nose has still to be determined and the family has been inbred for many years to maintain this quality. Over the years I have added collie blood in the form of Ahern's Rusty (a half-bred collie greyhound), Dai Fish's Merle (another half-bred collie greyhound) and Tully, a superbly bred collie greyhound who, to be perfectly honest, introduced a few traits I am now attempting to breed out. This collie blood has given the strain a sunny disposition – though Tully was anything but an affable dog and contributed a certain sullenness I have finally bred out. Furthermore, the collie blood has made the strain adaptable, easily trained and with a great willingness to please. I have seldom to speak to my lurchers and never to shout at them; in fact, should I ever attempt to shout the action leaves them confused and upset and I find that they blend with my ways rather than posing a challenge to my training techniques.

I have yet to see a saluki-blooded lurcher that was a suitable ferreter's dog and I have seen a great many saluki hybrids. The saluki-bred longdog or lurcher seldom has the ability to concentrate on the job in hand and when I trained my saluki greyhound hybrid Canaan to work with ferrets I found she was far too intent on watching rabbits moving in the next field to be able to unravel the cause of the sounds beneath her feet. I found I constantly needed to call her to hand rather than simply expecting her to fix or freeze, as I would my lurchers. Rabbits seldom run more than twenty-five yards to another hole when pushed out of their warrens by ferrets, so a lurcher must be able to strike quickly and deftly at bolting

A ferret has just engaged a rabbit and has fur clogging its feet.

conies to intercept their flights between burrows. Merab and Phaedra, my lurchers, are singularly adept at this technique, though neither could qualify for the title 'fast'. Canaan, however, simply failed to connect brain with limbs quickly enough to be a great ferreter's dog and was never happy working with ferrets, though she waited and froze after a fashion and caught a respectable number of rabbits during the two seasons I used her. She won well – no, quite magnificently – in the coursing field but lacked poke, thrust, drive, call it what you will, to be able to work well with ferrets. Frankly I have seen many saluki hybrids whose owners claimed them to be great ferreting dogs, but I have yet to see one I would give kennel space.

146

A ferret fitted with a harness.

Diminutive lurchers often find favour with ferreters, and once I saw a very small Italian greyhound × Shetland sheepdog that was supposed to be an excellent worker, while Moses Smith kept a pure-bred Italian greyhound that was an excellent marker and caught quite enormous rabbits with ease. The current trend to breed whippet Bedlington hybrids is easy to understand for these crossbreds are attractive little animals that seem to be in keeping with the image of ferreting. Frankly, I feel the pure-bred whippet could perform the task just as well as a hybrid and would be a great deal faster. I am, I confess, no great fan of whippet lurchers though I have seen many that were well trained and quite useful. It is argued that Bedlington blood gives nose to the hybrid, but I have observed whippets with truly excellent noses and the courage to face the deepest cover to secure rabbits.

Huge lurchers, dogs approaching deerhounds in size and shape, are seldom suitable as ferreter's companions and are usually too large and clumsy to be a lot of use at catching rabbits that are sprinting between burrows. Yet I have seen many huge lurchers that had fine noses and marked extremely well. During my National Service, two years which were ill spent I must add, a Lewis Atwell worked as a rabbit controller on one of the camps where I was stationed. Later that year Atwell was to be made redundant when myxomatosis wiped out most of Britain's rabbits, but Atwell had a fine lurcher for marking holes. The dog was supposedly an Airedale greyhound, but despite its black and tan colouring, it was too large to be a genuine first-cross hybrid. Atwell worked with ferrets and nets and so I was unable to determine how effective a catch dog the animal was, but it was an excellent marking dog and remarkably obedient. Brian Vesey Fitzgerald said that such dogs were not uncommonly found in Norfolk and many tricoloured collies with long silky coats were used by marsh shepherds, and it is possible that these were some of the almost legendary marsh collies that were the ancestors of Norfolk lurchers. Atwell's dog had, so he assured me, been obtained from a warrener called Beaumont who had known the Norfolk poacher Frederick Rolfe, the villainous hero/antihero of I *Walked By Night* but yet once more I digress.

No lurcher should ever be taken out ferreting without first making sure the lurcher is stock-steady with ferrets, and the place to steady a lurcher is in the yard not in the field. A lurcher that is heated by the chase and then introduced to ferrets is a dozen times more likely to hurt a ferret

Ferret boxes.

than a dog that is introduced to ferrets in its own yard. Such an animal is at ease in its environment and is at its calmest, and when introduced to ferrets is likely to regard these creatures with interest rather than hostility. These days I seldom undertake to train a lurcher for a client; I break only my own puppies to ferrets, and because young whelps are totally submissive the slightest hostility from a ferret is usually enough to ensure that never again will the lurcher take liberties with any hob or jill. I simply take the puppy to the ferret cage, allow the whelp to watch the antics of the ferrets within the cage, and then remove the ferret, placing it down before the puppy. If the puppy is hostile or even appears hostile the slightest slap followed by 'No' is usually enough to prevent the puppy following up its hostility with an attack on the ferret. A few sessions of this sort of training is all that is needed to produce a lurcher that's steady with ferrets.

Under no circumstances should the amateur trainer undertake the breaking of two or more lurchers simultaneously. In fact it is decidedly bad policy to attempt to train two lurchers to any task. A single lurcher puppy may well feel overmatched by the presence of a ferret and will

A lurcher must have a good relationship with a ferret.

149

often be too terrified to attempt to harm the creature. The presence of another dog of any breed or age may give the puppy extra courage, so much courage in fact that should the ferret chance to nip the puppy the whelp may choose to retaliate, and few ferrets will survive a bite from even a young lurcher. It is surprising to note how few lurchers are broken to ferret, and more surprising still how easily a lurcher might be made rock-steady in the company of ferrets. I am always sceptical about lurcher enthusiasts who, dogs on leashes, request I take them ferreting, particularly if the said owner states that while the dog has never been actually trained not to kill ferrets, such is the control of the handler that the dog can be prevented from causing havoc. Lurchers are usually easily broken to ferrets, but are seldom innately steady, and I wish I had a pound for every time I've heard, 'I'm sure he'll be fine with ferrets,' as a lurcher lunges at the tiny noses peering out of my ferret box. Frankly, if I find a dog is not steady with ferrets I am prepared to upset its owner by refusing to take the handler and dog ferreting.

A rock-steady ferreter's dog will allow a ferret to walk between its legs and take all manner of liberties with the lurcher and never think of retaliating. Likewise a dog must be prepared to take great liberties with a ferret. My own work very tightly with a ferret and should a ferret hold a rabbit in the mouth of a burrow thereby preventing its escape, my oldest bitch will reach into the burrow, seize the rabbit and extract both rabbit and ferret from the burrow. Yet she will never harm a ferret and will gently ease the ferret away from its captor and return that rabbit to hand. She never shows the slightest animosity towards the ferret and will tolerate ferrets crawling over her.

I cannot resist the following tale, and I have often wondered what caused the lurcher to act in the way it did. In 1971 a band of Irish tinkers came to stay in the lane on which my cottage was situated. They caused little trouble though they brawled among themselves and were often very drunk. Their dogs, however, were absolute liabilities and caused a great nuisance in the district. One of their lurchers, a medium-sized brindled dog, was a strange creature indeed. At that time I kept my ferrets in a chicken run near my cottage so that if a ferret escaped it would do damage to my stock rather than to a neighbour's poultry, and so I lived amicably with the rest of the hamlet. I frequently found this brindled lurcher attempting to break into my chicken pen and I was greatly worried about the brute killing my fowl, but it smacks of lunacy to request a tinker to keep his dog under control, so I suffered my problems in silence, though each morning before school I drove the dog away from my fowl enclosure. One morning the barking of my terriers awoke me and I raced

down to find the lurcher had broken into the enclosure, ignored the fowl, but was actively engaged in trying to tear the front from my ferret pen and kill its occupants. I was even more disconcerted to find that during the night the band had moved away and left the brute behind. I'll finish the tale. The animal actually served Tom Cope's collie, produced a litter of puppies and finally vanished as abruptly as it had arrived, but another band of tinkers, more aggressive and a lot more odious than the first, settled on the same camp site. Over the years the district was greatly troubled with marauding lurchers kept by itinerant families, but I have yet to see a lurcher that was quite as antipathetic to ferrets as was that brindled dog. It would have been interesting to trace the origin of the brute to discover what strange happening had generated the dog's antipathy.

Once a puppy is rock-steady with ferrets and is obedient to basic commands it is time to take the lurcher into the field to allow it to work alongside them. Training a puppy alongside an old-school master lurcher has both advantages and disadvantages. Puppies will often ape the behaviour of older dogs and sometimes learn to mark by doing so. Likewise the presence of an older dog may have a settling effect on the puppy. Conversely, a puppy will often come to rely on the marking ability of the older dog and thus may decline to mark inhabited burrows. Personally I try to enter a dog without the presence of a teacher dog for I believe bad as well as good habits are acquired by a puppy and the presence of another dog often acts as a deterrent to a puppy becoming net-steady – and I shall deal with this subject presently. Furthermore, a puppy chasing and seizing a rabbit that is caught by another dog can become decidedly hard-mouthed or reluctant to retrieve properly. Frankly I have yet to see a top-grade ferreting dog that has been trained in the company of another lurcher.

I enjoy watching a puppy learn how to mark an inhabited rabbit burrow or a spot in a dry-stone wall into which a rabbit has run, and experience great pleasure when I observe the marking technique improving. Furthermore I enjoy learning to read the messages I believe hunting dogs are capable of transmitting. I have a strange bond with Merab, my best lurcher, and can interpret the meaning of most of her marking techniques, and to date she has displayed some sixteen different signs. If I might be allowed to digress slightly, I have never understood the sort of person who changes his lurchers every few weeks. Such a dog swapper never obtains a worthwhile dog no matter how often he changes his dogs. The essential relationship between dog and permanent handler will never be forged by the dog swapper and the handler will never be able to interpret the signals a good hunting dog transmits to its handler. Should my own lurchers suddenly die or, horror of horrors, get stolen – an unfortunately frequent problem where lurchers are concerned – I should seek out a lurcher from the same family, not because I believe this

A ferreted rabbit tangles in a net.

153

family is superior to all others, but simply because I know both its virtues and vices and I can adapt my training programme accordingly.

As a lurcher matures the dog will run more rabbits to ground and eventually in its excitement attempt to scratch at the hole into which the rabbit has disappeared. The seeds of marking have now been sown and it requires only careful nurturing to produce a fine marking dog. It is, however, extremely bad policy to encourage dogs to check every hole and to praise their efforts if they dig. The seeds of false marking germinate all too easily if this method of training is practised. Dogs that are encouraged to check every hole and praised for marking these holes will often mark any hole just to please the owner.

I simply have to relate the following tale to illustrate the point. In 1973, just before lurchers became extremely popular, my home was visited by the most compulsive dog swapper I have ever met in my life. A dozen dogs a month passed through his hands, all were tried, all were found wanting and all were passed on to the next temporary home. Some were too tall, too small and too short in the back. Others were too long in the back to be able to lamp in the small fields around Lichfield, and some were poor retrievers. One poor brute, who was kept for three months, the longest I ever knew the man to keep a dog, was sold because quite suddenly the swapper realised the animal was the wrong colour! I can only assume that there were hundreds of the same ilk for the swapper seemed to know of an endless supply of wretched lurchers. One day he brought a ferreting dog to my premises and eulogised on the worth of the animal. I was barring out a root of a long-dead apple tree when he called and thrust the bar into the ground while my associate remarked on his good luck at the acquisition of his purchase, a refined, long-backed, elegant greyhoundy animal, but when I withdrew the bar from the soil the bitch promptly marked the hole from which I had lifted the crow bar. I said nothing for I had no desire to precipitate the departure of yet another lurcher, but by the weekend the lurcher had been sold. In the right hands the lurcher might have become a useful animal, but it had been encouraged to dig at any hole it encountered and had been ruined in the process.

Once the dog has marked decisively the mark must be 'honoured' if this marking technique is to be reinforced, and the only way to honour a mark is to ferret the burrow the dog has indicated is inhabited. The lurcher must experience pleasure as a result of the marking gesture so I never net the first warrens a young lurcher has marked. Few dogs experience pleasure at the sight of a rabbit struggling in the nets – a rabbit which incidentally they must be restrained from mouthing – but a

Lurcher restrained while a rabbit is withdrawn.

lurcher of any age enjoys (or experiences pleasure) at the sight of a rabbit bolting before a ferret and being allowed to chase and possibly capture the rabbit. A few pleasurable if unprofitable runs at bolted rabbit will establish this marking display permanently. I detest training a young dog with an uninitiated hunter in attendance for such a person is seldom *au fait* with the sacrifices a trainer must make to train a lurcher.

When I trained Merab to mark she indicated the presence of inhabited burrows fairly readily, but took an inordinate length of time to learn to catch rabbits. Rabbit after rabbit bolted from uninhabited burrows and I watched her try so hard but fail to catch. At that time a far from scientific hunter accompanied me on my forays and bleated piteously every time Merab failed to catch. 'She's losing all of them,' he would sob and almost tear his hair as the rabbits found the sanctuary of another burrow. If it is the reader's desire never to give a single rabbit a chance of escaping then I suggest he gives up hunting and simply buys rabbits from a game dealer. It will certainly be a more certain method of obtaining rabbits and far less stressful than hunting. A hunter must steel himself to accept that when he is training a puppy he will see many rabbits escape, rabbits that a man who relies only on ferret and nets will catch. Yet the time spent training a good marking dog is time well invested. A lamping dog is seldom worth keeping after its seventh season, a coursing dog burns up even faster, becoming a useless hunting dog before its seventh birthday. Fathom, one of the foundation bitches of my strain of lampers, still gave a great service into her dotage, and her last ferreting trip was conducted shortly after her twentieth birthday. She was still able to mark burrows and would have continued to function until shortly before her death in 1992, though after her twentieth year she developed a pained expression when she walked up hills or steep inclines. I kept her alive long after a person with some common sense would have put her down, but I have never been able to say goodbye to old friends and my kennels always resemble a home for geriatric dogs.

It is essential to keep the young lurcher near at hand while a ferret works its rabbit below ground, and a lurcher that wanders off and needs to be recalled can become a great pest and certainly not an aid to a pleasant day's ferreting. Hence it is wise to restrain young lurchers when a ferret is to ground, but just how to control such a dog is frequently debated by ferreters. It can be argued that a dog stationed at the down position when a ferret is put to ground is easily kept in its place, for the down position is easily maintained by a reasonably competent trainer. Likewise some advise that a dog placed at a sit position near the warren is easily controlled. However, a rabbit bolting between burrows does so at an incredible rate and a dog stationed at the down (or sit) position loses precious time getting to its feet to pursue the rabbit – and a split second is all that is required for a rabbit to escape capture. I tend to favour teaching a puppy to freeze above or near the burrow, for a dog so stationed is in a position to intercept a rabbit immediately it leaves the safety of a burrow. I simply station myself near, but not in view of, the burrow, for this might deter a rabbit from bolting, restraining my lurchers with a finger pressed against their sternums. The dog is held, albeit loosely, in this position and at the first sight of a rabbit pulls away in pursuit. After a while a dog will usually want to stay near the burrow and will develop its own style of positioning itself.

I am always criticised because I allow my dogs to stand near a burrow – indeed, I often allow Merab to stand with her feet upon the excavated soil. The notion that a dog standing directly in front of the burrow deters a rabbit from bolting is not without substance, yet I am convinced that while rabbits see movement and an indication of danger they are unable to connect danger with an immobile dog that will stand perfectly still without moving a muscle or an eyelid. Merab adopts just such a posture and catches many rabbits virtually as soon as they leave their burrows, and furthermore is able to perform her most spectacular feat of snatching out rabbits that are being held near the mouth of the burrow by the ferret that is working them. A dog should always be allowed to develop its own technique of stationing itself if, that is, that technique is not evidently counter-productive to the capture of rabbits – a dog that digs furiously at the mouth of a warren while the ferret is working should be stopped from doing so, for such actions are certainly not conducive to the bolting of rabbits. Likewise a dog that insists on crawling into the mouth of a warren should be deterred, though I have seen Merab catch many hundreds of rabbits by snatching them from the depths of the burrows where they are being held by the ferret. However, a dog that is not too excited will develop its own method of stationing itself at the mouth of the burrow and frankly is best left to its own devices to gauge the best place to stand. As a child I spent many hours attempting to station the lurcher near to where I believed the rabbit would bolt only to watch the rabbit bolt from a hole near which my dog had first stationed itself. A rigid, regimented technique of working a lurcher with ferrets is seldom successful, though it is lunacy to embark on a ferreting trip with a dog that has not been taught basic obedience.

Once the dog has developed the technique of marking inhabited burrows and being fairly efficient at the task, it is time to introduce the lurcher to purse nets and to prevent the dog seizing and damaging netted rabbits. Wildly excitable dogs seldom work well in conjunction with purse nets. I break dogs to nets fairly quickly despite the fact that I have never favoured heavy-handed techniques in the training of lurchers – in fact I have yet to see anyone succeed at lurcher training of any sort using harsh methods.

On the day I start to break lurchers to purse nets I leash up the dog immediately it has marked an inhabited burrow and then net every hole in the complex. A ferret is put to ground and with luck a rabbit bolts and is entangled in the nets. It is almost certain that the dog on seeing a rabbit entangle in the meshes will lunge at it. The leash is then jerked and the command 'No' is uttered sharply, upon which I will reach forward, kill the rabbit quickly and untangle the catch from the net while deterring the dog from mouthing the rabbit. If I can enlist the services of a fellow hunter who is prepared to leave his dog at home, my task is made considerably easier, but I would never attempt to train a dog to be steady to nets if a strange dog were present at the training session. Nothing can be more counter-productive to the training of a ferreter's dog during this period of its development than the presence of another dog, particularly if this dog is not yet steady with nets and attempts to seize the rabbit entrapped in the meshes. Lurchers are the most jealous of hunters and are reluctant to relinquish a catch to another dog, and the sight of a strange rival mouthing a netted rabbit is terribly counter-productive to training. Frankly I am decidedly chary of allowing any dog other than my own on a ferreting trip, for it is all too easy to allow a partially trained dog to slip into the habit of mouthing netted rabbits, for bad habits are terribly infectious and I have seen many net-steady dogs become a shade less steady when they have observed a wild, unruly lurcher attempting to seize a netted rabbit. At one time I bit my lip when a ferreting associate insisted on bringing along a wild, undisciplined dog that was clearly not steady with nets. These days I simply won't allow anyone whose dog is even slightly suspect to accompany me on any hunting venture, and if they insist on bringing the dog (or an unruly child for that matter) they are never again invited. I like to lead an orderly life, and any action that causes me stress or makes my dogs less efficient is avoided even if I offend long-time friends in the process. The current tendency of working groups of lurchers on a day's hunting is a ruinous practice and always results in badly trained dogs.

Thus the lurcher has been taught to respect the nets, is broken to ferret, will freeze while a ferret works below ground and has become an accurate marking dog, selecting each and every inhabited burrow on the land that is about to be hunted. Such a dog is a priceless asset to the ferreter, an asset that has taken an exceptionally long time to train, I should add. No one will be prepared to sell such a paragon and the ferreter's dogs that are offered for sale are without exception second-rate. If a hunter requires such a dog he must train it, and the process of training is a lengthy one, albeit a fascinating one. Such a dog will give service long after its youthful speed has left it and will be capable of working with ferrets until its dotage. Small wonder such a dog is rarely offered for sale.

13

The Single-handed Hare Courser

It is quite amazing that while lamping dogs can provide a lurcherman with perhaps more than pin money and a ferreting dog is a priceless treasure, the lurcher world seems to prize the single-handed hare-coursing dog, the dog that is capable of coursing and catching a strong winter hare that has been afforded fair law. In fact it is often believed by those who are new to the world of hunting that the only true test of a lurcher is its ability to catch a strong hare. Yet the single-handed pursuit of the hare is the task of the longdog rather than a lurcher and there are few strains of working lurcher that are capable of putting up a good performance in this area.

Amazing prices are often paid for single-handed hare-catching dogs that can perform this task with any regularity, for large sums are often wagered on such animals. In 1990 a shabby, untaxed Ford Transit van was stopped by the police and the van forced to disgorge its occupants, some nine men and two saluki-bred longdogs. The passengers were found to be carrying £23,000 in cash, money they were about to wager on a hare-catching contest that was to be staged between the two dogs. One dog had apparently been bought the week before for £5,000, while the owner of the other dog had refused a similar sum for his hound many times. In the same year the Gaskins, a family famous for its hare-coursing lurchers, purchased a longdog for £3,800, and this fact was given considerable coverage by the sporting press, but such sums are often recouped by a single weekend's coursing by those who seek to wager on the outcome of a best out of three or a best out of five hare-coursing event run on the huge fields of Lincolnshire and Cambridgeshire, and many times I have seen cars and lorries change hands after a single hare has been caught by one of the dogs competing in one of these events.

Readers, newcomers to the strange world of single-handed hare coursing who wish to enter such contests should ignore the ludicrous advertisement for puppies sired by or out of longdogs that regularly catch five out of six hares they run. These are mythical dogs, figments of the imagination, the fabric of ridiculous lies and exaggeration. Paul Sagar, one of the most successful of the saluki aficionados and one who has regularly beaten longdogs with his coursing salukis, once said that if the contest were properly organised, the hares strong and the law afforded the hare lengthy — a hundred or so yards perhaps — then the capture of a single hare in a best of three runs match was enough to ensure the victory of the dog. Tales of six hares captured in six runs by longdogs then become more than a little absurd and one assumes that the dog coursed the hares in a telephone kiosk to secure such a catch rate.

Brown hares are the greatest mammalian athletes imaginable. Few wild creatures can outrun them and once they have ceased to be young enough to be classed as leverets they are likely to be able to live to a great age unless they are caught napping by foxes or other predators. Eagles alone seem to be the only British birds capable of catching them, and foxes that spring a sleeping hare are seldom foolish enough to follow the hare once it has attained top speed. It is only the terrific mortality rate among the young of the species that ensures the British countryside is not overrun by hares — and there are few predators who disdain the flesh of newly born leverets. Cats frequently catch and kill them, foxes are particularly partial to them and slow, ponderous badgers will seek out and eat all the leverets a doe has secreted in her territory. Rabbits stamp newly born leverets to death, and even hedgehogs have been known to attack and devour young hares. Owls of all species relish leveret meat and stumpy-footed buzzards are capable of killing young hares. Black-back gulls enjoy the meat and even crows have been known to kill leverets. Truly the youth of a leveret is fraught with peril and few survive long enough to see the cutting of the corn that signals the end of the hare's breeding season.

Corn leverets, youngsters of a few months of age, are particularly vulnerable to dogs once the wheat or barley is cut. To the leveret that has sought sanctuary among the stalks, the reaping changes the nature of its world. No longer can it run for cover on fields where thick corn affords it protection and for a month or so the death rate among these youngsters is very high. A corn hare startled by a dog will run wildly to escape its pursuer and frequently runs back to the dog that is chasing it. If six hares are caught by a single dog they are corn hare leverets that are baffled and confused by the disappearance of the wheat and barley stocks that once protected them. In Alrewas near Burton-on-Trent there once lived a collie, a black and white unregistered brute, fierce with people, furious with other dogs and a poor worker. It was, however, a wizard at catching hares that took flight to evade the combine harvesters that cut the corn in which these leverets lived. I was travelling to school one morning and watched the dog catching leveret after leveret that raced from the cornfield to the grassland, and I arrived at school an hour late because of my interest in the collie – small wonder I was regarded as an oddball by the rest of the profession.

Yet as the autumn progresses and drifts to winter hares become more and more difficult to catch. The foolish, the unwary, the unsound hares have bitten the dust long before the first frosts and the hares that survive are master athletes. By Christmas the brown hare is at its strongest, its mind uncluttered with thoughts of courtship, its limbs well developed, its fatty tissue reduced to an acceptable minimum and so alert as to be almost paranoid. Such a hare knows its enemies, their strengths and their weaknesses, and knows just how to exploit these weaknesses. It is a match for any dog, except, of course, if it is caught napping or unaware. With a hundred-yard start it is capable of running any dog to a standstill, and Lorraine Syred, a journeyman greyhound trainer, tells of a Newmarket coursing meet where not even the strongest, fastest greyhound was able to come to terms with the hares.

Fen hares are the most difficult hares to catch and there are many theories as to why this is so. Don Southerd believes that the reason for the incredible vitality these hares are known to possess is due to their diet. Sugar beet is found in abundance on the peat soil of the reclaimed marshlands and sugar beet is rich in energy-giving carbohydrates. The great variety of crops grown on these fens also provides a rich and varied diet for these hares and there are few poorly grown, scrawny hares caught on the fens. Don's theory is, however, a shade too simplistic perhaps. While it is likely that the abundance of food found on the fens must contribute in part to the great strength of the hares found there, it is also likely that the savage culling inflicted by coursers and poachers alike has done much to assist the breeding of strong, vigorous hares, for the weak, the foolish, the slow-of-foot hares have been eliminated by the most ferocious method of culling known to man – coursing. For hundreds of years longdogs and sighthounds have coursed these fens; the strongest and fittest hares that have survived the winter's coursing have coupled and bred equally tenacious offspring.

The strongest hares seldom exceed eight pounds in weight. Huge brutes of hares, twelve pounds or so in weight, are usually among those culled early in the season. Small, weedy hares, no bigger than the blue

The New Complete Lurcher

hares of Scotland, are also early casualties once the season begins, and those which survive to perpetuate the species are usually more than half a stone in weight but are miracles of organic construction. I have caught some January hares with longdogs and a few unwary ones with lurchers, but I have yet to see a January hare that weighed more than eight and a half pounds. Yet these hares are the ones which will run the best of longdogs to a standstill and will leave greyhounds too exhausted to stand. Twice I have seen hares outrun the best of greyhounds, and as the dogs panted and swayed to a halt the hares started to browse two hundred yards from their pursuers. Hares are such incredible athletes that to dismiss them as easy meat for any longdog is little short of blasphemy.

And now to the dogs that are expected to course and catch these hares that are usually allowed a hundred or so yards' law to ensure a sporting course. Few conventionally bred lurchers are capable of performing this feat, for a lurcher is essentially a hunting dog rather than a coursing dog. Some three-quarter-bred collie greyhounds will put up a creditable performance against hares but it is usually longdogs and specifically bred longdogs that are prized as single-handed hare coursers and catchers. Most of the top-flight match dogs are in fact three-quarter greyhound and a quarter saluki, though sometimes a half-bred saluki greyhound has sufficient speed to win at these events – though the majority of these hybrids are a little too slow to be top-flight match dogs.

There are, of course, exceptional individual lurchers that will put up a better than just favourable show against even the best of longdogs. The one that comes most readily to mind is Tom Brown's Anna, a lurcher of dubious parentage despite many theories concerning her origin. Southerd, who competed against this bitch twice, winning one event and losing the other, describes Anna as a not particularly typey sort of animal but with great speed and even greater determination to get to her hare. Her career in the coursing field was little short of spectacular and top-class longdogs were simply grist to her mill, for she toppled many in the meets Brown attended. She eventually retired and her bloodlines are now mingled with those of longdogs, most of which were saluki greyhound bred.

The second exception to the rule is the strain of lurcher bred by Andrew 'Stat' Stainton of Lincolnshire, a strain that has been deliberately free of saluki blood and yet succeeds well at the testing sport of single-handed hare coursing. Stainton still wins regularly with these primitive Norfolk lurcher types that were once bred by Beaumont

Hares are difficult quarry.

nearly half a century ago. The origin of this type is obscure but sup-posedly deerhound, Bedlington terrier, whippet and greyhound conspired with marsh collie to produce what is loosely termed a Norfolk-type lurcher. These hounds are both speedy and surprisingly biddable and versatile, and are possibly examples of that chimera the all-round lurcher, for Stainton, who is the chairman of the coursing branch of The East of England Lurcher Club, lamps, courses and works his lurchers with ferrets.

Yet the majority of the top-flight single-handed hare-coursing dogs are longdogs, and these days it is only saluki hybrids that tend to become the coursing legends that fetch astronomical prices when sold. Virtually every major winner is a saluki greyhound composite, with more greyhound than saluki in its make-up. Many are now from fairly true breeding strains, though I feel that better could be bred by delib-erately created three-quarter-bred greyhound/saluki/greyhound hybrids and treating the hybrids as end products and discontinuing the line, but my views are decidedly heretical and many longdog buffs swear by their interbred saluki composites, most of which are derived from Jeff Smith's Fly and Winchat's Hoover, though the original blood has been much diluted with saluki greyhound lines.

Longdogs of this breeding are seldom trained in the conventional sense indeed most are unruly and disobedient, possibly due to their saluki ancestry and partly because few single-handed hare-coursing enthusiasts are particularly concerned if their wards are obedient provided that the dogs catch hares. This is indeed a rather short-sighted attitude for some basic training results in a longdog that is more tolerable than the wild-eyed brutes one sometimes sees at these meets. Some of these longdogs pursue a hare, lose the hare and then vanish over the horizon, returning only when they decide the time is right. However, lest the reader should come to believe that the realm of the longdog has the monopoly on chaos, a visit to the Waterloo Cup coursing event will convince the reader the training is equally as bad among greyhound aficionados and – frankly I find the sight of linesmen chasing after recalcitrant hounds lends an aura of crass amateurism to the world's greatest coursing event. Sighthounds of any breed are seldom properly trained. I would not tolerate this sort of behaviour from any breed of dog.

However, while it must be argued that few of these longdogs are trained in the conventional sense of the word, no one could argue that these dogs are conditioned to a nicety. In fact some of the most carefully tuned, well conditioned dogs are often found at single-handed hare-coursing meets, or matches as these contests are called. Forthwith it is necessary to debunk some of the popular myths about single-handed hare-catching dogs. The notion that a visit to a downmarket dog dealer's kennels on the Friday can result in the purchase of a longdog that will sweep all before it on Saturday is not only illogical but ludicrous, for a longdog must undergo a lengthy training period to allow it to perform well at such a meet.

To begin at the beginning. A young longdog should be taught basic obedience long before it is taken to the coursing field. It should return to hand quickly and be able to jump, and while I am a heretic regarding longdog training I teach even saluki hybrids to retrieve their catches to hand. Only when a dog is obedient should it be trained to live quarry. Once more it seems expedient to repeat the adage that a dog that is not trained in the yard won't be trained in the field, and I believe that many of the chaotic events one sees at matches – dogs running over the horizon, worried onlookers, lost dogs, landowners driven demented by the disobedience and wilful behaviour of longdogs – could be prevented if the handler subjected the whelps to some basic training.

There are, of course, many theories about how a match dog should be entered. E. G. Walsh's *Lurchers and Longdogs* believes that the youngster should not be run at rabbits, lest the sight of rabbits disappearing down a burrow sours the longdog. Walsh believes that a longdog should be left until it is eighteen months of age and then taken out with an old-school master dog, the sort of dog that still has speed and stamina enough to wind a hare, but seldom panache enough to capture it. When the older dog has tired the hare a little the youngster should be slipped and encouraged to chase and possibly catch the hare. Personally I have never favoured this method of entering, though no one could dispute Walsh's successes in the coursing field. I enter a longdog in much the same way as I enter lurchers, working them with ferrets and lamps and allowing them to chase and hunt up quarry during the daylight hours. I have found that such training not only allows the dog to learn the peculiarities of quarry species but also strengthens the relationship between dog and man.

Many match runners are decidedly shy about allowing a potential match dog to lamp. It is popularly believed that dogs that are trained on the lamp will not try when a hare approaches a hedge or a fence, losing the hare at the very moment when the dog should be trying the harder to push it off its well used runs. I have never been able to follow the logic behind such thinking and I am more than a little baffled when I hear match runners try to explain this notion. My own belief is that once a dog is deemed physically and mentally developed enough to catch rabbits or hares it must be given every chance to do so; just as the finest training for a fighter is a fight (Jack Dempsey) so the very best training for a hare-catching dog is work in the field – but I repeat, not all match runners share my opinions.

A dog needs to be really fit and in perfect health to put up even a reasonable show against a hare, and it is foolish to expect a dog to hold its form for an entire season, for like prizefighters, dogs must achieve the peak of their form on the day of a match. Southerd's method of getting a dog fit (a magnificent understatement) is both interesting and effective, and may serve as a model to those who wish to engage in this most testing and taxing of sports. Don's dogs enjoy a lazy summer, engaging in gentle exercise and play until some six weeks before the season begins. Exercise then becomes a little more taxing and the dogs are given quite a lot of roadwork along country lanes, trotting behind one of Don's four-wheel-drive vehicles. The work sessions are increased to fifteen minutes a day at fifteen miles an hour until the dogs are no longer panting with exhaustion when Don arrives at his home, and they are lamped frequently to give them the necessary enthusiasm for the sport that all match dogs need, for a listless, indifferent dog will seldom perform well in the field. Notions that dogs come to life on the day should be ignored and a dog should show increased enthusiasm for work as the start of the season approaches. If I might digress somewhat, I find that exhibitors who field a hard-muscled dog at the summer shows cannot produce the same condition on the field the following autumn and winter, and I feel that judges who demand that a working lurcher should be exhibited in 'match' condition are being a shade unrealistic for there is some evidence to suggest that canine athletes peak perhaps as seldom as six times a year. Summertime, the time of

Saluki greyhound puppy about to receive advance training.

shows and country fairs, should be lazy times for a longdog and judges must judge accordingly. A dog that is muscled up during the summer months is literally 'all dressed up with nowhere to go'.

As the exercise a dog is made to endure is increased, the diet of the hound should change. A dog at rest during the summer months needs a low-grade diet of perhaps 21% protein with a high carbohydrate content – the sort of meal sold as sheepdog meal – as exercise increases the amount of protein in the diet should also increase. Don achieves this shift in diet by boiling up lean meat and adding meal to the cooling mixture. Some longdog enthusiasts are fanatical about the diets of their wards and delicately prune all fat from the meat that is to be fed. This is a mistake, and one I urge the tyro longdog enthusiast not to make. Fats are an essential part of the diet of any dog and provided the meat is not too fatty it should be left intact and not stripped of fat. As to the source of the meat, pork is considered too fatty for longdogs, while horse meat seems to improve if it is 'hung' for two weeks before feeding to reduce the laxative effect.

As the coursing season approaches the longdog should be fed a protein-rich diet of perhaps 31% protein, and there are complete greyhound foods such as Wafcol that are ideal for a longdog that is approaching its peak. If complete diets are used it is rather pointless to add vitamins and mineral supplements to a mixture that is carefully balanced, and it is wise to heed the maker's advice when feeding these complete diets, though many longdogs will display voracious appetites as they begin to peak. I have seen some longdogs that prefer to exist on almost starvation rations and who spurn their feed trays if extra food is offered them. I have seen a few of these hounds that also succeeded well on the field, but the majority of longdogs will attack their food with gusto. Mo Smith once said that a longdog that is ready should cast longing glances at the crisp, white substance beneath its feed – the plate. Yet some longdogs, even fit longdogs, will eat slowly and unenthusiastically, yet perform well in the field. Saluki hybrids, particularly saluki-saturated longdogs, will often display what is known as a 'picky' appetite, while longdogs with a high proportion of greyhound in their make-up are usually furious trenchers. It is good policy to feed 'in training' longdogs immediately after they have excercised, though it is wise to allow a cooling time before feeding or watering these hounds. I enjoy watching fit dogs eat and gain quite a lot of knowledge from my observations. A dog that ignores its feed and seeks its bed is clearly unwell, and I am deeply suspicious of a dog that displays an excessive thirst when it returns from its exercise period. If it does the trainer has overdone the exercise, or else the dog is unwell.

Some six weeks after the autumnal training of the longdog has begun the dog should be approaching a state where it can be matched against a hare, and once again impromptu forays must be avoided for a strong hare is much too fleet a creature for a partially fit dog or a dog that has been fed then taken onto the field. Match runners must learn to ignore visitors who arrive, often univited, and request that their dogs be matched against the householder's longdogs. An unplanned match is, in fact, a recipe for disaster and more dogs finish blown up or damaged after such meets than the reader might imagine. A game dog coursing its hare will often tear muscles, damage its heart, blitz its lungs and distort its diaphragm in its efforts to catch a hare. An unfit dog subjected to unplanned courses is almost certain to injure itself. In fact it is unwise to exercise an unfit longdog in country that is unknown.

I always worm and dip both lurchers and longdogs immediately prior to the start of their training for the winter's hunting. Modern practice seems to ignore worm segments wriggling in the dog's droppings until the infestation becomes heavy, but I'm afraid I disagree with this practice. I dose twice with diochlorophen to clear worm infestations and then dip my dogs in a mangicide which kills not only mange mites but the fleas that often harbour tapeworm eggs, and only when I am sure that my dogs are free of parasites do I proceed with training.

The day prior to a coursing meet or match is all-important to the welfare of the dog and the success of the course. Some weeks prior to the first course of the season I give my hounds an egg or so at night-time, and immediately prior to the course only an egg or so is fed to the hound competing. The longdog certainly needs an empty belly to be able to run its hare and give of its best during the course, and raw eggs are easily digested. I have known some coursers who believe that a hound needs to be starved for forty-eight hours before a course, but I believe this to be a ruinous practice. A hound going into the slips in a famished condition, its blood sugar level low, its stomach and bowels totally empty and its kidneys taxed by having to remove the breakdown products of body fat (oxybutyric acid etc.) will certainly not perform as well as a hound that is conditioned by a more sensible handler. Conversely, dogs fed immediately prior to a course will perform badly on the day and suffer considerable discomfort during and after the course. A successful courser is usually a sensible courser, one who adapts his training methods to the needs of the dog he is training and disregards advice that is patently ridiculous.

I am very much against the notion that a longdog needs to be fielded in a paper-thin condition if it is to succeed well in a contest with a hare, though once again, a glutinous brute will do rather less well in such a contest. A dog that carries virtually no body fat will suffer greatly during its courses, and once again might I resort to a tale to illustrate a point. At one of the East of England coursing events of 1992, admittedly some of the most testing and meticulously organised events, Canaan, my own longdog, began the day weighing 62lb. She endured (the correct word considering the strong hares she coursed) three hard courses, one of which continued for over four minutes. When she returned home that night she weighed in at a shade under 57lb. A dog that has no such fat resources to lose will suffer badly when run at strong hares, and will not only return looking jaded and emaciated but fade badly during the courses. The phenomenon known as 'pulling up' or failing to stay with the hare when the course becomes long or extremely hard is usually due to the hound being prepared badly for the course rather than some disinclination to give of its best. A fit dog with virtually no fat reserves will usually try but not have sufficient energy to come to terms with its hare. Some dogs that have been 'run out' look simply awful when they return from their runs, and if their blood sugar levels have been greatly reduced will appear unsteady on their feet. Such animals need to be rugged, treated and returned home. To run them yet again in this condition is to court disaster.

A dog that is clearly distressed at the end of a day's hard coursing needs careful attention if it is to recover quickly and compete again the following week. I avoid allowing a dog access to water after a hard coursing meet until it has cooled and is no longer panting badly, and only when the day's coursing is over do I allow it a chance to drink its fill. No dog with its stomach full of water should be allowed to run yet one more course. I am very much in favour of allowing a coursing hound, or a lurcher that has undergone a strenuous day's hunting, to drink an electrolyte solution to facilitate its recovery. These solutions often appear to work miracles in aiding the recovery of a jaded hound or lurcher, and I have seen hounds that have faded badly on the field, looking decidedly off colour and out of condition, recover in hours after drinking such a solution.

Three hard courses at hares that have been afforded fair law are usually enough to tax the energy of a good longdog to its limits, and the newcomer to coursing would do well to close his ears to tales of sixteen runs at strong hares. A greyhound fielded in top condition is seldom capable of three ninety-second courses at strong hares, and all the magical mixtures of saluki or deerhound blood in the world are unlikely to produce a longdog that is capable of the feats described in the beer tent by lurcher-toting liars. When housed near Six Mile Bottom in Cambridge I frequently saw dogs bested by hares to such an extent that the dogs were so exhausted they needed to be lifted into the cars that had brought them to the meet, and few dogs were capable of running three strong hares in these conditions. A tyro longdog owner would do well to ignore the stupid tales that are all too common among lurcher enthusiasts and observe how the same liars are all too ready to sell their super dogs for a song. A hare is the most testing adversary for a longdog to run.

I have never regarded the rugging of a longdog before or after a course as a sign that both the courser and his hound are in any way effete. A hound that is warmed up before a course will perform better than a hound that stands shivering in the slips immediately before it begins its course. It is good sense to observe the athlete limbering up before an event to warm up his or her muscles, to observe a boxer shadow boxing before he begins his contest, to realise how important it is to keep a dog warm before it is released at a hare. Human beings are capable of assessing just how much they must exercise to acquire the correct degree of warming up. A dog is not capable of understanding the machinations of its own constitution and needs to be rugged before a course.

As to the practice of rugging up a dog that has just undergone a traumatic course and is both hot and panting, it is logical to believe that rugging such an animal is the best way of preventing the animal chilling. It is interesting to note that lurcher buffs who believe that such careful treatment of a coursing animal is both unnecessary and undesirable are seldom successful in the coursing field and are usually only too willing to pass on dogs that fail to perform well on the said field. Time and care spent on training and conditioning a coursing dog is well spent, and the proper care and management of the said hound is amply rewarded by improved performance in the field.

14

Lurcher Shows

Lurcher shows are great fun and can often be a great day out for the entire family. To some it is a *raison d'être*, however, and I cannot but feel that anyone that is unable to accept a win or loss at such a show in good grace is rather spoiling the ethos engendered by a pleasant summer's afternoon. Yet there are people who religiously travel to every lurcher show in the country, either as spectators or exhibitors, and prize the rosettes and ribands they win. Man is indeed a highly competitive animal and once an interest in some hobby is developed it is certain that events to determine who is best at the said hobby will be staged.

Lurcher shows are relatively recent events. In 1974 a group of lurcher enthusiasts met to stage the first all-lurcher show at Lambourn, and this event produced a great many exhibitors and an even greater number of spectators. For the next eight years at least the show went from strength to strength, and it was obligatory for any lurcher enthusiast to set aside the first Sunday in September as the day to make a pilgrimage to the fields just outside the village of Lambourn. The show was, to say the least, superbly organised, and for the eight years the show was run the weather was always hot and sunny so the event always attracted a huge crowd and few went home unhappy with the day's events. Lambourn attracted not only lurcher enthusiasts but also stallholders who sold fieldsports equipment, artists who specialised in dog portraits and photographers with an interest in faces, both canine and human.

However, the seeds of self-destruction were sown as soon as the show became more popular and eventually a far from desirable element began to make its presence felt at Lambourn. Lurchers have always attracted the attentions of travellers and their bedfellows and a host of unpleasant characters to boot, and hordes of such undesirables descending on the village of Lambourn caused considerable alarm among the natives of that fashionable village. Bands of raffish characters descended on Lambourn weeks before the show, camping out on the downs adjacent to the village and causing little short of bedlam. Sheep were, apparently, worried and thug-like creatures began to terrorise the district. Thus long before the show was terminated there were moves afoot to prevent the event being staged at Lambourn.

In 1982 matters came to a head when a band of travellers sought to stage a bare-knuckle fight at the show and a series of unpleasant incidents preceded the Sunday spectacular. As I watched the two louts batter and bruise each other while their supporters raced around the spectators smashing cameras and threatening those who were drawn to the gladia-torial spectacle, I made a vow not to attend the show again and to avoid Lambourn as I avoid Appleby at mid-summer. I have every sympathy with residents who object to such behaviour and I am of the opinion that the natives of Appleby should live rate-free as some sort of compensa-tion for the nuisance the fair causes shortly before and shortly after the

Lurcher judging at a southern Welsh show.

Lurcher judging.

solstice. My vow, however, was not to be tested for the national press made much of the incidents at the show. Accounts of badger baiting and cock fighting were published – I never saw any indication that these events were staged and I spent the entire day at the show – but the photographs of blood-bespattered louts mindlessly resolving their problems in public appeared in most newspapers and this delivered the *coup de grâce* to the organisers. It was a great pity for I really enjoyed Lambourn and made many friends at the show. Indeed in 1981 I judged my one and only lurcher show at Lambourn and met Michael Lyne, the coursing artist, and my co-judge at this lurcher meet.

Nevertheless, Lambourn served as a pattern for other lurcher shows and there were many more to follow. Whaddon Chase soon became the Mecca for all lurcher enthusiasts, but later Chatsworth was to surpass it as the premier lurcher show, as indeed was Weston Park, a strategically placed lurcher show staged in September near the A5 and the M6 motorway. It has to be mentioned that despite the fact both shows are well organised and well attended they lack the ethos the ill-fated Lambourn Lurcher Show once engendered. What a great pity that a small band of louts should destroy the entertainment for so many, but then in the early days of lurcher showing there were many louts with a passing interest in lurchers. These days such characters are seldom seen at lurcher shows and the sight of drunken brawlers roaming about making themselves pests to all and sundry is uncommon.

Lambourn certainly set the parameters within which a lurcher show should be run, and while there are no separate classes for lurchers and longdogs (most lurchers/longdogs are far too mongrelly to be classified anyway) there are usually classes for small and large lurchers. It can be argued that the larger lurchers are more versatile and more capable of taking hares, but this is far from the truth for many twenty-two-inch lurchers are fine hare catchers, but the more classes staged for lurchers the more satisfied exhibitors, for a greater number of show enthusiasts will win rosettes and most shows stage a contest between the winners of the small and large classes to determine best in show. There are usually classes for puppies as well as adult lurchers, and in the larger shows classes for intermediate or sapling lurchers and longdogs, but for obvious reasons it is rare to find a young lurcher winning the coveted Best In Show award, for it is argued that the attractive youngster may grow into an unattractive adult. Yet if the hounds are judged on their merits on the day and the judge makes an attempt to predict the aesthetic progress of the whelp it is perfectly reasonable for a judge to award the B.I.S. award to a puppy, though it would be a very brave judge who would commit this heresy.

It would also be a very brave judge who awarded a B.I.S. prize to a dog with a strong baseline, though due to its whippet-like shape a Bedlington terrier will often breed good typey first-cross lurchers when mated to greyhounds or whippets. Collie hybrids, or at least collie/greyhound or collie/whippet first crosses, are seldom typey enough to be placed, and it usually requires a further dash of sighthound blood to produce a suitable collie-bred show lurcher. During the early 1960s the versatility enjoyed by collie hybrids encouraged show organisers to stage classes for collie hybrids, but these were usually disastrous affairs; without guidelines by which to judge few of the show judges, who were usually sighthound aficionados, knew what to look for in a good collie lurcher – and for that matter neither would I. These days most of the collie-bred show-winning lurchers are three-quarter-bred collie/greyhound/ greyhound composites, though few collie lurchers are as aesthetically pleasing as longdogs or supersaturated sighthound-bred lurchers, and most successful show winners have a percentage of deerhound blood in their ancestry.

I am always baffled to hear ringside critics uttering the usual sour grapes comment, 'The judge isn't putting up working lurchers', for I am uncertain what actually constitutes a working lurcher. Furthermore, I am baffled as to how to define a working lurcher. Most dogs with a dash of sighthound blood in their ancestry will work or chase and attempt to capture game, but while I have seen some decidedly ugly and aesthetically unpleasing brutes that were excellent workers, I have also seen some very attractive lurchers that were also extremely good at their jobs. Might I quote as an example the longdog Benson, owned by Sarah Smith, that is not only an attractive dog but also a fine worker to all quarry – and such all-round yet attractive show-winning lurchers are legion. I am in fact unable to define what is meant by a working lurcher and I would advise judges simply to select their winners from the most aesthetically pleasing exhibits in the show ring. It is virtually impossible

Sarah's Smith's Benson, an excellent all-rounder and a show champion.

to tell which of the exhibits work and which don't, and, furthermore, the show ring is a place where dogs of a pleasing shape should be selected regardless of whether or not the exhibits perform any sort of work. Virtually any lurcher will, if given a chance, work, and if a person chooses not to allow his or her hound to work then this decision should not debar the lurcher from being placed in the show ring. Yet the rebel yell, 'He don't work 'em' rings out every time a judge places a good-looking animal that certain members of the audience consider is a shade too aesthetically pleasing to be classified a 'worker'. What a load of nonsense, and such nonsense does little to improve the image of the lurcher enthusiast.

At one time only the most bizarre of people were deemed suitable to judge lurcher shows. It was believed by early show organisers that the lurcher was the dog of the poacher and the companion of the traveller, so it was argued that only the traveller and the most incredibly seedy disreputables were suitable to judge lurcher shows. In those days it was not uncommon to see the most disgusting-looking louts judging the exhibits, men whose only qualification for judging a show was a string of poaching convictions mingled with sundry burglaries. Other judges often resembled hillbilly comic-book characters or New Age travellers, and many of the judges manifested questionable personal hygiene and, frankly, stank. Some were the precursors of New Age travellers, others simply dog dealers who traded in canine misery but had such a multitude of sighthound waifs and strays pass through their hands that the uninitiated show committees considered them 'experts'.

Thankfully, these people are no longer as liable to judge and are seldom seen at lurcher shows, though dog dealers with a host of run-down beasts in their trucks are still far too common at the less well organised country fairs. A new type of judge has emerged, selected or conscripted from the ranks of successful lurcher exhibitors, and possessing not only a good eye but an excelled knowledge of conformation and type. The evolution of this new breed of judges is both interesting and worthy of mention. At the time when traveller poacher judges were in vogue and certain judges put in a spot of lurcher assessing between prison engagements, a band of stalwart sighthound enthusiasts, Kennel Club exhibitors and breeders of registered sighthounds had the temerity to judge alongside the bizarre riffraff. These sighthound exhibitors/breeders did in fact survive long after the lurcher world had started to reject the filthy exhibitionists, and by dint of good judging sensible selection stimulated the genesis of judges who knew little of pure-bred sighthounds but were experts on lurcher conformation.

Typical of this new breed of judges is Lana Gadzer, a horse wrangler and racehorse trainer who is possibly one of the most successful of the new breed of lurcher judge.

A good guide for the ideal conformation of the show lurcher is that described by the Abbess Juliana Berner, author of the *Boke of St. Albans*, and this piece of rhyming wisdom should always be borne in mind when a young lurcher judge steps gingerly into the lurcher show ring to adjudicate:

> A greyhound should be:
> headed like a snake
> necked like a drake
> backed like a beam
> sided like a bream
> footed like a cat
> tailed like a rat

And the judge should make certain allowances to this standard, accepting that a lurcher needs to be a shade broader in the head than a greyhound, to accommodate a greater brain perhaps, or simply to indicate the presence of blood other than pure-bred greyhound blood in the hybrid about to be judged. A judge should also realise that the rat tail is sometimes disguised by long hair.

Few of the older lurcher judges, the New Age traveller experts, were concerned with the mouths of exhibits. Indeed, few of these people knew the difference between the correct scissor bite and undershot or overshot mouths, hence many of the early winners had far from satisfactory dentition. These days the modern judges are far more *au fait* with canine dentition and most show winners have excellent mouths, though the occasional slightly overshot dog does pass through from time to time. Undershot mouths are in fact extremely rare in lurchers, or sighthounds for that matter, though in 1981 I saw a smooth-coated lurcher bred from a greyhound dam and an American pit bull terrier male with a very bad pig (undershot) mouth.

'A lurcher is only as good as its feet' is a commonly used epigram among coursing enthusiasts, and a dog that manifests poor feet, knocked-up toes or badly flattened feet should never be placed in preference to an exhibit that has good, sound feet. Road work or much exercise in a large concrete run will usually improve bad feet a little but a dog with long, untrimmed nails is sooner or later a lame dog, and one that cannot work as a lurcher or longdog should. Should I wish to judge or be offered an

A winning three-quarter greyhound one-quarter collie hybrid.

opportunity to do so I should not place a dog with weak or defective hare feet – and having said that I received a very bad whipping in 1967 when I entered my lurchers in a coursing match against some saluki hybrids that had simply terrible feet but performed wonderfully well on the field.

Short, stuffy necks, such as are found on some collie hybrid lurchers (first-cross or reverse three-quarter-bred collie/greyhound/collie) seldom find favour with lurcher judges and very few first-cross collie/greyhound hybrids win at lurcher shows. An exception was Ian Porter's Mel, a collie/greyhound bitch bred by mating a greyhound male with a merle collie bitch (the mother of Hancock's Richard Jones, a famous beardie border hybrid), but Mel was one of those exceptional animals that won well at shows, obedience tests and put up a fair perfor-

178

mance against longdogs in the field. She resembled a greyhound as much as a lurcher and was often placed when she ran on some of the unlicensed greyhound racing tracks, but animals of this type and breeding are indeed rare. My own strain of lurcher is heavily laced with collie blood and is decidedly stuffy in the neck and very cloddy, and should I wish to breed out these aesthetically unpleasing characteristics (and I do not, I must add) then I should need to cross this strain with a typey pure-bred grey-hound.

Deep-chested dogs (sided like a bream) are not only very successful in the show ring but equally successful in the coursing field, if, that is, these chests are broad and capable of housing large, spacious lungs. The type of chest sported by the exhibition greyhound – and I must confess I find these huge hounds very beautiful – is seldom spacious enough to be functional, for such chests lack volume. Some of the deepest chests are found on dogs with a strong trace of deerhound in their ancestry, and K.C.-type whippets (quite distinct from some of the track-bred stock in shape) will produce lurchers with very deep chests. Collie crosses are rarely deep-chested, not unless, that is, the hybrids are supersaturated greyhound crosses with threequarters or more of their genetic make-up sighthound blood. Half-bred collie hybrids usually have notoriously shallow chests and this lends them a decidedly untypey appearance that seldom attracts the attention of a judge.

The tail sported by a lurcher attracts considerable attention from a judge for some reason or another, and most tend to favour the long, whiplike rat tails described by the Abbess Juliana Berner. The tail is one of the devices a dog uses to steer it during its flight and is quite an impor-tant extension of the dog's spine. It may be, however, that the importance of a hound's tail has been grossly overvalued. Several hounds with tails truncated by accidents have performed well on the track and the coursing field. If I might be allowed to digress somewhat, one of the most common causes of loss of caudal vertebrae in sighthound, lurcher or longdog is tail whip. Sighthounds and their composites are happy dogs and wag their tails incessantly at any opportunity. Thus the ends of the tails of kennelled hounds lash against the walls and wires of the kennels and bleed, and unless treated the caudal vertebrae at the ends of the tails of these hounds bruise, die, wither and fall off. It is not uncommon to visit greyhound kennels and to find hounds with the tips of their tails plastered and bandaged to prevent further damage. Tail whip is, I believe, as distressing to the owners of these hounds as to the hounds themselves, for the kennels in which these hounds are housed are frequently daubed with blood. Hounds that are missing a few vertebrae either by atrophy or surgery are seldom incapacitated on the track or coursing field, yet they look badly balanced, and few judges will place a hound that has had the end of its tail removed.

Gay tails, tails that sweep upwards or curl, are seldom favoured by show judges, though such tails are rarely a hindrance to the lurcher in the field. Some strains of greyhound sport this peculiarity and Edwardes Clarke was particularly antipathetic to this type of tail and stated that if he owned a gay-tailed greyhound he would have the tail broken and reset – a somewhat extreme practice I've always thought, for such a tail carriage does not impede the flight of the greyhounds in the slightest. Once again, collie blood, particularly Border collie blood, tends to produce gay tails in the lurchers produced from this breed, though this type of tail is seldom seen in three-quarter-bred hybrids or in lurchers with only a tiny dash of collie blood in their make-up. A gay tail,

Jayne Drakeford – a
top lurcher judge.

however, gives the hybrid a very cur-like appearance and thus this type of tail is seldom liked by show judges. My own strain of lurcher is not only gay-tailed but has a decided kink in the extreme portion of the tail. Thus, while I have not found this type of tail hinders the lurcher in the slightest I believe it would be a very unwise judge who would place a lurcher with a gay or kinked tail.

On the subject of tails, a newcomer to lurcher shows might be surprised to see lurcher judges pulling the tails of an exhibit between the hound's hind leg and assessing the distance the tail extends along the dog's sternum. This is simply a display of histrionics on the part of the judge, a pointless, though harmless, display that serves no purpose other than to create an image or to entertain the crowd. In all probability the judge has chosen the winner within the first few seconds of the dog entering the show ring.

Other idiosyncrasies are also evident at these shows. Judges will often examine the cranial structure of these hounds as intently as would a phrenologist and state that they are searching for signs of concussion in the dog. Magnificent hokum, no more, no less, as is the swinging of the dog's wrist to assess how flexible the joint is, but the crowd loves such histrionics even if an experienced Kennel Club sighthound judge would be baffled by such displays.

The oft repeated quote of Abraham Lincoln 'You can fool all of the people some of the time, and some of the people all the time, but you cannot fool all of the people all the time.' should always be borne in mind by those who have the temerity to judge a lurcher show, for only three of the exhibitors will agree with the judge's decision and a great many disappointed exhibitors will curse and vilify him. Some poor losers will often give a more outlandish display of histrionics than the judges themselves, shouting execrations, cursing lineages and swearing death and destruction to those who have won the coveted rosettes – value ten pence. Spectators at the show may claim to be shocked, disgusted or horrified at this display of bad sportsmanship, yet such strutting is simply part and parcel of lurcher shows and should be regarded as part of the weekend's entertainment – and it would be difficult to imagine better value for one's money than a ticket to a lurcher show.

15

Other Lurcher Events

These days country fairs stage a great many events to attract the lurcher enthusiast who is not really interested in showing his dogs or, like me, is blissfully aware of the aesthetic shortcomings of his animals. During the early Lambourn shows only lurcher racing events were staged to entertain those with no interest in the parade of glamorous hounds. These days, however, there are a myriad events to captivate even the lurcherman who believes that the only place for the lurcher is in the field, and these events are run largely through the good auspices of the National Lurcher and Racing Club.

I must confess that while I was not hostile to this club when it was first formed by the McCurry brothers in the early 1980s, I certainly did not promote the organisation. A speedy lurcher without use or brain was certainly not what I desired and a club that promoted only the speed of a lurcher by staging whippet-type races was, in my opinion, an organisation that spelt disaster for the working lurcher. Hence, while I refrained from attacking the said organisation, I also refrained from joining for I felt it offered little for me and nothing for the world of the working lurcher.

These days the club offers far more diverse events to please its members and cater for their interests, and because of the club the lot of the lurcher and the image of a lurcher being only a slip-and-run dog has been ameliorated. More to the point, the club has started to stage properly organised field events – quite distinct from some of the chaotic illegal affairs that are the curse of fenland farmers – and these events have done much to elevate the status of the lurcher owner in the eyes of other field-sports enthusiasts who had hitherto regarded lurchers as wild, untrained brutes as much of a nuisance as the people who owned them.

At first the obedience tests, first staged in the early 1980s, attracted little attention from the lurcher fraternity, for these tests, while they were watered-down editions of the K.C.-type tests, were far too testing for the average lurcher owner. At this stage – the early 1980s – the dog swapper and the downmarket dog dealer were still held in some esteem by the average lurcher owner, and the man who materialised at a show with some twelve lurchers on leashes was credited with being a good lurcherman. A tale will readily illustrate this point. During this period of time I competed regularly at jumping events and with more than average success. One day a young lurcher enthusiast turned up at my cottage and engaged me in conversation and asked just how many lurchers I owned. I replied that I owned two (one too many, perhaps) and the attitude of my interrogator changed to derision. 'So and so owns fifty-eight,' he exclaimed as if the said number indicated the value of the dog dealer, who would have had no knowledge of how to train any dog of any breed and whose kennels were simply transit camps where a dog spent an unhappy few days until it found a new, if temporary, home. Such was the attitude of the lurcher buff at that time, so these obedience tests found little favour.

Yet another reason for the lack of interest in these tests was the evolution of what I choose to call the 'instant expert'. The sporting press has a surfeit of educated, talented writers wishing to write about the merits, training and working of gundogs, but there are few such writers who wish to attempt a weekly article on the subject of lurchers. From time to time various people with an interest in lurchers experience a meteoric rise to fame before being eclipsed and passing into obscurity. The evolution of these writers is interesting, if predictable. A letter to a sporting magazine will usually create interest among the friends of the writer who is prompted by this adulation to pen yet another letter. An invitation to judge a show is usually issued to the writer at this point, who, goaded to greater efforts, pens his first thousand-word article, usually a junior school type 'what I did in the holidays' tale about a day out with a favourite dog and an amazing haul of rabbits. Fame is a heady drug and in no time the writer is recognised at shows, and such recognition prompts a spate of further articles which are replicas of the first, but by now the writer is aware of his limitations as a fieldsports scribe. Yet such is the heady nature of success that he finds it impossible to discontinue writing, and as he has no experience and no ability to train dogs simply lashes out in print at any activities at which he cannot hope to compete and ridicules those who are able to take part. Such a writer must never attempt to enter any form of competition where his credibility will be questioned and his incompetence exposed. Hence, such a writer, before his inevitable eclipse, which is as certain as his rise to temporary fame, will heap contempt on the competitive events he has no possible chance of winning, and as such embryonic competitions can seldom stand bad publicity they too cease to exist. Such was the reason for the decline of these events in the early 1980s.

Fortunately the N.L. & R.C. revived these competitions and gave them credibility. Lurcher obedience tests are now well attended and attract large audiences. Most of the lurchers used in these competitions are collie-bred, though in recent years G.S.D. crosses are becoming quite popular. Longdogs are seldom used to compete in these contests, though from time to time one finds the odd deerhound hybrid not only competing but winning in this sort of competition.

The tests are remarkably simple and consist of encouraging the lurcher to walk at heel, to retrieve, to sit, to lie, to stay while the owner vanishes from sight for a few seconds, and to jump fairly low hurdles. Yet few lurchers seem able to perform these simple tasks, and in the early competitions a handful of competitors turned up to take part in these contests despite the fact that some shows boasted five or six hundred lurchers competing in the less taxing beauty classes. In recent years more and more interest is being paid to these obedience classes and it is now prestigious to win such an event.

At one time competition jumping events were the only competitions to be staged at lurcher shows, and I must confess I was besotted with these events and competed at any opportunity. In recent years there has been a revival in interest in the event and now the jumping contests are staged far more efficiently than hitherto. In the early days of competition lurcher jumping dogs were often damaged when they leapt from perhaps ten feet onto hard ground, though some organisers softened the landing area by adding quantities of water to the hard soil. These patches soon became mud and exacerbated the danger of landing rather than improving the condition of the landing place. These days the landing spots are buffered by rubber gym mats or mattresses, and few dogs are injured at these events. At one time it was by no means uncommon to see dogs limping away from these events, and I know of many trainers with quite excellent jumping dogs who refrained from entering these contests because of the damage their lurchers might sustain. One of the best jumping dogs I have ever seen was a fine-boned Norfolk type owned by an out-of-work warrener called Jim Cornell or Jim Corner (his accent was very strong and I often failed to understand him). Jim owned a pale straw-coloured Norfolk type, a curious-looking animal which had little body fur but heavy facial furnishings. I saw this dog leap ditches and fences that would have deterred steeplechasers, but Jim refrained from jumping the animal competitively because of the way some of these events were run. Jim died of cancer in 1982 and I missed seeing this great character and his highly unusual-looking dog. I once watched the dog retrieve a goose egg over a five-bar gate without breaking the shell.

A very popular event at many country shows is simulated coursing, a sporting event which consists of a pair of dogs pursuing a dummy that is manoeuvred in such a way as to make it follow an irregular path, such as is run by a wild brown hare perhaps. I have only twice watched this event but did not find it exciting or exhilarating. Obviously I am alone in my views for the activity attracts a huge number of spectators and so many potential competitors that I have observed lurcher enthusiasts queuing to secure a place in these events. Simulated coursing is therefore a big fund-raising event, and more and more shows seem to be staging these contests. Indeed, a country fair that caters for lurchers and lurcher owners offers considerable value for money and an excellent afternoon's entertainment for all the family.

16

Catching Foxes with Lurchers

The most amazing-looking lurchers will catch foxes and there seems to be no common denominator that determines that a lurcher will catch foxes. Some quite impressive-looking lurchers pursue foxes with indifference (most lurchers will chase foxes even if they refuse to tackle them) and other less typey lurchers catch foxes with great enthusiasm. Yet is is impossible to evaluate what will grow into a good fox-catching lurcher and some dogs will take to the activity without being formally entered or introduced to foxes. Some months ago, during the spring of 1993, Don Southerd was returning home with my longdog Canaan after attending a coursing meet on the Welsh

A lurcher runs a fox.

borders. Canaan had been subjected to an intensive training session in Caithness and had been taught to come to hand, retrieve, jump and to mark rabbit burrows, but had not seen a fox during her stay in Caithness. Don turned out the hound to exercise for a while and a fox sprang up in front of her. Canaan ran the fox, caught the animal and killed it with the aplomb of a trained fox-catching borzoi. Her litter brother apparently shows no interest in foxes though he will run alongside them and views them with interest. Furthermore, my two lurchers, Merab and Phaedra, which have been given exactly the same training as Canaan (and have responded to the training a hundred times better), show no interest in foxes and are not inclined to chase them.

Greyhounds, even game greyhounds that will come to grips with red deer, are often disinclined to catch foxes. Yet some hounds possess a devastating flair for fox catching. Just recently a greyhound bitch came to the Highlands drifting north, changing hands repeatedly, as is the way with Highland lurchers and longdogs I'm afraid, until her condition plummeted and she became a far cry from the track athlete of a few years before. Her speed had waned until a good lurcher could have bested her and her feet were terribly damaged because no doubt her present owners insisted on running her on hares on the tarmac runways of our local aerodrome. Yet she caught foxes with great enthusiasm and killed them deftly and with gusto. Yet sporting writers since the days of John Caius have remarked how reluctant even the best greyhounds can be to tangle with foxes.

Somewhere in the limbo between breeding and initial entering lies the secret of entering a dog to fox, and while it would be a very unwise lurcher breeder who would guarantee a puppy to be able to catch foxes in its later years, there is no doubt some lurchers regularly produce puppies that enter easily to fox, or more easily than other lurchers perhaps. David Hancock has a great variety of lurcher and collie stud dogs but finds one stud dog, Richard Jones, produces a larger number of fox-killing dogs than his other stud dogs. Yet sometimes formidable fox-killing dogs are unable to pass on this inclination to their progeny. One of the most ferocious lurchers I have ever known was Ahern's Grip, an enormous and quite hideous hybrid bred by mating an Ardkinglas deerhound to a very strong and game coursing greyhound bitch. Grip would tackle just about any creature and once killed a Dobermann that had invaded Terry's garden. He killed foxes as a terrier would a rat and ignored their retaliatory bites. Yet though the dog bred many, many puppies he bred no offspring that displayed the same animosity to fox – though many of his ancestors were fierce fox killers and utterly game.

While it is true that many foxes are killed during daylight hours after being disturbed and coursed by lurchers, most are killed by lamping lurchers or are bolted by terriers and coursed by lurchers and long-dogs that are stationed near the earths from which the fox is likely to bolt. However, whatever the method used by the hunter to catch foxes, lurchers need some preparatory training before they are entered to foxes.

While I know instances of dogs whose first catches have been adult foxes – Hancock's Romulus (Fish's Merle × greyhound) is a good example – I believe that quite a lot of training and entering on rabbits and hares should precede the dog's first course at a fox. Lurchers should know how to pick up a speedy though harmless species long before they encounter a speedy quarry that bites and retaliates furiously. I should like my ideal fox-catching dog to have experienced a successful season pursuing rabbits or possibly hares before it sees its first fox, though I will concede that if one is regularly hunting during daylight hours it is usually only a matter of time before a lurcher accidentally encounters a fox.

I confess that I am a cadaver gatherer and often excite the interest of passing motorists when I stop to pick up road casualty animals. Rabbits and hares are fed to my ferrets, or if there is a superabundance of these bodies available, to my puppies, but foxes killed on the road or given to me by my local pest control officers are treasured as training aids. I tie them to lengths of twine, tow them in front of the lurchers and en-courage the hounds to attack the carcasses. I also tie the carcasses just out of reach of the lurchers and encourage them to jump at and seize the bodies and try to encourage hostility to foxes and all things vulpine. A fox carcass is, however, a haven for mange mites. In fact more foxes die as a result of red mange (caused by the tiny mite *Sarcoptis communis*) than are killed by hounds, and at one time shire foxhound packs encouraged badgers to clean out fox earths that were known to harbour mange mites. Lurchers engaged in worrying fox carcasses will often develop skin infections that can be transmitted to both children and other dogs, and the would-be fox hunter must be vigilant concerning the treatment of these mange infestations.

It may seem a shade unsporting but I believe that young cubs are the best vulpine quarry on which to start a young lurcher that is to be used to catch foxes. At one time I lived near a breeding earth where cubs were produced every year and they were abundant in the district around my cottage. Each night I would return from school and walk any lurcher I was sent to train between the fox earth and the rabbit-infested grounds on which these cubs were known to feed in the hope that a cub would

be encountered on its way home to one of the earths on the embankment. When a cub appeared I slipped the lurcher and I trained few dogs
that failed to wed to fox by this method. When the embankment was
bulldozed to provide access to a housing estate I felt as though I had been
robbed or someone had violated the land I treasured.

A lamper who spies the huge saucer-like eyes of a fox appearing in
the beam must gauge the distance the fox has to run to find sanctuary
before the longdog or lurcher is slipped. Foxes are wary creatures,
which explains why they are so abundant perhaps, and will rarely, if
ever, deliberately afford a lurcher a sporting chance of catching them.
My best fox lamping spot was a turkey farm where the viscera from
drawn turkeys was spread on the midden pile. I would gather up the
viscera and carry it to the centre of a large field near the farm and wait,
lurcher on slip, while the foxes came to dine on the disgusting mess.
Once I deemed the foxes were sufficiently far from the hedges to afford
the dogs a chance of catching them, I slipped a lurcher. Once I caught
and dispatched the fox I left the cadaver in the middle of the field, for
if anything attracts foxes more than decaying turkey bowels it is the
presence of a freshly killed fox cadaver. A fox so placed will attract both
dogs and vixens, which approach the body gingerly, sniff it carefully
and then usually attempt to haul the corpse away to dine on it in peace.
Foxes thus preoccupied are often oblivious to the fact a lurcher is speeding towards them. One night in 1979, a bitterly cold night with driving
sleet to add to the misery I felt, I caught seven foxes, six of which were
attracted to the presence of their comrades. Foxes were a terrible pest in
the district at the time, for though the area was situated between
Meynell and Atherstone hunt country neither pack hunted the district,
and I am fairly certain that foxes were driven into the district by both
packs.

Lurchers soon learn how to deal with lamped foxes and avoid the
retaliatory bites, but the learning process is sometimes a painful one.
Penguin never really learned how to avoid getting bitten and simply
ploughed into foxes with gusto and venom. She caught several hundred foxes during her lifetime and I'm afraid her face was often bitten.
In her youth I ran her with her grandsire, a doughty fox killer, but I
soon realised this was a mistake. While the old dog launched into his
foxes and shook them fiercely, killing them quickly, if not instantly,
Penguin gripped the fox's flanks; this prevented the almost instanta-
neous death of the fox and wreaked havoc on Penguin's face. Once I
realised the damage it did I stopped running Penguin with her grandsire, but the damage had already been done and Penguin went to her

grave many years later bearing the scars from those early encounters. Her descendants would not have endured such treatment, particularly after the bloodline had been ameliorated with the blood of Ahern's Rusty, an excellent worker but never a brave dog, but Penguin became totally wed to foxes henceforth. At the sight of one a curious buzzing noise seemed to generate in her chest (I never heard her bark) and her body quivered with excitement.

It is the moral duty of the lamper to terminate the battle between dog and fox as soon as the dog has secured its catch. A prolonged battle, a protracted struggle, is unnecessary and totally undesirable and a fox so caught should be killed instantly and painlessly. I have an intense dislike for any unnecessary cruelty; anyway, a fox can inflict terrific damage to a dog during a protracted battle. In the early 1980s I worked a merle half-bred collie greyhound that was utterly game and extremely biddable and he caught over a hundred lamped foxes. Only once did I allow him to test his mettle in protracted struggle and that incident occurred by accident. I seldom ventured out of the district to catch foxes for they were plentiful around my cottage at that time. One night a fox ran out of the field and Merle caught it as it passed through a hawthorn hedge and I ran to intercept and terminate the battle. I knew the fields well – I had hunted them for nearly twelve years – but in my haste and excitement I somehow overlooked a slime-filled ditch near the hedge and sank up to my chest in the ooze. I dropped my lamp which sank out of sight, the light suddenly giving out as the equipment disappeared in the filthy mess that drained from the nearby poultry houses, and the night suddenly became intensely black. I took several minutes to extricate myself from the mess and left one of my shoes behind in the slime. Meanwhile, the battle twixt dog and fox continued in the next field.

Soaked and chilled, I was prepared to leave Merle to his own devices as I limped home in the darkness, chilled to the bone, my foot stinging from contact with the 'plough' over which I was required to walk. I reached the house half an hour later having taken that time to walk per-haps less than a mile. Merle killed and carried the fox to hand and arrived with his burden almost as soon as I did, but he was fearfully bitten as a result of the encounter and out of action for a full month. I vowed never again to allow such a battle to proceed and he never again received such punishment from a fox. Yet to terminate a battle between dog and fox while holding a lamp is never easy and I have been bitten by my own dogs as I attempted to kill a fox my dogs had captured. It is only on such occasions that I appreciate the terrific biting power of a

A bob-tailed lurcher closes on its fox.

lurcher. On one occasion while I endeavoured to separate Penguin from a fox she had caught, she struck out blindly and bit me on my upper arm. At the time I wore a very thick leather jacket made from quarter-inch thick leather by a saddler friend of mine, so Penguin's bite did not pierce the flesh, but I found myself bruised from shoulder to elbow by the encounter.

I am always a little wary of working with someone else's dogs in such a situation and I received a terrific bite from a friend's dog when I endeavoured to take a live fox from it. The dog in question, an inert and apparently lifeless saluki hybrid, lived indoors and accepted the attentions of four children, a cat and a tortoise that was wont to crawl into the dog's basket at night. Yet when I tried to take its fox and dispatch the animal the dog erupted, struck at my face wildly and sought to follow up the attack with a vengeance. Since that time I have been very chary about taking a fox from an unknown lurcher in pitch darkness, particularly when that lurcher is heated by the conflict.

Calling in foxes by squeaking or imitating the sound of a stricken creature is impressive to watch, but a lot more easy than the process

A soft-coated Wheaten terrier, a popular base line for fox-catching lurchers.

appears. I have no imitative skills, but I can call foxes from a great distance to investigate the sounds I am making. I have, however, met people who are capable of making the cries of trapped or injured animals and birds that are amazingly life-like, and these cries are reputed to be particularly efficacious in luring foxes. Still, I repeat that despite my lack of imitative skills I have never experienced any problems calling in foxes close enough to allow a lurcher I have been holding a reasonable chance. A cry similar to the scream of a frightened rabbit is usually most efficacious in attracting foxes. When I regularly lamped the land between the Meynell and the Atherstone hunt country – a triangle that was rich in foxes – I many times watched a lurcher carry back a squealing rabbit and watched foxes rush close to the lurcher to investigate the source of the squealing, only to be astonished to find my lurcher involved in the scenario. Foxes are such intensely curious creatures (as indeed are all carnivores) that while it is said that curiosity killed the cat, it often brings about the death of the fox.

I have called in foxes using a variety of methods, ranging from tapping two pebbles together at regular intervals to 'squeaking' the back of my hand in my mouth, a cry that certainly would not fool the most naive of people but caused the fox to come close to investigate, and I have called foxes to within fifteen feet of where I have been crouched. Why countrymen make such a display of fox calling is interesting, and I am half inclined to believe that all countrymen seek to shroud their activities in a certain mystique to confound city dwellers.

What is difficult, however, is keeping a dog still while a fox illuminated by a beam of light approaches the lamper who is making the strange sounds. Young dogs particularly become very excited, and even the most mute of lurchers is prone to give a slight 'yip' in such circumstances. A few foxes are bound to be lost in the training of a lamping lurcher as a young lurcher can no longer contain itself when a fox approaches and lets fly a battle cry and endeavours to engage the fox. Yet lurchers are perspicacious animals where their presence of quarry is concerned anyway, and soon learn to adjust to this technique of hunting. I have trained quite a few lamping lurchers which will wait with baited breath, as excited as the lamper perhaps, but without moving a muscle or uttering a cry while a fox comes closer and closer to investigate the sound of the strange cries. However, the evolution of such a lurcher takes time and those who chop and change as soon as it manifests a fault will never train a fox-killing lurcher properly. I expect half a season of mistakes before a youngster comes to learn what I expect of it and I ignore the most incredible errors in the dog's judgement during that time. I have lost a great many foxes as a youngster no longer capable of controlling its excitement has cartwheeled on its leash to attempt to catch a fox that is creeping towards it, and many times have I heard very steady, reliable, mute lurchers bark when they are placed in such a situation. Ahern's Grip, a remarkably fierce fox catcher who made no bones about catching foxes even if they were in a position to bite him savagely, was quite incredible to watch as a lamped fox approached him. The dog's body generated a strange, almost electrical, dynamism, a force that flittered up his slip into the hands of a lamper when a fox approached the team. He was virtually silent apart from a strange bee-like buzzing that seeped from his badly bitten nose, but remained totally stationary until slipped at his fox. It would be impossible to imagine a dog that tried harder to catch its fox. He was a truly ferocious animal, a danger perhaps to any creature that appeared in the beam, be it a fox, dog, deer or cat, yet he was wonderfully tolerant of Terry's children, and of puppies.

I have left the subject of red filters fitted over the lamper's beam until this chapter, and now it becomes expedient to discuss their use. A red filter or sheet of red cellophane fitted over the beam of light will afford the lamper a curious Forbidden Planet-like picture of the fields he is lamping, but will not alert either the fox (or rabbit) or the dog on the leash to the presence of the fox, for animals are, at the risk of being unscientific, unable to see red light, and the lamper armed with such a filter may thus approach a fox or the rabbit which is less able to sense the presence of the lamper. This is, however, what the majority of lampers believe. There are numerous schisms between theory and practice, and after a while some dogs are able to detect the presence of a rabbit or fox that appears in a beam of red light, though some lurchers never seem to be able to see the movement of an animal that is illuminated by this filtered light. Whether or not foxes ever have the opportunity to adjust their vision to sense this red light is questionable, though they learn quickly enough the dangers of a lamper's beam and certainly learn to distinguish between a lamper's beam and a similar beam of light from an oncoming car.

I have observed some curious reactions from both rabbits and foxes when a lamper who has approached the creatures silently and stealthily suddenly removes the red filter and the quarry is bathed in white light. Some rabbits will leap vertically in the air, and I have seen foxes turn and hiss at the beam of light that has suddenly enveloped them. Yet the efficacy of using a red filter is debated by many lampers, some of whom abhor its use, while others swear by it. Many fox hunters have taken to using these filters in the last few years and fieldsports suppliers find a great market for such equipment. The filter, if properly used, will often give a lamper an 'edge' – a few seconds' advantage – in catching the fox.

Foxes enjoy feeding on carrion, hence the bites inflicted by them tend to fester badly if they are not treated immediately the lamper arrives home or has light enough to see the extent of the damage, and few medium-sized predators are capable of biting with more fury than a fox. When I lamped foxes regularly – so regularly in fact that my job suffered as a result of my obsession – I followed the practice of cleaning minor wounds with salt water and then giving them a further cleaning with Milton, and then treating the deeper, more ugly bites with an antibiotic ointment. I found that dogs that were newcomers to foxes often suffered badly from some infection or other when they were first bitten; some of the lurchers I trained were badly bitten during their first encounters and their heads swelled to ludicrous proportions two days after the skirmish. As the season progressed, however, either the dog's technique of catching foxes improved or else the dog became more immune to streptococcal and staphylococcal infections, for they seldom suffered badly from the results of fox bites.

Once more I cannot resist a tale, I'm afraid. During the time when there was a huge market for red fox pelts, an acquaintance of mine bought a huge smooth-coated saluki greyhound composite (heaven knows what else was in the dog's make-up) from South Wales. The vendor had sold the dog as eighteen months of age, guaranteed to fox. Yet while it was obvious the hound was a great deal older than eighteen months, it was certainly a doughty fox-catcher and caught many foxes for his handler. One night the handler came to my house and in a panic announced that the dog was choking, and this too was patently obvious. The beast's head resembled that of Cerberus for it had swelled so badly that the animal had become unrecognisable to the handler. The throat and neck of the beast had also puffed up so badly that the thick bull terrier-type collar was virtually lost in the swollen tissue. Yet once the collar was released the dog began to breathe more easily. I injected the beast with some penicillin donated by a local farmer, and almost as I watched the swelling began to subside. I shall finish the tale. As dextrous as the beast was with foxes, it proved more dextrous at killing sheep and I suspect this is the reason the animal was offered for sale in the first place, for fox pelts fetched twenty or so pounds each in those years. My associate had few scruples and once he discovered the dog's fondness for mutton he too passed on the brute to the next unsuspecting buyer. *Caveat emptor* indeed, for there are very few honest, properly trained, vice-free lurchers offered for sale.

Hancock of Sutton Coldfield, the world's largest breeder of collie lurchers, states that while he sells many lurchers to lampers who wish to catch foxes, the majority of would-be fox-killing lurcher puppies are sold to those who wish to work lurchers in conjunction with terriers, and if the use of the red filter is a controversial subject the use of terriers to bolt and flush quarry is more so. I must confess that working lurchers in conjunction with terriers is a topic that sets my teeth on edge, and I freely admit that while I keep both lurchers and terriers I refrain from allowing the two types to exercise together, let alone work in conjunction with each other. Frankly, I have never seen a satisfactory rabbit-catching lurcher and terrier team. In theory the terrier works rabbits out of deep cover for the lurcher which is waiting close at hand to catch and retrieve to hand. In practice the use of both terriers and lurchers to hunt rabbits is a chaotic affair. Both lurchers and terriers are jealous hunters and never deliberately work in conjunction with each other. A terrier will hunt up cover readily and cause a rabbit to bolt, perhaps thereby enabling the lurcher to chase and catch the coney. However, once the lurcher has secured its catch the terrier usually races out and attempts to snatch the catch the lurcher is carrying. This action then sends the lurcher racing around the field to evade the terrier, and retrieving is bound to suffer in such circumstances. Some desperate fights, even between dogs and bitches, have been known to result over the ownership of the rabbits, and I have yet to meet any hunter who has control or charisma enough to prevent such combinations developing into riotous situations. I must confess that if I am on a rabbiting foray and a friend brings a terrier I will not take my lurchers out of the van to engage in the bedlam that is certain to follow.

The only use of the terrier-lurcher combination seems to be as a fox-hunting team – and even if this combination is to be used both the participants must be kept under control. In this practice the terrier sim-ply replaces the ferret as a creature tailored to bolt underground quarry so that the lurcher might chase and catch it, and frankly if one examines this method carefully there is little difference in the training of a fox-catching lurcher and the training of a ferreting lurcher – the same care is required to produce a top-grade fox-catching lurcher that is required to work with terriers. Before even considering this combination it is wise for the lurcher enthusiast to acquaint the lurcher with the terrier with which it is required to work, and if possible to establish a good work-ing relationship between the pair. There is in fact much to be said for the notion that a lurcher works best with a terrier of the opposite sex, for there is less chance of animosity between the two participants. Ahern's Grip was a wonderful fox catcher but was extremely spiteful if the terrier with which he was required to work was a male. My own bitch Penguin was equally antipathetic to bitches, and when I worked a bitch I called Chance, a truly excellent fox bolter who could nip and panic almost any fox into bolting, I could not bring Penguin out with her for the pair were decidedly hateful to each other. The best type of terrier for working alongside a lurcher at fox catching is the noisy, vociferous terrier that will bay at but not tackle the fox. An annoying, chanting bay of the sort that keeps a neighbour awake at night is equally irritating to any fox the terrier encounters underground, and foxes read-ily bolt when faced with such a dog. A dog that tackles its fox, engaging it in a to-the-death struggle so beloved by some terrier enthusiasts, is not efficient at bolting foxes for lurchers to chase. My ideal sort of fox hunt would be a terrier bolting a fox within seconds of encountering it followed by a quick chase by a lurcher, whether that chase was success-ful or not. Frankly I question the sanity of anyone who relishes a sixteen-foot dig to catch a fox, particularly when one considers that if some precautions are observed most foxes will bolt rather than slug it out with a terrier.

When a lurcher is first introduced to the sound and sight of a terrier working a fox below ground, it is wise to restrain the lurcher with a quick-release slip lead, and if possible station the lurcher near to the spot whence the fox seems likely to bolt. A young lurcher, particularly a youngster flushed with success carried over from a previous fox hunt, can often be an unmitigated nuisance if not restrained, for it will often try to crawl into the earth to reach the source of the conflict and thereby deter the fox from bolting. The longest rescue dig I have ever been invited to attend was in Derby and occurred simply because a fox attempting to bolt encountered a lurcher creeping into the earth and attempting to seize the fox. The fox, which apparently was only too willing to bolt, promptly shot back into the earth, sought sanctuary under the roots of a hedge and sat out the storm. Three days later the terrier was recovered but the fox apparently lived to fight another day. Frankly, I could tell a dozen such tales of over-enthusiastic lurchers spoiling a fox hunt in similar ways to those described.

As a lurcher matures, however, it acquires what must be the canine equivalent of wisdom, or develops a technique to deal with foxes that are ready to bolt. Penguin had a remarkable style of dealing with foxes a terrier was working below ground. She would walk on tip-toe

A fox drive using lurchers as catchdogs.

above the earth, as silently and delicately as would a cat, and wait at a half crouch until the fox decided to bolt. Most of her catches were achieved within a dozen yards of the earth and her speed at moving such short distances was amazing. Her great-great-granddaughter Merab has no inclination to tackle foxes, but adopts the self-same style when ferreting and achieves equal success at catching rabbits in the mouths of warrens. I cannot but feel sorry for people who swap and sell lurchers, one week keeping saluki longdogs, the next collie hybrids, only to settle for Bedlington greyhound hybrids the following week. I have experienced such pleasure observing how the twelve generations I have bred from one dog have developed, how sometime the line peaks then produces slightly less suitable progeny, and then peaks again, each generation contributing something to the next, but each time improving in its quality – but I digress.

Some of the best fox-catching dogs, or rather dogs that work in conjunction with terriers to catch foxes, I have ever seen have been pedigree unknown breeding but with a strong trace of sighthound. One particular dog that comes to mind is Beynon's Nell, described by Dan Russell as an oversized whippet but with a broad, sagacious head that suggested something else contributed to the incredible skills the bitch manifested. She had an uncanny knack of marking an inhabited earth, whining softly to indicate a fox was at home, and then following the progress of the terrier below ground as silently and as pussy-footed as a leopard. She tackled foxes fearlessly and would hunt up and course again any fox that reached cover and vanished from sight. This bitch was reputedly sired by John Mason's dog Sabre, but this coursing legend had died long before Nell was born so she justly deserves the sobriquet 'breeding unknown'. She died in 1981, one of the first victims of Parvo virus, or perhaps from some form of gastro enteritis, for few vets could determine the difference between the two diseases at that time.

Another very successful fox-catching dog was Paul Thomas's Max, a Hancock-bred half-bred sired by Richard Jones (beardie Border collie) out of a Hardly Ever-bred greyhound bitch. Max was an untypey, unattractive half-bred, broken-coated with an ugly ruff, but he was an incredible fox-catcher. Not only could he mark a fox to ground with alacrity but he would draw a fox from a difficult place no matter how badly he was bitten doing so. His haul of foxes was high and I have little doubt that the reputation this dog achieved did much to promote the Sutton Coldfield kennel, for Max was one of the first half-bred collie/greyhounds produced there. He had a truly flawless nose, and if he had faults they were that he never developed a technique of catch-

ing foxes without suffering from a retaliatory bite. I believe Max is still
alive, but though he mated a variety of mongrel lurcher bitches Max
bred little of outstanding worth, though I believe two of his brothers
were brilliant workers and breeders.

Longdogs are often formidable fox-catching dogs, if, that is, they can
be persuaded to tolerate the terriers that are used for fox bolting. Ahern's
Grip was a formidable fox-killer but a devil with any terrier that upset
him, and few dogs of any breed fared well when they upset this ferocious dog. One of the most spectacular fox-catching longdogs I have ever
seen was in fact one of Nuttall's breeding, a composite with more than
a touch of deerhound in its ancestry and possibly almost a pure-bred
deerhound despite the lack of stature. I cannot remember the bitch's
name but one Alan Dawson owned her and took her to New Zealand
when he emigrated there. This bitch was totally steady with ferrets and
allowed terriers to take terrible liberties with her. She enjoyed the role of
children's pet and towed trolleys carrying the Dawson children with
great patience. In the pursuit of hare she was a sluggard and became more
sluggish as she experienced repeated failures on the coursing field. Yet I
have seldom seen a more enthusiastic worker to fox, and her attention
span while a terrier worked below ground was incredible. She would
stand head down, ears cocked while the terrier battled beneath her feet,
and I rarely saw her out of position when a fox bolted. I once saw her
catch five grown cubs as they bolted in rapid succession, and she often
put lurchers to shame at her chosen sport. Before she left for New Zealand
she was mated to a full brother of Letesia (dam of the fabulous Minisotta
brothers Yank and Miller) and I believe quite a number of her puppies
took prizes at Lambourn lurcher shows. I have often wondered why
Nuttall ceased to breed this type of longdog, they seemed so tremen-
dously popular and successful at the work for which Nuttall intended
them. At one time most of Britain's top-rate fox-coursing dogs came
from this kennel in Clitheroe, and I saw few of these dogs that were not
utterly game yet had a steady disposition.

I cannot emphasise too much the importance of getting lurchers stock-
steady with terriers before taking them in the field to work together.
Despite ridiculous stories told by some terriermen there can be only one
outcome of a battle between a crazed lurcher and an angry terrier, and
woe betide the hand that comes between the antagonists. Cue for a tale.
In 1977 I visited an old airfield owned by Abbott Brothers, the Norfolk
ferret breeders, and coursed with Alan Bryant, the fieldsports supplier,
who owned a particularly ferocious Irish terrier. In the team was a fairly
docile deerhound hybrid who normally avoided trouble and was

regarded by many as inert – useful at coursing, quite good at fox-catching, but reluctant to bite. Irish terriers are, however, famed for their ability to ferment trouble, and this one launched several attacks on the lurchers before one retaliated, whereupon the inert deerhound hybrid eventually exploded, lifting the terrier clear of the ground. Alan, realising that the action could cause the death of his terrier, rushed to intercept, only to be badly bitten by the terrier. A far more unpleasant incident occurred at a Scottish lurcher and terrier show in 1992 when a terrier/lurcher battle escalated into a bloodbath that resulted in a badly damaged terrier and a spectator with a lacerated throat. I simply avoid taking terriers or lurchers to country shows because I find such skirmishes not only upsetting, but distasteful.

At one time it was extremely common to find certain country shows prohibiting lurcher classes, partly because these shows often attracted what can accurately be described as unsavoury louts and partly because the battles between terriers and lurchers upset contestants and families seeking to enjoy a day out in the company of others with similar interests. Fortunately the incidence of louts at such shows has decreased, yet battles between terriers and lurchers are still the bane of many show organisers. I cannot believe that lurchers which are hostile to terriers in a show situation would be any less hostile in the hunting field. Enough, however, of the subject of working lurchers with terriers, and I shall proceed with an even more controversial subject – the pursuit of deer.

17

The Pursuit of Deer with Longdogs and Lurchers

have always questioned the wisdom of Richard Grant Renwick, who published that compendium of tales *Coursing*, for the book starts with a highly controversial tale superbly written by one Thomas Hope. Hope recalls an incident where his wife, exercising a diminutive whippet Crossbow Jason, springs a roe deer and the whippet latches onto the throat of the animal, remaining thus fixed until Thomas Hope returned some fifteen minutes later to shoot the deer. An emotive chapter, and one that was sure to sway public opinion against the use of longdogs and lurchers, but a chapter that certainly illustrates that even small longdogs and lurchers can and do catch small deer.

I have always cherished the notion that the greyhound and the deerhound are one and the same breed, and the dichotomy between the types only began when certain types of greyhound began to be developed specifically to course hares. Certainly most sighthounds, from the great Irish wolfhound to the diminutive Italian greyhound, show a marked desire to pursue deer of all species. It is also true that hounds that are hesitant about taking foxes will pursue and capture deer with great enthusiasm. My present lurcher Merab shows absolutely no interest in the pursuit of foxes; they will spring from under her feet and she will watch them run with some interest but show no desire to chase them. Should a roe deer appear, however – and they are plentiful near my croft – she needs to be restrained for it is illegal to hunt deer with dogs north of Carlisle.

Pattison, also writing in *Coursing*, states that while lurchers will chase deer they regard the activity as only a form of amusement and that he has never seen a deer captured by a lurcher. Pattison could not be more wrong, for I have seldom seen a lurcher of any breeding that will not do its utmost to catch deer. In 1979 I received a letter from a distraught *Shooting News* reader who obtained a diminutive lurcher from a rescue society. On one of the local nature club rambles her dog flushed a roe and brought down the beast in front of the horrified club members. Yet the lurcher had never been entered or encouraged to catch deer and had been dissuaded (I'm not quite sure what this means) from chasing rabbits. The truth is most lurchers show a natural inclination not only to chase deer but to seize and catch them.

Britain harbours an amazing number of deer of a great many species, but only two species, the red and the roe, are indigenous to Britain. Roe are plentiful but are such shy, suspicious creatures that they are seldom seen, though many live on the suburbs of large towns. I live a great distance from civilisation and my visits south entail journeys through the night, so I frequently pass the network of motorways surrounding large towns and cities. Roe abound on the verges of such motorways and are far more numerous than the general public would believe. The land around Carlisle and Glasgow must harbour an enormous roe deer population, yet the country around both conurbations is regularly lamped by lurcher enthusiasts who seem to make little difference to the numbers of deer.

Roe seldom appear during daylight hours unless disturbed by some activity, and usually venture forth to feed at night. As the sun rises roe will usually seek out dense cover and blend so well with the undergrowth that they pass unnoticed. Near my present cottage the roe deer seek sanctuary in deep antique heather that has somehow escaped the burning that controls the growth of heather on the Highland moors. I frequently pass deer hidden in such heather, undetectable to the human eye, and it is only when my terriers disturb them that I notice their presence. They are fast-moving creatures but not as fleet as fallow, which vie with the hare for the title 'Britain's Speediest Mammal'. Yet to consider roe as easy meat for a lurcher would be a mistake. If such a beast were to be sprung on a golf course or in the centre of one of the fenland fields the chances are most lurchers would be able to outrun them. Roe, however, are furtive creatures, which explains why so many abound in Britain, and seldom place themselves in positions where they can be easily coursed by dogs. When disturbed the roe living on the heather behind my croft disappear into the deep heather or hot-foot it across the marshland over which they seem to be able to pass like water skaters, though even terrier-sized dogs sink up to their bellies when they attempt to negotiate such terrain. Roe seldom feed far from deep cover in the woodlands of the south of England, and once they find sanctuary in the deep bramble and undergrowth are rarely caught by lurchers or longdogs.

Lamped roe deer often fall victim to the poacher, for deer, unlike rabbits, seem unable to adjust to lampers' techniques. It is, of course, illegal to lamp deer – I shall explain the law regarding this practice at a later stage in the book – but indifferent lurchers are usually capable of pulling over a deer that is both illuminated and confused by the lamper's beam. Most roe deer are killed after dark and therefore are killed illegally, but few roe are more than seventy pounds in weight (I found a large seventy-pound roe killed by a lorry near Slocht Summit, hence the figure I have mentioned) and are often brought down by quite small lamping lurchers.

Before proceeding to the subject of other species of deer found in Britain, perhaps it is wise to tender some advice to the lurcher keeper. During my walks I frequently find very young roe deer fawns apparently abandoned by their dams and it is very tempting to the lurcherman to bring one home to rear the tiny, very appealing mite. Under no circumstances should the hunter do this. The chances are the doe has merely left the fawn to lure the hunter and his dogs away, and she will return to the creature as soon as all danger has passed. Furthermore, a roe deer can be the very devil of a creature to own as a pet, and if the fawn is a male it can create a great danger to the would-be pet keeper. Some years ago I knew a young laboratory technician called Elgan Phillips (now Dr Elgan Phillips, I believe). Elgan had a great gift for rearing exotica and often hatched parrot eggs in the laboratory incubator. His home assumed a zoo-like appearance where jackdaws and thrushes swarmed over his clothes as soon as he appeared, and a visit to his premises resembled a set for the film *The Birds*. I gave him numerous small creatures as pets including fox, badger and a single three-legged otter cub I found in the Lake District, a cub that was always vicious and unpredictable and damaged Elgan badly on New Year's Eve 1970, but that is another story.

One autumn I found a young roebuck fawn, the cutest, most attractive beast I have ever seen, and gave the tiny creature to Elgan, but it was an ill advised present and on reflection should have been left where my dogs found it. Elgan kept the tiny creature in a warm box and fed it on a sheep milk mixture, and it grew rapidly. At ten weeks of age (or, rather, what I gauged to be ten weeks of age) the fawn played at butting my dogs and was totally unafraid of Penguin who was a good deer-catcher and viewed the fawn with great suspicion. However, it was to grow out of its appealing ways all too soon. By the summer of the following year the buck was almost fully grown and perhaps more than half the size of the giant roe I found at Slocht. It pursued dogs, butting them less playfully than hitherto and causing Elgan to roar with laughter. As the summer progressed, however, Elgan had less cause for mirth. The beast started attacking not only dogs of which it had no fear but also strangers, and by the end of the summer had become so dangerous that Elgan built a special secure compound to house the brute. The following year the buck gored Elgan badly and followed up each charge with great fury. Elgan offered the buck to a zoo some fifty miles distant and neglected to inform the new owners of the beast's peculiarities, though a competent zookeeper should know of the problems that attend the rearing and keeping of a roebuck. The buck refused to breed but savagely attacked females introduced to him. The creature developed a ferocious temper with anyone who approached him, even when the intruder brought food, and later Elgan was told the buck had contracted some disease and died – but I suspect otherwise! To keep such a beast is utter lunacy and certain to produce a tragedy. Frankly I consider this digression far from a waste of time. Most lurcher owners are natural pet keepers and it is so very tempting to attempt to adopt an orphaned fawn. I beg the reader to forestall the desire to do so.

Red deer present an entirely different and more formidable species for the longdog or lurcher. Traditionally two large and powerful deerhounds were required to bring down a large stag, though there are tales of a single hound bringing about the capture of one of these eighteen-stone cervids. A stag brought to bay by hounds of any sort will defend itself mightily and wreak red ruin with its antlers, maiming and killing any hound foolish enough to come within reach of these terrible appendages. Over the years it appears as though the red deer has become progressively smaller and specimens which would be considered trophy-size today would have attracted little interest in Norman England. Today's deer are usually denizens of open moorland where feed is scarce and of a poor quality, but in Norman times the great forests of Britain harboured these elegant beasts which fed on the best of grazing supplemented by the fruits of deciduous trees in winter. Huge beasts, more than a match for a single hound, lived in these forests and from Norman times were the quarry of kings and perhaps the clergy.

Sparse grazing and the culling of trophy specimens has reduced the average size of the red deer, but in recent years deer farms have sprung up offering the deer supplementary feed in winter and during the growing period of the calves, and specimens of the same dimensions as Landseer's *Monarch Of The Glen* are commonly seen once again. Some of the farmed stags are magnificent and weigh in at nearly twenty stone, while the hinds are considerably smaller. Today, truly wild red deer are confined to Scotland (the Highlands boasts a huge population of red deer), the West Country and the New Forest a wooded area deliberately created by Norman and Angevin kings so that wild deer could breed and be hunted, but it is highly unlikely that any lurcher owner would obtain permission to hunt red deer in any of these locations. In Scotland it is strictly forbidden to hunt deer with dogs of any kind, though the Scottish deerhound was specifically developed from the old Celtic hound to course and kill this species of deer. Landowners outside Scotland may, however, kill deer with dogs if the said deer are causing damage to crops, gardens or forestry, provided the deer are not killed at night, and I shall deal with this subject later.

Contrary to tales told in public houses few lurchers are capable of catching and holding red deer single-handed. Poachers usually arrive by car or van to a spot where red deer are feeding and stop the car to allow the deer to experience a false sense of security before slipping half a dozen or so lurchers. The result is usually bloody and unpleasant, and certainly not conducive to encouraging the public to accept or tolerate the existence of fieldsports. A furious, bloody skirmish might have been much admired by ancient Celtic bards who immortalised such scenes in ballads and verse, but it is certainly not desirable in a more modern age where there is decided antipathy to scenes of this nature.

Few single-handed lurchers are capable of holding an eighteen-stone stag and are usually dragged, trampled or gored badly long before the lurcher owner can come to the assistance of the dog. It should always be remembered that antique, pure-bred deerhounds were more powerful, though perhaps the same size as a modern lurcher (few working deerhounds were above twenty-eight inches at the shoulder before the Kennel Club embraced the breed) and were considered worth a small fortune if single-handed they were capable of pulling down a stag, though admittedly it does seem likely that the stags of yesteryear nourished on a diet gleaned from deciduous woodlands were larger and more powerful than the stags that have been forced to forage on the bleak moorland that is alien to their true natural habitat.

It is in fact extremely unlikely that the majority of lurcher buffs will acquire permission to hunt this, the largest species of British deer, with lurchers, longdogs or pure-bred sighthounds, hence it is perhaps not only expedient but wise to pass on to other species of deer, for the image of the hardened poacher killing both farmed and wild deer alike is one the lurcher fraternity no longer seems to wish to foster, though some twenty years ago a person had but to secure a host of criminal convictions and a few prison sentences to be classed as a qualified person to judge a lurcher show! Fortunately such ludicrous notions are now a thing of the past. It is also highly unlikely that the majority of lurcher keepers will ever acquire permission to hunt fallow deer, the graceful, elegant, fleet-footed deer that were once part and parcel of the decor of the grounds of most stately country homes. Unlike the red deer and the diminutive roe deer, the fallow is not a native of Britain, though there is evidence that long before the Ice Age froze out all life forms in these islands fallow deer may well have flourished in Britain, and perhaps served as part of the diets of whatever hominids dwelt in these islands.

It is generally believed that the fallow deer was introduced into Britain from southern Europe, though exactly who introduced the deer is subject to some speculation. Peter E. Millais, inaccurate as only Millais is allowed to be, suggests that the Phoenicians were responsible for the introduction, and offers proof of his theory that these Semitic explorers were great travellers and certainly visited Britain. I am always baffled as to why Millais achieved a reputation as a scientific naturalist! Yet this deer was certainly numerous in Britain fairly early in the days following the Roman conquest. Gordian I exhibited deer during the Roman games, and if I might digress, there are accounts of chariots being drawn by fallow deer in much the same way as the demented Lord Orford harnessed his phaeton to a team of red deer – an extremely dangerous practice as many dogs display a natural antipathy to cervids of any sort, as Orford was to discover! During Elizabethan times over seven hundred parks fostered these deer, and to quote Christopher Lever, each county in Britain harboured more fallow deer than the rest of Europe. The presence of these deer in the wild is explained by the fact that during the English Civil War the fences and walls that enclosed these deer parks fell into such disrepair that many deer escaped and bred in the country surrounding the parks. These days fallow abound in the south-east of England and apparently are spreading north to the Midlands. In Scotland isolated pockets of these deer are sometimes encountered, the descendants of deer introduced by enthusiastic sporting lairds with a penchant for the exotic.

Once again it should be mentioned that is is highly unlikely that any lurcher enthusiast will acquire permission to hunt fallow deer, though I have encountered two landowners who were troubled by fallow and did encourage lurcher owners to deal with the problem. The tale has an unfortunate ending for in both instances the landowners had cause to regret granting permission. Within weeks of the lurcher enthusiasts arriving damage to nearby pheasant stocks had been reported and three sheep had been killed. This is but one of the instances that has served to alienate the lurcherman.

Fallow are gregarious, they feed together in medium-size groups, and certain members of the group serve as sentinels to help protect the welfare of the rest of the group. When disturbed or startled the herd race off noisily, their hooves making a sound akin to distant thunder when they run. I believe this noisy style of running to be purposeful, for dogs which are only too keen to attack and hold the fleet-footed but silent-running roe deer are often reluctant to face the rumbling cacophony made by the hooves of fleeing fallow deer. Few natural activities are entirely without purpose or do not assist the survival of a particular species. The whirring sound of partridge exploding from the grass deters a canine, musteline or feline hunter by a split-second, thereby allowing the partridge to escape its attackers. Likewise, a woodpigeon disturbed while perching noisily flaps into flight, the sound of the wing beats disconcerting or confusing an avian or mammalian attacker. Many times I have watched quite formidable lurchers back down from the sound made by startled fallow deer running over dusty and dry ground.

It would of course be impossible to mention the subject of the pursuit of fallow deer with lurchers without referring to the infamous Attingham Park escapade of the early 1980s, a caper the press instantly labelled the Attingham Park Slaughter. Some superb fallow deer had been collected in the park for breeding purposes, a collection so fine that visitors from abroad came and photographed the herd. Deer had been reported missing by keepers for some five or so weeks before the actual poaching event and keepers and police had lain in wait for the arrival of the poaching gang. The gang, one man from Lichfield and two from Wolverhampton, were caught red-handed, though while one pleaded guilty to the offence, the Wolverhampton men pleaded their innocence to the last. The press reported that the carnage the trio created was terrific, thereby exaggerating the damage wrought by the group, but all three received prison sentences of eighteen months apiece and the deer were unmolested for several seasons after this.

On the subject of deer poaching, it would be impossible not to mention Geoffrey Battans of Leighton Buzzard whose escapades in and around Woburn Abbey attracted great interest from the national press. Battans pleaded guilty to the poaching of some two hundred and sixteen deer including specimens of the rare Pere David deer, a species of imported deer that had been extinct in the wild for some three thousand years. Battans too received a prison sentence for his offences.

More interesting perhaps than the fallow deer is the Japanese sika deer, which resembles an undersized red deer, the stags weighing in at about 120lb while the hinds rarely exceed 80lb and are roughly the height of a deerhound bitch. Yet despite their small size the sika is one of the deer that will on occasion stand its ground against man and is at times possibly dangerous to approach. Yet the same deer are often terrified of quite small dogs. The tale of Maud Beddows is frequently related, but well worth repeating. In September the sika stag attempts to gather a small harem of hinds together and the rut lasts until late October. During this time sika males become furiously aggressive and will take the battle to any human that approaches the seraglio. Mrs Beddows, a mycologist with a special interest in the boletus fungus, stumbled upon a male sika jealously guarding his harem. The deer rushed Mrs Beddows, knocking her over but not goring her as the newspapers reported, but a tiny mongrel terrier belonging to a nearby picnicking couple heard the tumult and furiously attacked the deer. Whether or not the deer would have followed up its charge on Mrs Beddows is questionable, but there have been incidents of damage done to unwary human intruders near Vladivostok where this type of deer is particularly numerous. It is also worth noting that this species appears to be particularly terrified by the presence of dogs even when the rut is on, and the stags seem almost oblivious to danger from human beings. It has been suggested that the deer still retains racial memories of wolves for it has existed in Britain for less than a century and a half, but this is a somewhat fanciful explanation for its fear of dogs.

The deer was supposedly imported to Britain in 1860 and a single pair presented to the Zoological Society of London where the species enjoyed some notoriety on account of its cross and furious expression, a facial expression exacerbated by the deer's prominent angular facial bones. In the same year the animal dealer Johann Carl Jamrach, one of the most colourful collectors of exotica of the nineteenth century, who kept an amazing collection of strange and curious animals, birds and reptiles in his premises near the London docks, imported three hinds and a stag which were sold to Enniskerry, County Wicklow. These were the original breeding stock the progeny of which were used to stock several parks in England and Scotland.

Sika will mate with red deer and there is some evidence that hybrid sika/red deer have appeared in untamed areas of Scotland. Whether these hybrids are as fertile as the pure-bred sika or red deer is debated by naturalists, though it is true that the sika seems well adapted to the more remote areas of Scotland which resemble the district of Manchuria in which sika abound. In passing I must state that I have tasted both the venison of sika and red deer, and have been given meat from what is considered the hybrid of red and sika deer; I find it impossible to tell which meat is which.

It is unlikely that the owner of a lurcher or longdog will obtain permission to hunt these deer – and certainly not in Scotland – but a strong, powerful, determined lurcher finds no difficulty in holding a hind, though the larger more powerful stags are a more testing foe for a lurcher. Sika are so terribly wary of dogs that it is difficult for a hunter to secure a reasonable slip at a deer.

Few lurcher owners living in the south-east of England and East Anglia have not encountered muntjac deer, small creatures that on first impression resemble a large hare and are now very numerous in these districts and are rapidly spreading north. Muntjac are tiny deer standing at roughly seventeen inches at the shoulder and seldom more than 25lb in weight when.fully grown. In colour they resemble a mature brown hare and are often mistaken for late-born leverets by legitimate coursers, particularly as in winter the hair on the back of the adult deer is darker than the rest of the pelt. Add to this the fact that the word 'muntjac' is derived from the Sunda Island dialect meaning 'springing' or 'graceful', and the resemblance to the hare is apparent.

Despite the fact that a great many muntjac fall prey to lurchers and the breeding rate of all cervids is not great, the muntjac continues to increase in numbers in the south-east of England and East Anglia and is rapidly spreading to areas in the Midlands. These deer are shy and usually spend their days in deep gorse and bramble through which they seem to establish well trodden runs along which they try to escape if frightened or pursued. Fawns have been found even in mid-winter and are carefully hidden in the dense cover, with which the spotted coat of the young blends admirably. It is a little known fact but there are actually two species of muntjac living in Britain, the Indian muntjac, an aggressive species that at certain times of the year (possibly during the time when does are in season) will sometimes face down a small dog, and the less aggressive Reeves or Chinese muntjac, which is extremely timid and will run or hide at the sight of any predator.

Whippet-sized lurchers, and diminutive whippet lurchers at that, regularly catch muntjac if the deer are disturbed by a lamping party. The flight of this tiny deer is swift but no match for even a moderately fast lurcher, if, that is, the deer is unable to find refuge in deep cover. Should this deer manage to find its well trampled runs before the hound comes to grips with it, it is unlikely that a lurcher or longdog will catch it, for muntjac, both the Chinese and Indian and the hybrids that are intermediate between the two species, are wonderfully adept at losing a dog in gorse or bramble. I have many times watched hounds that are determined catch dogs and fine strikers lose a muntjac that has managed to find sanctuary in small patches of woodland, and I am baffled at just how dextrous these deer are in evading a pursuer. Most muntjac are taken by lampers and if these deer are sprung away from cover they can be taken by quite indifferent lurchers.

For some reason the Chinese water deer has never become as numerous as the muntjac and there are authorities who believe that the hybridising of the two species of muntjac – the Reeves or Chinese and the Indian – has produced more vigorous, more fertile hybrids which are able to survive and prosper more readily than the pure-bred stock. Only one species of Chinese water deer exists, however, and these are confined to pockets in the south and east of England, and for some reason on the Welsh borders.

The introduction of these deer to Britain is attributed to the 11th Duke of Bedford who tried unsuccessfully at first to introduce deer to Woburn Park. The first pair died, but the second imports soon produced a breeding herd. In 1944 the duke sent specimens to two Hampshire estates where they were reported by the author Brian Vesey Fitzgerald, who shot one specimen near Farnham, Surrey in 1945. Later, Noel Stevens transferred a small herd to his home near Ludlow and this nucleus seems to have flourished.

Water deer are slightly larger than muntjac, shy and timid, and are equally at home in woodland and deep reed beds into which they vanish as soon as danger presents itself. It is in fact possible to live near to these deer without even noticing them, though at night water deer are quite vocal and bark or yelp rather like small basenji rather than deer. These deer too are easily overmatched by even whippet-sized lurchers, and a Mrs Harvey of Ludlow once reported that a pair of Italian greyhounds caught and killed a water deer that had strayed into her garden at night and failed to find its way out. It should be pointed out, however, that some Italian greyhounds are extremely game and have a strong coursing instinct. I have seen several which were devils for cat worrying and were the scourge of the district in which they lived.

Thus the deer that dwell in Britain, their habitat, their feeding habits and their behaviour. As to the legality of hunting these creatures, I shall deal with the subject in a later chapter. However, it should be stated that it is illegal in Scotland and generally perceived as unacceptable, even in those parts of the UK where it is not actually unlawful. The use of lurchers to pursue deer is best left as a matter of history.

18

Breeding Lurchers

B efore the breeder embarks on a breeding project, indeed before the breeder even considers breeding a litter, I ask him to conduct the following survey. Firstly he should buy one of the sporting papers which deals with the subject of lurchers – I suggest *Shooting News*. He should then peruse the 'Puppies For Sale' column, and not only the number of puppies offered for sale, but the frequency with which the same advertisement appears in the magazine over successive weeks. Next, if the would-be breeder has the stomach to face the next project, I ask him to visit the kennels of some downmarket dog dealer who specialises in the sale of lurchers, both young and adult stock. The often wretched denizens of such places have seldom been bred by the dealer but have been bought in from some breeder who, full of hope, has produced a litter of puppies in the mistaken notion such puppies will be snapped up by buyers long before they are able to leave the nest. The hopes of the said breeder have plummeted as each and every advertisement in each and every sporting paper has failed to sell the puppies until finally, in desperation, the breeder has sought out a downmarket dog dealer and asked him to sell the litter. There has, in fact, never been a lurcher bitch whose puppies have not been spoken for long before the bitch conceives. Likewise there are few owners who once the bitch produces the litter have not observed friends and acquaintances cancel their orders, offering somewhat lame excuses for doing so, or in some cases vanishing like the dew in the morning, leaving the breeder with a batch of perfectly delightful but totally unsaleable lurcher puppies.

The third initiation trial has yet to start, however. I ask the reader to visit a summer country fair and take some time off from watching the magnificent specimens parading in the lurcher ring to observe the often pitiful creatures disgorging from the dog dealer's van, dogs packed as tightly as the equipment in the Tardis, for I have often thought that is is physically impossible to stow so many hapless beasts into such a small space. Observe these specimens a while before embarking on the next part of the project I have set the reader, and count the number of rather wretched lurchers bearing 'For Sale' signs around their necks being toted around the shows by less than caring owners who have tired of their wards. Each and every one of these dispirited, unhappy creatures has started its life as a delightful, friendly puppy who expected little of life but received even less. I ask the reader to consider these points before embarking on the project of breeding a litter of lurcher puppies.

Yet, as always, there is hope, squeaking rather pitifully perhaps, from the bottom of Pandora's box. There is a good if hard-earned living to be made breeding top-class specimens of specific and popular cross-bred lurchers and longdogs, for there is certainly a market for the said product. A reputable breeder who sets up a well organised kennel breeding deerhound/greyhound composites, or saluki/greyhound hybrids, or better still, genuine Bedlington/greyhound or Bedlington/whippet crossbreds, would be able to make a good living,

Whippet Bedlingtons — the most popular small lurchers.

213

A very unusual German Wire-haired Pointer greyhound lurcher.

if, that is, he is situated in a centrally placed district easily accessible from any part of the country, and if he is prepared to tolerate the human derelicts who from time to time would visit the kennels to buy puppies or waste a day or so. I must confess I would not tolerate some of the human debris I have seen visiting lurcher shows near my home, and so I have no desire to start a commercial lurcher-breeding kennel. Yet if the reader wishes to start a commercial lurcher-breeding kennel he must learn not only to tolerate this sort of person but to treat such people politely and courteously, for if I might quote David Hancock, the world's most successful lurcher breeder, 'Each visitor is a potential client.' However, the reader must be made aware that if he or she intends to start a lurcher-breeding establishment, while the majority of the clients will be perfectly delightful people, a small minority will be trash that scarcely deserve the sobriquet *Homo sapiens*.

I suggest that long before the reader breeds a litter he or she should examine the reasons for the production of such a litter carefully. If the breeder wishes to perpetuate a particularly successful bloodline of lurchers, then by all means breed a litter, if, that is, he or she can ensure permanent and happy homes for the surplus puppies long before they are born – and I have already warned the reader of the problems attendant on disposing of a litter to friends and acquaintances who have promised to home puppies. If, however, the would-be breeder acquires a bitch of questionable origin and the said bitch comes into season, should the potential breeder seek to breed a litter by mating the bitch to a convenient dog simply to produce puppies to make a small profit, the project is doomed from the start. All the eulogies, all the exaggerations, all the false accolades imaginable will not produce a profit from the sale of such a litter and it is almost inevitable that the puppies will gravitate to one of the downmarket dog dealers who exist on the periphery of human decency just out of reach of environmental health officers in every large town in Britain. The would-be breeder who attempts such a breeding project is doomed to financial disaster from the onset of the scheme and in all probability has sentenced the puppies to a lifetime of being swapped, sold, run out of condition, with only the prospect of premature death as a release from this purgatory. If the reader believes that I exaggerate the problems of disposing of a

Head study of a Whippet Bedlington lurcher.

215

litter of lurcher puppies, let me assure him, I don't. I avoid breeding surplus lurchers and spend some time placing those puppies I breed with associates I know will love and care for the dogs, and above all give them a good permanent home.

I may well have dissuaded the reader from breeding a litter in the last thousand words. Indeed, I may well have dissuaded him from reading the rest of this chapter, concerned as it is with breeding a litter, but for those who wish to persist and breed another litter of lurchers I shall continue with the subject.

Basically there are four methods of breeding lurchers or longdogs: the mating of lurcher to lurcher, the most commonly practised method of breeding as well as the least successful, though my own strain of lurcher is bred in this manner; the mating of base-blooded dogs, collies, Bedlingtons to pure-bred sighthounds; the mating of lurchers to sighthounds to increase the speed of the progeny of the mating, and this method of producing lurchers is fraught with perils if the breeder is uncertain of the origin of the lurcher he intends to use for breeding; and the experimental crosses bred by mating lurchers to base-blooded dogs – and I shall explore this subject at some length as the production of these somewhat unsightly if useful lurchers is a highly controversial subject.

Let us assume that the would-be lurcher breeder has a much loved, much valued lurcher bitch that is the epitome of all a lurcher should be. In her youth she has been fast, a good striker with a wonderful nose and natural tendency to carry to hand. She has been, in fact, the ideal lurcher, but has since grown old and her owner desires to breed a similar paragon as a replacement for the dam. Let us now examine the options open to continue the bloodline and produce an animal as good as, if not better, than the dam.

Firstly, the breeder can mate his bitch to a greyhound, the fastest of dogs and certainly the most readily available of sighthounds. The progeny of this mating will certainly be as fast, if not faster, than the dam. However, it is highly unlikely that the greyhound will confer brain, nose or that most enigmatic of qualities 'field sense' to the puppies, and frankly I have seen many good strains of lurcher ruined by further additions of greyhound blood. I once attempted to speed up my own strain of lurcher with greyhound blood and the result was little short of disastrous. I lost nose, sense and much of the natural retrieving instinct for which the family is justly famous. I abandoned my project, placed the whelp I kept back with a reliable friend, who kept the bitch to her dotage I must add, and resumed line breeding to the fastest of the strain

I kept. I have never regretted abandoning the addition of greyhound blood to the strain and the stock I breed is now everything I desire.

I shall not repeat the reference to adding saluki blood, either neat saluki blood or saluki hybrid, to a fine strain of working lurcher other than to state that such a mating is the most certain method of ruining any strain of working lurcher, and producing puppies that are neither fish nor fowl, not capable of performing the work of a longdog nor a lurcher, canine messes that are of little use to anyone other than the least demanding running dog owner.

If I owned the bitch in question I would do my utmost to seek out a close relative of similar type and with similar sterling qualities. Failing that I would seek out a dog of similar type with equally good qualities (and I would need to watch the dog work in the field to ascertain if it had the qualities I desired). If, however, I knew the breeding of the lurcher bitch I owned and knew it had a very strong base line (a collie/greyhound of a Bedlington/greyhound) and realised it lacked

Lurcher to Lurcher hybrid.

Hancock's Zebedee, a bearded/border hybrid and the sire of many lurchers.

speed, I might consider using a further dash of greyhound blood or perhaps a dog of similar type or disposition that had the qualities I desired in a lurcher – but mating together lurchers with strong base-lines is an almost certain way of producing a percentage of puppies that are too cloddy to be versatile. In the early days of the creation of my own strain of lurcher I regularly produced brindled collie-type dogs that were biddable, often very game but seldom fast enough to do the work I required of them. Dogs of this type are referred to as litter wastage by lurcher breeders, though such dogs often make fine hunting dogs that lack just a little of the edge required of a top-grade lurcher. However, the process of adding more and more greyhound to a strain of lurcher has an equally ruinous effect, producing speedy animals that possess little of the qualities required of a good lurcher, and frankly far too many lurchers are too sighthound saturated to be really efficient hunters.

It is a popular practice to mate pure-bred base breeds such as collies and Bedlington terriers to produce working lurchers, and some of these hybrids are first-class workers though seldom enough to put up a speedy show against a hare that is afforded fair law. Indeed few lurchers of any breed are capable of catching such hares anyway, for such a task is the role of the longdog. If the breeder is aware of the limitations of such hybrids they make fine and serviceable lurchers that are superior at warrening and lamp work to lurchers with a greater proportion of sighthound blood in their make-up.

To breed these first-cross hybrids is simplicity itself for greyhound bitches are easily obtainable, and once they are past their prime are invariably free to a good home. Perhaps at this point it is expedient to evaluate the qualities of a greyhound that is to be used as a dam for breeding lurchers. Few greyhounds are physically or mentally defective and virtually any cast track or coursing greyhound (as opposed to the elegant exhibition-bred hounds) is suitable for breeding first-cross lurchers. The fact the the bitch held the track record at such and such a stadium makes not the slightest difference to the first-cross hybrid bred from her for any superior speed the bitch may have is diffused when crossed with collie or Bedlington. I dislike hounds that are frequently lame or have suspect feet but I am aware that few first-cross lurchers bred from such a bitch will be troubled with the same type of foot disorders. Hancock places greater importance on the choice of sire than he does on the quality of the greyhound dam, and certainly has produced some phenomenal workers from quite ordinary track-bred bitches. Some of the most successful competition dogs he has produced were from a quite ordinary track greyhound that refused to chase a mechanical hare. Thus the breeder who wishes to breed a first-cross collie/greyhound or a first-cross Bedlington/greyhound litter and who spends his money buying a track-winning or coursing-winning greyhound bitch is wasting his money, for a perfectly suitable bitch can be obtained free of charge, and will almost certainly breed a litter as serviceable as the one bred by a top-flight greyhound. Still, I will defend with my life a breeder's desire to waste his money on any animal he chooses to buy.

There is certainly a good market for genuine first-cross lurchers, particularly if the lurchers are Bedlington/greyhound hybrids which are in short supply at the time of writing. Most of the supposed first-cross Bedlington/greyhound or Bedlington/whippet hybrids offered for sale are in fact hybrids between Bedlington-bred lurchers of various types and are quite likely to manifest copper toxicosis, for many Bedlington terriers carry this distressing malady. Breeders intending to produce these genuine hybrids are almost certain to find a market for their surplus stock.

Whatever the method of producing lurchers, the process of dog breeding is basically the same. Lurcher bitches with strong baselines bred from collies, Bedlington terriers etc. will usually come into season quite early in their lives, some before their first birthdays, though long-dogs and sighthound saturated types of lurcher may not be sexually mature before their third year. There is some, albeit slight, evidence to suggest that greyhounds may well be deliberately bred not to come into season regularly in order to facilitate a successful racing and coursing career (greyhounds are not allowed to race or course when they are coming into or just going out of season), but this is a fanciful notion that has never been scientifically substantiated. Certainly no lurcher or greyhound owner should be concerned if their bitch has not come into season before its second birthday and Phaedra, my youngest lurcher bitch, did not come into season until shortly before her sixth birthday.

However, even if the bitch comes into season at twelve months of age it is certainly not good policy to breed from such a young animal even though bitches will produce perfectly healthy puppies when they are only a year old. It is not good stockmanship to breed from either greyhound or a lurcher at such a young age. Firstly it is unlikely that the greyhound that is to be used as a brood will be fully grown before she is perhaps eighteen months of age, and secondly I should be reluctant to breed from any lurcher before it has proved its worth and few lurchers have proved their worth before their third or fourth year. If the reader questions this statement because he or she has been told otherwise I suggest the reader observes the steady improvement of a lurcher after its third year until it reaches its peak at four years of age, the improvement is usually quite remarkable. Hence a bitch that has proved her worth as a matriarch fit to continue her bloodlines is usually at least four years old before she is really ready to breed, though a bitch that is severely injured might well be used as a brood at an earlier date, if, that is, her breeding is exceptional and her early performance considerably above average.

Lurcher and greyhound bitches often come into season only once a year; my own strain, which has not been bred for fecundity, comes into season even less frequently. Hancock of Sutton Coldfield, who keeps a very accurate record of the performance and behaviour of his broods, states that he has noted that while a greyhound or sighthound saturated lurcher or a longdog may in her virginal state only come into season once a year, once she has been mated and produced a normal litter she will come into season twice a year as with any other domesticated breed of dog, and continue to do so until she is too old to be considered worthwhile as a brood bitch.

As a bitch approaches season her vulva will swell and she will usually become skittish with both male and female dogs. After a few days the vulva will secrete a bloody fluid and male dogs will become attracted to the bitch, and even attempt to mate her, but while the bloody discharge continues to flow the bitch, while she may tolerate considerable foreplay from the dog, will not allow the dog to serve her. Only when the bloody discharge changes to a pinky hue and the bitch's vulva is swollen to its maximum size will the bitch accept the services of a dog.

Some male lurchers and greyhounds are notoriously difficult to mate to bitches and it was a popular notion among Black Country lurcher owners that the only suitable greyhounds to use for breeding were those that had run the streets and had gained some sexual experience attempting to mate cur bitches. Hancock believes that with much patience and a great deal of time any greyhound male can become a useful and efficient stud dog, and he has little difficulty encouraging his hounds to serve visiting bitches.

A bitch needs some preparation before she is mated, and I shall deal with the process of mating presently. I seldom breed except to produce replacements for much loved workers, but when I suspect I have a bitch approaching season I dose her with diochlorophen to clear her of tapeworm and dip her to ensure she is free of fleas and mites – and fleas will harbour tapeworm eggs, I must add. The old foxhound kennel adage that a brood should be wormed and dipped three weeks before mating and three weeks after whelping is probably a good one, despite the fact that modern mangicides and vermifuges have improved dramatically since the days of Nimrod Capel. A bitch should, however, be clear of fleas, lice and worms before she is mated if she is to give of her best at producing puppies.

Hancock takes the process one stage further and breeds so many litters his advice is well worth heeding regarding the breeding of lurchers. Dave doses each bitch with an antibiotic immediately prior to the bitch coming into season so that the bitch's genital tracts are free from any bacterial infection that may discourage conception or hinder the development of the foeti. Hancock claims that the average litter size has increased since he first adopted this method in the late 1980s. He is of the opinion that so harsh and tough is the life of a typical lurcher that the whelp needs all the help it can get from conception until weaning.

A bitch that is ready to receive the dog will usually turn her tail and push her vulva towards her suitor, and it is good sense to allow a short courtship ritual display before the bitch is encouraged to receive the dog. I hold lurcher and greyhound bitches that are to be mated and muzzle the bitch before the dog is allowed to serve her as this prevents damage not only to the dog serving her but to me, as some bitches, particularly maiden bitches, bite with great savagery when a dog penetrates them. I learned about muzzling the bitch the hard way, I'm afraid, for I had been terribly bitten by a greyhound bitch when my lurcher dog attempted to serve her. Henceforth I insist on a bitch being muzzled even if the muzzle is simply a piece of tape used to clamp the jaws together. This type of muzzle presents only a temporary inconvenience and is totally painless to the bitch. I have never been a brave man and have never invited disaster since I was first badly bitten by a terrified greyhound bitch. If it is any consolation I may add that the mating resulted in the production of Peter Newton's excellent lurcher bitch – and I still have the scars from the wound the greyhound created.

The dog will usually mount the bitch and with a series of pelvic thrusts attempt to penetrate her. When he succeeds in doing so the frequency and force of the pelvic thrusts increase and the bitch may become wildly excited as the dog's penis swells within her. At this point I would advise holding the bitch, but avoid touching the dog's back or rear for this action may cause the dog to withdraw its penis and discontinue the mating. A bitch might also try to struggle wildly and if not held may rupture the dog. It can be argued that street matings are usually conducted without help from human agencies – quite the reverse in fact – but then many curs that are allowed to roam are damaged when the bitches they are in the process of mating attempt to struggle while tied to the dog.

Once a dog's penis is swollen inside the bitch the dog may attempt to adopt a back to back position by shifting his hind leg over the back of the bitch. This curious position is often referred to as 'a tie' and a tie will usually last from five to thirty minutes, though I have heard of ties lasting for more than two hours – though this is an abnormally lengthy period. During this period of time it is wise to gently restrain the participants to prevent damage to either party.

Just how many times a bitch should be mated is a matter of some debate. There is every chance the bitch will conceive after just one mating, particularly if she seems particularly eager to mate – a sign of sexual readiness – but it is more likely the bitch will conceive if mated several times during her season. Hancock, who maintains a huge force

Bearded border lurcher puppies.

of collie and collie/greyhounds studs, allows his bitches to mate every two days of their season until they refuse to stand for the male, and he has very few bitches which fail to conceive after such treatment.

It can also be argued that a dog that is infrequently used at stud is less fertile that one used regularly, for such a sparsely used dog will ejaculate semen with a lower viable sperm count. Hence a dog that is used to mate a bitch every few days will produce a large quantity of viable and healthy sperm. An experienced stud dog is indeed a treasure; my own studs get few opportunities to mate whereas some of Hancock's studs mate dozens of bitches a year, and are extremely proficient stud dogs that need little encouragement to mate. Yet it requires a great deal of patience to encourage a young and gauche dog to serve a bitch and even more patience to encourage an older dog that has in the past been actively discouraged from mating bitches, as are some track and coursing greyhounds prior to their retirement. As I write David Hancock has taken a bitch to the fabulous Sam The Man, a truly great Waterloo Cup winner which, because of its successful, if celibate, coursing career, was quite difficult to mate to the virgin greyhound Hancock took to the dog.

It is, therefore, fairly obvious that it is best to take the bitch to be mated to a fairly experienced, frequently used stud dog, for such a dog is often able to mate a bitch quickly, efficiently and with little damage to the bitch. Bitches taken to a variety of inexperienced dogs are often so bruised by frequent but unsuccessful assaults as to be unwilling to stand for mating by an experienced stud. When I owned an efficient and very fertile stud dog – and I no longer do – I rather dreaded a visit from a bitch that had been tried with a variety of local would-be

A Dartmoor collie - a dam of many useful rabbiting lurchers.

Lotharios but had failed to mate. The vulvas of these bitches had often been so terribly bruised that while the bitch turned her tail and showed a readiness to mate, when my stud dog prepared to penetrate her she screamed in agony and sometimes had to be strongly restrained to prevent her savaging the male and myself. Personally I should be very careful about taking a bitch to a stud dog that had never sired a litter for not only would such a dog sometimes be difficult to get to mate, but I would have no idea of the progeny the dog was likely to breed. I have many times seen quite indifferent stud dogs, both greyhounds and lurchers, that have produced some excellent field dogs. Conversely, I have seen some excellent field performers that were incapable of replicating their qualities in their progeny. One of Fathom's brothers was an excellent worker and a fine athlete but I discontinued using him when I realised how squat and unsightly his puppies were, and more to the point, how poor were their noses. Yet the same dog owned by Peter Owen of Derbyshire was an incredibly good worker and put the rest of his litter to shame in the field. He bred perhaps ten litters of puppies, some to related lurchers others to track greyhounds, yet never produced a puppy I would have considered keeping. The value of a stud dog lies in the quality of the progeny he can produce, not in the apparent virtue of the dog himself.

A bitch once mated needs little special treatment to ensure the birth of her litter, though the owner of the animal would do well to adopt a common sense approach to the pregnancy. A bitch will seldom indicate that she is in whelp until her fifth week after mating, but will show obvious signs after that time. There is little to be gained by taking a bitch to a veterinary surgeon for his expert opinion on whether or not the bitch is pregnant, for she either is or is not, and there is nothing the vet can do to alter this. However, after the fifth week after mating pregnancy is usually discernible.

Extra feeding of the possibly pregnant bitch is not only unnecessary but inadvisable, for at five weeks after mating the foeti are scarcely the size of a marble and need little food to maintain them. A good diet rich in protein, minerals, vitamins, carbohydrates and fats is usually enough to ensure the perfect development of the puppies. Some high-grade dog foods are ideal for feeding a pregnant bitch, though I still favour a flesh-based diet balanced with a high-calcium meal. As the bitch increases in girth there is a tendency to overfeed her rather than deny her, I'm afraid, but while the would-be brood needs extra food it is wise to give her several small meals rather than allow her to gorge herself once a day in the manner of a fit and healthy lamping lurcher. The growth of puppies causes the stomach walls to contract slightly, and the bitch cannot fill her stomach in the manner of a fit but unmated animal. Several small feeds of high-protein food are best for a pregnant bitch as she nears parturition.

When a bitch is seven weeks pregnant it is good policy to cleanse her of roundworms, which become particularly active at this stage and migrate across the placenta to infect the puppies. It is highly unlikely that any worming will completely clear the bitch of these parasites, but if a bitch is wormed at this stage of her pregnancy the medication will certainly reduce the incidence of roundworms in the puppies she is carrying. A cheap proprietary worming medicine obtainable from any chemist or pet shop is sufficient, for most roundworm medicines contain piperazine-type chemicals which are unlikely to harm the bitch or the puppies she is carrying.

Puppies usually gestate from fifty-eight to sixty-three days in duration and few lurchers, longdogs or pure-bred sighthounds experience any problems during parturition. The sighthounds and their composites are some of the most perfectly formed creatures in the world and are seldom troubled by the problems which seem to plague other less selectively bred types of animals. Yet because the lurcher or longdog is unlikely to experience any problems in parturition, this does not mean that the whelping bitch should be placed in a pen and left to her own devices. Careful stockmanship can result in the saving of several puppies, and even large-scale professional breeders of Hancock's calibre are reluctant to allow a bitch to whelp unattended.

A heat lamp is an excellent investment for any lurcher keeper whether or not the lurcher enthusiast wishes to breed puppies. A sick dog, an unwell dog, a dog run to a state of exhaustion will recover more quickly if placed under a heat lamp and allowed to recuperate, for the therapeutic value of gentle warmth has long been realised. Frankly, puppies whelped outside in sheds or kennels need to be born under a heat lamp unless, that is, the country is experiencing a heatwave at the time. Many puppies can be saved if a heat lamp is placed above a bitch that is in the process of whelping. The temperature within the bitch's uterus is 101.5°F (37°C) and puppies emerging from such a cosseted environment into a cold and less friendly world are hardly likely to prosper. A heat lamp suspended above the bitch producing a temperature that is warm but not too hot for the bitch to tolerate creates a favourable environment for the bitch and her newly born litter, and a happy, warm, contented litter will grow far better than a chilled litter that is hugging the bitch, desperately seeking her body warmth.

A classy collie hybrid and a fine catch dog.

It is argued by some who favour a somewhat curious Darwinian survival-of-the-fittest doctrine that lurchers that are tailored to lead the harsh, stark life need to be reared in a harsh and tough atmosphere, and those puppies that fail to survive would be unsuitable for the life a lurcher is required to lead anyway. This is totally illogical thinking by any standards. No athletic coach would deliberately seek out a hostile environment to rear a protégé and top-class athletes need the best of starts in life to give of their best on the field or track. A single puppy that survives when the rest of the litter chill to death is highly unlikely to have benefited from the treatment that has caused the death of its litter mates, and in later life the check the puppy has received is sure to manifest itself, particularly if the dog is worked hard. A hard-working animal needs the best of starts in its life and proper rearing. Sufficient to say that I have seen litters reared in cold kennels without artificial heat and litters of the same age reared in warm conditions, and there is no question as to which are the better puppies.

Should a bitch experience some difficulty in producing her litter – and few greyhound-blooded dogs will, for such bitches usually

227

whelp easily – allow a little time and then get the bitch to a veterinary surgeon. More often than not a shot of calcium oleate will give the bitch the Dutch courage to proceed in the parturition, but if this fails vets may resort to a carefully measured dose of pituitrin – a substance made from the posterior lobe of the pituitary gland of some domesticated animal – though the use of this substance to assist parturition has often been likened to adjusting your carburettor with a sledgehammer. However, should both the calcium oleate shot and the pituitrin shot fail to produce puppies, the veterinary surgeon may consider a caesarean section. This is quite a simple operation if one has the knowledge, the equipment and sterile conditions, but it is an operation no lay person should ever consider attempting, though in the hands of a competent vet the operation is performed simply and safely. I have seen many caesarean sections conducted on my bitches and have observed few casualties either among the dams or the puppies.

A maiden bitch may be deeply suspicious about her owner handling her puppies and even more suspicious about having strangers touch her whelps. Others may accept the action with little concern, but should a bitch take offence or appear upset it is wise to leave her in peace to settle down for a few days. If one examines the practice of checking the puppies in the cold light of reason there is little to be gained from it, for there is nothing one can do to change the gender of the puppies and a bitch or dog is certain to retain its sexual characteristics for a few more days, after which the bitch will accept the examination of her puppies more willingly. I feel a terrible hypocrite writing this last statement for I cannot resist checking the sexes of the puppies as soon as they are born, but I can see the logic of waiting a while so as not to disturb the bitch. Some bitches are decidedly unconcerned about the examination of their puppies anyway, but it is good sense to prevent strangers distressing the bitches.

Puppies gain little from being handled before the tenth day following their birth and should be left in peace to suckle and grow. Most puppies open their eyes at roughly ten days of age, but there is nothing unusual about puppies opening their eyes before or after this time. I have seen puppies thirteen days old with their eyes tightly shut and puppies with their eyes open at eight days of age. Neither litter grew into strange nor peculiar lurchers, and yet newcomers to dog breeding are prone to pay far too much attention to minute details concerning the development of puppies and record every stage of development of the litter as if each is of monumental importance to the future of the dogs. However, this almost neurotic attention to detail is a far better indication of stockmanship than the couldn't care less attitude of many lurcher breeders.

At roughly three weeks of age a whelp will start to take solid food. If the litter is large or the bitch is short of milk then the whelps may show an interest in solid food somewhat earlier than this. Conversely, if the litter is small and the bitch well endowed with an adequate supply of milk puppies will often show little interest in solid food before they are three weeks old. When a puppy is ready to take solid food, however, it will show its interest in no uncertain manner. I find the very best food on which to wean a puppy away from its mother's milk is scraped meat or pulverised kidney, kidney that has been pounded to a fine pulp or, if the lurcher owner is more sophisticated than I am, processed in a liquidiser. Scraped meat is simply raw meat that has been scraped with a sharp knife to extract the bloody, meaty tissue but leaving the fibre still attached to the original chunk of flesh. Puppies that are ready to eat solid food will suck at this bloody pulp voraciously, and this is an ideal food with which to start. Hancock does not agree with this method, or rather does not practise it, for it takes a lengthy period of time to pre-pare and feed this pulp to a litter. Hancock allows his whelps to explore the meat/meal mixture he feeds to his bitches and in time to partake of the food in the dishes – a less time-consuming method, particularly as Hancock breeds a great many litters a year. However, such a practice is fraught with danger. Many greyhounds and lurchers will snap at very young puppies that attempt to feed at the dish the bitch considers her own, and unless care is exercised bitches can kill puppies which seek to feed at the dish. I deliberately feed puppies separately, keeping them well away from the bitches at feeding time. This is a time-consuming practice, but since I breed only a litter or so every few years it is not too demanding of my time besides which I enjoy watching puppies feed.

If I might return to the subject of roundworms yet again. Most proprietary worming medicines purchased at chemist's shops or pet shops contain a set of instructions that usually advise leaving a puppy until it is six weeks old before attempting to worm it. My personal opinion concerning this practice is to worm puppies with a liquid wormer when the whelps are three weeks of age and to worm them again when they are six weeks of age. At one time I followed the worming instructions to the letter but found I produced better puppies when I wormed the whelps earlier. Incidentally, it is policy to burn the worm-ridden excreta passed by the puppies immediately after worming. Worm eggs are unaffected by the piperazine and will remain dormant in the soil for many months, and can infect adults and

The author's lurchers Merab and Phaedra — granddaughter and grandmother.

children alike. It is in fact good policy not to allow children to handle unwormed puppies.

Once puppies are partially weaned and are regularly taking solid food it is policy to feed them four times a day and to feed them as much as they will readily eat in a sitting. Should the puppies leave their food they are obviously being fed too much. If they are clearly still hungry after they have been fed then they need larger meals. At the risk of appearing a Job's comforter it should be pointed out that lurcher puppies will eat enormous quantities of food and grow at an alarming rate, and good-quality food is never cheap. Puppies need a diet with a protein level of not less than 27% to grow well, and a good proprietary dog meal is certainly the best way to feed a single litter of puppies.

Hancock adopts a fairly elaborate method of feeding puppies, but does not deliberately attempt to wean them. He feeds a brood bitch nursing a litter a boiled meat and meal mixture of 27% protein and allows the puppies to start to feed on the mixture when they seem ready to do so, and eschews the scraped meat, pulped liver method I tend to favour. My own method is certainly more labour intensive and would be outrageously time-consuming for breeders with two or more brood bitches simultaneously nursing puppies. However, the method used by Hancock is not without its hazards. Greyhounds are furious trenchers and will certainly clear a huge dish of food in one sitting, particularly if they are nursing a litter of whelps. They are also very protective of their food and are all too likely to snap at whelps which intrude at the feeding bowl. Some greyhound bitches are savagely protective with their food and it is wise for the breeder to stay with the bitch and her litter until the bitch has fed and to observe how she behaves when her whelps approach the feeding bowl. Greyhounds are also protective over chunks of meat or bones they are gnawing and can damage or kill puppies that intrude. It is good policy to take out a bitch from the brood until after her whelps have fed, or to feed her separately and then allow her to eat the food the whelps have left.

A good mixed diet of meal and meat will need few synthetic additives to ensure the growth of healthy puppies, though a pinch of bonemeal or dicalcium phosphate doesn't come amiss at feeding times. Raw, lean meat is deficient in calcium, but meal produced from grain will compensate for this deficiency. If milk can be obtained cheaply by all means add it to the feed; if it has to be bought at shop prices it is usually not worthwhile buying. I feed eggs – I hatch many chickens and have many still eggs – but fed in excess eggs can have a deleterious effect on the growth of puppies. I use my lurchers as dustbins I'm afraid where still eggs are concerned, but I feed puppies with care, and one egg per day fed raw or cooked does no harm.

Rabbit meat is a bit of a mixed blessing for the carcass of the wild rabbit, particularly the viscera, is an excellent breeding ground for tapeworms, though these together with their eggs are killed if the flesh is boiled for twenty minutes. I have never experienced the slightest problem feeding rabbit bones, particularly green raw rabbit bones, though most books advise against feeding any fragments of the skeleton that may splinter and cause damage to the alimentary tract. Personally I like rabbit meat as a feed for puppies, though my tendency to feed plenty of rabbits is due to the fact that they are so abundant in the district where I live. The whole carcass supplies protein, fat, minerals and certainly bone-producing substances.

It is always recommended that puppies should be fed at least four and possibly five times a day, and this is good advice, particularly in the case of sighthound puppies which because of their slim-waisted structure have small stomachs which are incapable of holding the quantity of food that a mastiff puppy is capable of ingesting at one sitting. Yet if the food is not eaten in five or so minutes the plate should be removed and the food scrapped or given to the brood bitch, which is invariably more than willing to oblige by cleaning up food trays. Stale food is likely to ferment and putrefying food is a guarantee of gastric disorders, and gastric disorders are the scourge of young litters of puppies.

On the subject of inoculating young puppies against Parvo virus before they leave their homes, the practice is excellent policy for several reasons. Firstly, the first few days after a puppy leaves its dam it will invariably scour or produce loose droppings, and its resistance to disease will almost certainly lower slightly. A puppy dies so easily from Parvo virus and it is almost certain that a client who has bought a puppy will not only request the return of his purchase price but also bring the cadaver of the diseased puppy to show the breeder. When this happens any remaining puppies are almost certain to contract the disease, for the fresh cadaver is a rich source of infection. I am particularly scared of Parvo virus possibly because I have seen the ravages of the disease, and I inject my whelps at three weeks and six weeks of age, and since I have followed this practice I have experienced little trouble. Might I suggest that anyone who believes I am over-zealous about the injections is unlikely to have seen the disease devastate a litter of puppies. I believe Hancock of Sutton Coldfield is even more thorough in his inoculation programme as David has perhaps five hundred visitors (all of whom are capable of carrying Parvo virus to the kennels) each year.

Selling one's surplus puppies, or even finding homes for whelps, is never easy particularly if one remembers that there is a strong chance that one in every five puppies is likely to change hands within a month of purchase – and this is unfortunately true of all types of longdogs and lurchers a person is likely to breed. I confess I do not sell or give puppies to particular types of people, nor will any form of legislation persuade me to cease or reject my prejudice, even though I am aware that I can be prosecuted under British law for my discrimination against these people. However, there are absolutely no guarantees that any group of people, family or single person will not abuse, ill treat or swap the puppies the breeder is offering for sale, so a person who wishes to sell a litter of lurcher puppies must harden his heart before he advertises, or seek out reliable friends who will home the litter. In such times the breeder may also come to realise how few suitable friends there are who will home a lurcher puppy.

232

Bedlington lurchers, a
useful lurcher base line.

I am always amazed when I see advertisements for lurchers affixed
with the proviso 'working homes only'. Lurchers make quite good pets
whether or not they are worked (I am fairly certain that my puppies
would dearly love a family-type lifestyle whether or not they were ever
allowed to see a rabbit). Furthermore, some of these working homes
are fairly damnable affairs where a dog is run to exhaustion when it is
the owner's pleasure to hunt, and allowed to vegetate when it is not.
Many of these working homes are extremely temporary affairs where a
puppy is passed on if a grown or trained (what a deliciously inaccurate
word where lurchers are concerned) dog is offered the owner. Some of
these puppies that survive to adulthood or age prematurely after such
treatment are passed on by working homes to places that are somewhat

undesirable as retirement homes. In fact I wish I had a penny for every time I have bitten my lip when I have heard the owner of a lurcher that has gone to a working home state, 'Old Ruby/Gyp/Ben got too old to work so I sold him to some lampers.' What a glorious ending to a life-time of good service, one that smacks of cutting down public spending by running the Chelsea pensioners to death in the London marathon. I must confess my observations regarding the lurcher fraternity have made me suspicious of breeding dogs until I have homes for an entire litter, and a few homes to spare. I am also more than willing to place a puppy in a pet home than in some of the working homes I have seen from time to time.

It is no longer an easy matter to sell litters of lurchers and if one is set on the policy of advertising puppies it is perhaps well to place one's advertisement in a sporting paper when the puppies are five weeks of age. It will take possibly three weeks for the advertisement to appear in the papers, by which time the puppies will be eight weeks of age and of a suitable age to sell. Older puppies are less appealing and eat an inordinate amount of food after they are eight weeks of age, thereby costing the breeder a sum of money he is unlikely to be able to recoup by the sale of the older whelp. I shall refrain from suggesting the price one should ask for a whelp, except to say that I am puzzled by a vendor's advertisement which states the puppies are for sale at a 'work-ing man's price', or uses some other equally curious sales gimmick to sell his wares. Advertisements that guarantee the performance of a puppy – 'These dogs will catch two out of every three hares they run by the time they are two years of age' – are not only inadvisable but ludicrous and will deter any client with an intelligence level superior to that of a gerbil from buying one's puppies. Preposterous claims should always be avoided by the vendor who is attempting to sell puppies for they afford the vendor a bizarre aura. For instance, an advertisement that dealt in glowing eulogies would have a thinking person blushing with embarrassment rather than reaching for the telephone to enquire about the puppies.

It is unlikely that the lurcher fraternity has a monopoly on time-wasters, though at times it must seem so to the lurcher vendor for an advertisement for lurcher puppies will invariably produce an amazing spate of time-wasters and sometimes near lunatics who have absolutely no intention of buying a puppy but are anxious to talk to someone. In fact I have often wondered as to whether some sporting paper adver-tisements serve a function similar to that served by the Samaritans. Many of those answering the advertisement will engage the advertiser in lengthy telephone calls only to ring off, and if the advertiser is lucky, never phone again. More irritating by far is the type I refer to as the 'hold the front page' enquirer. This particular type of lunatic is all too common in the lurcher world. The phone will ring and the caller in a breathless, urgent voice will enquire as to whether there are still puppies for sale. He (women are seldom such pests) will then make the vendor promise not to sell a single puppy until he arrives and will promise that he is setting out on the journey to the vendor's house as soon as he replaces the receiver. Like the Rapunzel fairy he is unlikely to be seen or heard from again, until, that is, one places yet another advertisement for lurchers in a sporting paper.

Some of the enquiries will be so ridiculous as to make the vendor wonder how the person on the other end of the telephone is able to dial, restricted as he is by his straitjacket. Phone calls in the early hours of the morning are by no means uncommon after one places an advertisement in a sporting paper, and the placing of a single advertisement is usually enough to persuade a lurcher owner never again to place an advertisement in the sporting press, or for that matter to breed another litter of lurchers.

Sprinkled among the hosts of buffoons, social inadequates and out and out idiots who will answer the advertisement will be those who are genuine clients, anxious and willing to buy a lurcher puppy, and it is the unenviable task of the vendor to sort out the wheat from the all too bountiful chaff. I must admit I find no pleasure in advertising a litter of puppies, though the lunatic callers have furnished me with copy for many articles, and I file the accounts of the more bizarre letters under the heading 'Keep taking the tablets'.

I cannot but admire the way in which David Hancock deals with such phone calls. David treats even what is patently a demented sot with cool aplomb and absolute courtesy and never loses his temper with someone who answers his advertisement. He treats the most outrageous lout with the same tact and courtesy as he would a refined, titled lady out to buy a family pet. I have yet to see him ruffled, angered or upset, even though I have at times heard him vilified and verbally abused by people I consider to be a near miss on the evolutionary development of men. He is polite to time-wasters, and some of his visitors are blatant time-wasters who have absolutely no intention of buying a dog but persist in ridiculing the stock David has for sale. I have seen him treat with total courtesy creatures the like of which I would have been embarrassed to know, and never once have I seen him act in anything other than a totally civil manner with crazed idiots who accost him at home or at shows. This, of course, explains why David is the world's most successful lurcher breeder, and I am content to remain an impoverished breeder of hunting dogs – and on this point I shall end my chapter concerning the breeding of lurcher puppies.

19

In Health and Sickness

Despite the reputation the greyhound has for being the dog of kings, the reference to 'no mean man may own a greyhound' falsely attributed to Canute, the greyhound is one of the most hardy and ailment-free dogs in the world. Three thousand years of selection for speed, tenacity and endurance has produced a miracle of physical prowess, a dog free of the hideous maladies that are part and parcel of the production of modern pure-bred dogs. Hip dysplasia is unknown among track or coursing greyhounds, epilepsy so rare as to be newsworthy, and copper toxicosis has yet to be reported, yet the malaise is not only the scourge of the Bedlington terrier but becoming increasingly common in Dobermanns and Skye terriers. Modern pure-bred dogs become more and more plagued by genetic disorders and it is often wise to counsel a potential dog breeder as to what problems he or she may encounter when purchasing a specimen of a particular breed. Yet defective greyhounds are rare, so rare in fact as to be extraordinary. Lurchers and longdogs derived from such paragons are equally tough and disease-free, more so perhaps for that indefinable quality known as hybrid vigour has added yet more vitality to an already vital type of dog.

Frankly, if a lurcher or longdog is injected against the five deadly ills – Parvo virus, distemper, canine infectious hepatitis, leptospirosis and canicola fever – and given a booster injection every year or so, the type seems almost indestructible, at least as far as common infections are concerned, the sort of common infections that may well incapacitate other breeds of dog. So anyone purchasing a lurcher puppy and inoculating it against the diseases described can look forward to a virtually disease-free dog, an animal that will seldom become acquainted with a veterinary surgery. Thus if the lurcher is to be kept either as a pet or as a working dog it is unlikely to be such an expense or a worry to its owner as would most pure dogs of registered breeds. Lurchers and longdogs are singularly undemanding dogs and have over the years existed on the poorest of viands, the most mean of conditions, and yet endured hard work without complaint.

Yet of course from time to time a dog that lives the lifestyle of a lurcher is bound to contract certain infections or sustain certain injuries, particularly since that most hellish of inventions barbed wire – a machination of the devil no matter how advantageous it has been to the agriculturalist. A lurcher leads a strenuous lifestyle, a life pock-marked with terrible jeopardy as it pursues its quarry over the British countryside at speeds approaching and sometimes exceeding thirty miles an hour.

However, let us forget the injuries that can be sustained during the perils of the chase and discuss the common parasites that can plague any dog that enjoys a rural lifestyle, and a coursing dog will be very lucky if it finishes its life injury-free and blessed with amazing fortune if it doesn't acquire both internal and external parasites before its demise.

Many strains, sprains and muscle injuries can be avoided if the handler exercises a little common sense during training. A hound taken from its kennel without preparation and considerable conditioning and required to run a strong winter hare experiences great pain during the course and tears, strains and pulls a variety of muscles that have the hound in agony by the end of a day and unable to stand the morning after. A hound needs gradual conditioning before being allowed to run a hare, or for that matter to undertake a lengthy lamping period. My own hounds, lurchers and longdogs start the season terribly unfit. They have spent the summer in kennels with exercise in a quarter-acre concrete run twice a day. They start training in early August and are allowed to run around my holding for an hour or so each night, an action that not only gets the dogs fit but deters foxes from troubling my poultry. After a week I extend their exercise period for a few minutes a day until they are spending some four hours a night wandering on the moor behind my croft. Still I expect them to be tired, exhausted and only too willing to climb on their benches after their first serious ferreting foray, which is conducted on some of the roughest country in Scotland. If they were to be taken unfit then I would expect them to limp home from their first trips out and to be *hors de combat* for a fort-night afterwards, particularly as my September hunts are on the rocky shore of the extreme north of Scotland.

Still my dogs experience strains and sprains, particularly in the early part of the season, and the finest treatment for these is quite simply rest. Other panaceas such as liniment rubs etc. may help the healing process, but rest alone allows tissues to heal and swellings to subside. A dog with a particularly badly wrenched shoulder certainly benefits from a few days under a heat lamp. In 1991, when Phaedra was starting to become quite a useful dog, she developed a technique to increase her haul of rabbits when we hunted on the rocky coastline east of Tongue. As a rabbit increased its pace and then suddenly began to slow down as it neared its warren (this practice always gives the lurcher owner the impression his dog has only narrowly missed a rabbit), Phaedra would attempt what can best be described as a rugby tackle and quite often came out of the rolling dive with the rabbit in her mouth. I have observed many dogs in this family perform this caper which, while I must agree the technique is spectacular, I have found it is only a matter of time before a dog becomes injured when it adopts this technique of catching. Phaedra took a terrific tumble and even released the rabbit she had caught as she bowled headlong down the beach. She lay stock still as I approached her and at first I thought her dead. She struggled to her feet, fell, groaned quite a lot, and I rushed her to the vet as I thought she must have broken every bone in her body. She was clearly in great pain, but examination revealed no bones had been broken, and after a week of total rest under a heat lamp she was walking around the yard, a little stiffly perhaps, but not in great pain. She resumed her hunting a fortnight later and has since modified her style of catching – it is perhaps a style that is slightly less effective at catching rabbits but certainly not as dangerous to the dog.

If I might digress slightly, I cannot help but be baffled by the boasts of lurcher enthusiasts who proudly claim their hounds would rather die than miss a rabbit, and can only conclude that such aficionados either hunt in country where rabbits are scarce or that these people value the life and safety of their dogs lightly. I live in a country that is blessed, some would say cursed, with an abundant rabbit population and I catch many thousands of rabbits each season, yet my best bitch, the best bitch I have ever owned, will ignore rabbits that are darting in and out of barbed wire tangles. I would not tolerate a foolhardy dog with the do or die temperament so beloved by some hunters, owners who possibly seldom see rabbits and whose dogs are so wildly excited as to behave in a crazed manner every time they encounter one. A sensible, well conditioned, experienced dog is seldom injured by a day or night's hunting in the same way as a journeyman boxer is rarely hurt in a contest with an up and coming potential champion. Both athletes, dog and human, know what they are capable of doing and are only too keen to avoid situations that may injure them sorely.

Yet rips and tears are commonly encountered by lurchers in a country where tree stumps are abundant and the land is criss-crossed with barbed wire. Tiny rips and tears can be treated by a layman simply by cleaning the wound with a suitable antiseptic, keeping the wound open and free from straw shavings or other detritus, but the very act of stitching even a tiny rip is fraught with danger. For a layman to stitch a wound, even a tiny wound, could cause him to step into one of the shadowy grey areas of British law which, while I believe British justice is the best in the world, has certain aspects that are open to various interpretations. Under the Protection of Animals Act 1911 Section 1 (1) e it is an offence to subject any animal to an operation which is performed without due care or humanity. Thus for an unqualified person to stitch a wound on any animal the action may constitute an offence. It could also be argued that for unqualified persons to dock tails (this will be illegal by the time this book is published) or to rip off the tiny dew claws from a puppy or to dub (to cut the combs and wattles on game cocks) is illegal. Now, to be perfectly honest, I am quite good at stitching up fleshy tissue – my training as a biologist has given me much practice on the bodies of dead animals and hence I might consider myself a qualified person to stitch a wound, or at least a minor wound. However, whether those who are in a position to ascertain what is or what is not legal would agree is a moot point. So I refrain from stitching wounds in my dogs and get the dog to a veterinary surgeon, though frankly I have seen stitching performed by qualified vets that is far inferior to that which I could perform at home.

On the other side of the coin I have seen lurchers that manifested the signs of lay stitching of the very worst order proudly paraded around lurcher shows, the owners of the dogs literally inviting a private prosecution from some enraged person who sees such an outrageous liberty inflicted on some animal. Frankly, some of these illegal operations (I can think of better descriptions of such stitching) are enough to sicken any sane person and to ensure a conviction from any member of the bench that saw such a hideous mess.

Certainly in some circumstances it might be perfectly legal to stitch up even quite a bad wound on a dog, but those circumstances must be few and far between. If, for instance, a blizzard shut off the west coast of Scotland or the Grampians and conditions were so bad that a stock keeper could not contact a veterinary surgeon or a veterinary surgeon could not come to the assistance of the beast, these might constitute extenuating circumstances that allow a layman to stitch up a wounded animal. Conversely, a court might find against a person who conducted such an act even in these circumstance, though I doubt even magistrates courts would make such a stupid decision.

Many lurchers suffer from foot troubles, particularly lurchers and longdogs that have a high proportion of greyhound or whippet blood in their make-up. The speed of a greyhound or whippet is astonishing, and I never fail to gaze in wonder at the performance of a good greyhound on the track or on the coursing field, but the feet of these hounds are ill-equipped to pursue hares over rock or to run on flint. Worse still is the effect of running such animals on tarmac strips or roads or airplane runways, an all too common practice among some Caithnessian lurcher owners I'm afraid. A collie or a lurcher with a strong trace of collie in its make-up and whose feet resemble those of a herding dog rather than a sighthound might not be sorely damaged by running over such surfaces (though such a practice will certainly not do the dog much good), but a lurcher whose feet favour a sighthound rather than a collie will suffer dreadfully.

I will concede that it is justifiable for a layman to treat some of a lurcher's minor injuries, but a lurcher with damaged feed needs expert treatment, and sadly few qualified vets seem capable of treating a sighthound's damaged feet without resorting to amputating toes at the first sign that all is not well. Frankly, I cannot see how any lurcher or greyhound can give even a fraction of its best on the track or, particularly on the coursing field with some of its toes missing. A hound that runs, brakes and swerves at high speed needs all its toes and I regard amputation of a toe as a last resort rather than a matter of course. I freely admit that I avoid taking a running dog to any veterinary surgeon who is not *au fait* with greyhound ailments and who knows a great deal about how to treat a running dog's injured feet. Such a veterinary surgeon will suggest various modes of treatment before he decides on the instant and irreversible panacea of amputating offending toes. Many badly injured toes will heal if given special treatment and veterinary surgeons who specialise in treating greyhounds or have practices near to greyhound tracks will certainly be the best people to treat a lurcher or longdog that has sustained damage to its feet. In horse racing circles the statement 'a horse is only as good as its feet' is frequently used. The cliché is equally appropriate to running dogs of all types, and no aficionados of the breed type should ever neglect injuries to a running dog's feet or attempt to treat the injuries himself, or take the dog to some lay practitioner whose remedies possibly smack of witchcraft. Lurchers are passed on to new owners for various reasons and a number of lame dogs stagger and totter between one downmarket dog dealer and another which would have been sound, injury-free animals if the injuries to their feet had been properly treated as soon as they had manifested themselves.

Few dogs that enjoy a rural lifestyle or make frequent trips into the countryside are ever free from internal and external parasites, and the most commonly acquired parasites are fleas. I experienced one of the worst infestations of fleas I have ever seen in 1983 when a hot dry summer somehow triggered a flea population explosion in my kennels. Until that time I had dipped my dogs in a sheep dip solution containing gamma benzene hexachloride and seldom experienced a single problem with fleas, despite the fact my terriers hunted rats with regularity, and rats are renowned carriers of many species of fleas. It is a little known fact that rats and dogs are known to harbour both human and a variety of animal fleas so dogs should be kept free of fleas, particularly if they are required to live indoors. Fleas, or at least certain species of fleas, are also known to harbour tapeworm eggs, and as dogs are frequently biting at the irritated areas caused by flea bites, fleas and the tapeworm eggs are often ingested by the dog. Hence a dog that is not free of fleas is hardly likely to be free of tapeworms, and now I shall return to the tale of that summer in 1983. During that year I had failed to buy a drum of sheep dip containing the active ingredient Gamma B.H.C. and the dogs were left unprotected, so to speak. I have never known any creature take advantage of such a situation and my dogs teemed with fleas, fleas that I attempted to eradicate with insecticidal dog shampoos which had little effect but gave my dogs a delicious though slightly cloying scent. A dip in Gamma B.H.C., however, worked like magic and I combed out over a gram of dead fleas and flea dirt (the bloody droppings of fleas) from one of my G.S.D. bitches which was particularly heavily infested. A dip two weeks later killed off fleas that had existed as eggs (almost immune to B.H.C.) but had hatched just in time to be destroyed by the second dipping.

The flea is a great host for numerous diseases – the Black Death was initially spread by the flea, though the pneumonic form was not. So also are a variety of unsavoury and unpleasant canine infections, so it is wise to treat any dog with a pesticidal powder or dip from time to time. Alas, this is not as easy as it sounds for it is no longer possible to buy insecticides which contain Gamma B.H.C. and some of the organophosphate insecticides which replaced B.H.C. have also been removed from the market. There are, of course, effective flea-killing chemicals still available but they are not as toxic (nor do they seem as effective) as some of the older remedies, which were both cheap and reliable. I keep a large number of dogs and purchasing sachets of proprietary flea killer would be slightly ludicrous and ridiculously expensive. So I use a sheep dip which kills a variety of insects and other external parasites, and certainly eradicates fleas for two or three months.

Ticks are great pests and are all too common on lurchers that make regular forays into the countryside. These are vile, unpleasant creatures that anchor to a dog's skin, become bloated with the dog's blood and then sometime fall off to infect another host. If the dog owner attempts to pull off one of these insects its body, bloated with partly digested blood, is readily detached but the head remains firmly anchored in the dog's flesh and usually causes a festering wound before the portions of the head are rejected by the dog's body. Some advocate that a hot iron or a piece of red-hot wood applied to the body of the tick is effective in causing the tick to release its hold, and there are now mechanical tick removers available from most pet shops. Personally I have found neither the homespun nor the pet-shop remedies are particularly useful, and tend to favour either dipping the animal in sheep dip or dabbing the tick with tincture of iodine, which I find poisons the tick and causes it to release its hold on the dog. The moor around my croft teems with ticks, but as I dip my dogs regularly in the sheep dip solution kept in barrels adjacent to my kennels, I have little trouble with ticks or mange mites.

Mange, or rather sarcoptic mange, is an ever-present problem if the lurcher is used to catch fox, for foxes are great carriers of mange. Two types of sarcoptic mange mites can cause mange, or scabies as the complaint is known when it infects human beings. Mange seems to be endemic among foxes and the great Isaac Bell once stated that he encouraged badgers in the country he hunted because badgers cleaned out fox earths and repeatedly reduced the incidence of mange among foxes. Whether or not this is true should not concern the lurcher keeper, but a fox hunter must constantly be aware of the symptoms of mange among his lurchers and terriers.

Some people are particularly prone to scabies infections if they handle foxes or dogs which are affected with mange. At one time when I lamped foxes regularly I was plagued by the most maddening itches imaginable and found it virtually impossible to sleep because the heat trapped by the bedclothes exacerbated the itch. It was during the Christmas holidays so fortunately I was not troubled with the prospect of teaching a difficult class the following day. One weekend I suffered the tortures of the damned and on the Monday I daubed myself with benzyl benzoate emulsion which stopped the itching instantly, and henceforth until I left the teaching profession and travelled north I bathed in Derbac or Bob Martin's Dog Soap which prevented further infection, but I shall never forget that weekend when I felt driven to distraction by the itching.

As a result I am particularly sensitive about and very observant of any mange infection that plagues my dogs. Dogs that are infected with sarcoptic mange, which can be caused by either sarcoptic communis or carcoptic scabie (two very similar mites), will scratch madly and by dint of their incessant scratching puncture their skins. Some dogs will scratch away huge areas of fur in an effort to ease the pruritus, and sometimes but only very rarely will the host become so infected that the mites will virtually leave a sinking ship and the dog will clear up without any treatment. However, more often the animal will become a bleeding scabrous mess as each puncture caused by its incessant scratching opens yet new wounds which become infected and fester. Sarcoptic mange was once referred to as red mange, and with good reason, for the skin of the infected animal becomes red and fiery, not so much because of the action of the mite but simply because the mite causes such a maddening itch that the dog scratches frantically to ease it and hence causes the inflammation of the skin.

Localised mange patches may be treated as I have mentioned, with benzyl benzoate, an emulsion obtainable from any chemist, but I have never favoured treating tiny patches of mange. Infected dogs need treatment by dipping if the treatment is to be effective, and a visit to a veterinary surgeon will usually produce a suitable solution in which to dip an infected dog. I must confess I use sheep dip that has been tailored to treat sheep scab, for the mite that causes scab is very similar to the mange mite and I have yet to find a dog ever sicken after treatment with sheep dip. Usually two dips at fortnightly intervals are enough to kill all mange mites, but the fur denuded by the ravages of the mite and scratching will take six weeks to grow back to its normal length and thickness. Hancock of Sutton Coldfield, who owns a great many greyhounds, collies and greyhound/collie composites, dips his dogs regularly as a matter of course to avoid any mange or flea infestations and his dogs are seldom troubled by external parasites. In summer dogs are dipped two or three times, but in the colder months less frequently for obvious reasons.

In passing it should be noted that the parasite fungus that causes the complaint known as ringworm produces symptoms that are very similar to those produced by certain types of mange, and the difference between these types of infection can only be determined by taking a skin scraping and examining the scraping under a microscope. Ringworm, like mange, is highly contagious and can infect not only other dogs but also their handlers. It is of interest to the handler that if diseased hairs of an animal infected with ringworm are placed under a light some of the hairs appear fluorescent, though the Wood's Lamp method is by no means foolproof. There are a great many highly effective fungicides available for the treatment of ringworm, but the spores of the fungus that cause the disease are so resistant to a variety of chemicals that treatment for the ailment should continue long after the symptoms of ringworm have disappeared. The bedding on which an infected animal has been allowed to rest should also be burned and the walls, floors and grids of the kennel cleaned with a fairly strong solution of bleach.

Ear mites, or otodectic mites to be a shade more scientific, are similar in type to the mite that causes scabies or sheep scab, and while it is fair to say that ears infected with mites are more delicate than some other areas of the body that are prone to mange attacks, when the dog is totally immersed in a dip some of the liquid enters the outer ear and usually eradicates any otodectic mites residing there. Sometimes, however, these mites are protected by a waxy substance and this must be removed, and removed carefully (for the ears are delicate organs that need careful treatment), before the dog is dipped. I dip all my dogs regularly and I am never plagued with what is commonly known as ear canker, though I once experienced great difficulty in treating an infected bitch puppy that was greatly troubled by otodectic mites.

Follicular mange is a far more insidious disease and extremely difficult to cure. This is the dreaded black mange of veterinary dog books, and some of the cures suggested for this malady are entertaining if a little laughable. Frankly, while mixtures of axle grease and the fat from obese bacon pigs mixed with wormwood might seem ludicrous to the reader, such remedies are no more nor no less effective than some of the treatments dispensed by modern veterinary surgeons, for follicular mange is a baffling malady that is extremely difficult to treat even by a competent veterinary surgeon. The disease will usually manifest itself with the dog experiencing some form of stress, when a puppy is teething or when a bitch is lactating heavily, and as the degenerate mite that is causing the illness lives deep beneath the animal's skin the parasite is very difficult to kill. Veterinary treatment is very costly and, frankly, invariably ineffective, and if the dog's condition is kept high the disease will sometimes clear of its own accord. I have yet to see any remedy that has any effect on the progress of the disease, and I have seen many cases of follicular mange. Some hounds will experience seasonal attacks of the illness and appear to recover as the weather becomes cooler or warmer, but hounds that are susceptible to the infection should always be kept in high physical condition to minimise the incidence of the disease.

There are considerable differences of opinion as to how the disease is spread, for an animal with quite serious follicular mange can often be kennelled in pens with other dogs without infecting its kennel mates. My views on how the disease is spread are to say the least heretical and would not find favour with many veterinary surgeons. It has been suggested that puppies suckling their dams are infected either by ingesting the demodectic mite or by intimate or constant contact with the dam. I feel it is equally likely that certain families of animals are more prone to the infection than others, and certainly some strains of dog appear to be totally immune to the infection. In the early part of this century certain strains of smooth-haired dachshund, and good typey strains at that, became extinct because the high incidence of follicular mange among the progeny made it unwise to perpetuate these strains, while other strains appeared virtually immune to the infection.

To return to the subject of endoparasites, or parasites that live within the dog, the tapeworm or several species of tapeworm are the most commonly encountered. These vile creatures anchor themselves in the gut of the dog by dint of a hooked head-like structure known as the scolex, and simply hang in the dog's gut absorbing the food the dog is in the process of digesting. The amount of food such an organism, that neither moves nor attacks its host as does a flea, absorbs must be minimal but the toxic substances tapeworm secrete to maintain their position in the dog's gut certainly do not help the dog to flourish. In recent years a school of thought has emerged among biologists that believes that few organisms are truly parasitic but rather enjoy a strange symbiotic relationship with the host, a relationship that benefits both the host and the creature that is dependent on the functions of the host. There is some evidence (I confess that I am not convinced) that mice that have mild tapeworm infestations grow more rapidly than mice that are completely free of this loathsome parasite. Hancock of Sutton Coldfield does in fact believe that provided a lurcher, greyhound or collie he owns is not obviously in low physical condition as a result of tapeworm infestation it is wise not to worm the dog for tapeworms. I cannot share David's beliefs, however, for I find tapeworms quite repulsive and worm any dog that passes faeces with a single tapeworm segment in its stools. I find the presence of a segment cast off by the body of the tapeworm wriggling on the fur near a dog's anus disgusting, so, unscientific as it may seem, I reject the notion that any dog can benefit from a single tapeworm anchored to its gut.

Rabbits are great carriers of tapeworms and the gut or abdominal cavity of the rabbit is a haven for these sickening brutes. Hence dogs that catch rabbits, or more particularly dogs that eat uncooked rabbit meat, are particularly prone to tapeworm infestation. Both lurchers and longdogs suffer from tapeworm infestations particularly as rabbit fleas harbour tapeworms, and it is a very lucky dog that can carry a rabbit without ingesting at least some fleas which abound on the creature's fur. These eggs, when triggered by the dog's gastric juices, will hatch and anchor themselves to the dog's gut, and once more the dog becomes infected. A rabbit-hunting lurcher is seldom free from tapeworm at various stages of development, and whatever the current scientific opinion regarding the relationship of parasite and host I worm my dogs as soon as I see tapeworm section (a gravid segment is usually filled with eggs ready to be ingested and to infect another host) wriggling in a stool one of my dogs has passed.

Remedies that will rid the dog of tapeworms are many and varied and frankly a book written on some of the remedies would resemble a script sanctioned by Roger Corman. I have met travellers who swear by dosing the dog with a hell brew of powdered glass and cod liver oil, a deadly mixture that must scar and damage both the gut and the tapeworm suspended in it, however efficacious this abrasive mess may be at ridding the dog of its parasites. Quite an effective remedy for ridding a dog of tapeworms is the chemical dichlorophen which has replaced areca nut, areca oil and extracts of male fern as the most popular and readily available worming remedy. Unlike the vegetable extracts previously mentioned, which caused the tapeworm or at least the portions of the tapeworm to leave the gut by dint of a violent purgative action – and some dogs were woefully ill after dosing with male fern and areca – dichlorophen simply removes the tapeworm's protective covering and the alimentary tract's enzymes virtually dissolve it so that there is no trace of the parasite in the stool passed by the dog. Over the years I have changed my mind about the use of dichlorophen for I once insisted on seeing evidence that the bowels had voided tapeworms. Since that time I have come to accept how effective dichlorophen can be as an anthelmintic, but it should be borne in mind a dog needs frequent worming to keep it free of these disgusting parasites. One seldom sees any anthelmintic other than dichlorophen offered for sale these days, and old-fashioned remedies such as areca nut (or even its derivative, arecolune) can only be found by seeking out herbalists who still specialise in selling antique but natural remedies.

Roundworms are quite different from tapeworms but are equally injurious to the welfare of the dog. These wire-like nematoids have hooked extremities and may often be vomited or passed in the faeces of infected dogs. I have dealt with the subject of roundworms rather more fully in the chapter concerning the breeding of lurchers and feel that repetition is unnecessary. It is, however, of interest to note that some of the older remedies for ridding a puppy of these distressing parasites advocated pressing a cud of masticated chewing tobacco down the puppy's gullet, whereupon the puppy usually went into a state of shock or vomited a mass of tangled roundworms. Bad scouring usually followed such a barbaric method of worming, and some roundworms were passed in the liquid faecal matter voided by the whelp. Many puppies were made desperately ill by such treatment and not a few died. Modern roundworm medicines are usually piperazine-based and cause both adults and puppies little discomfort. Piperazine citrate or hydrate, the most commonly used forms of the chemical, are readily available in pet shops where the worming tablets or liquid are inexpensive to buy.

20

The Lurcher and the Law

Traditionally the lurcher has been the companion dog of the Autolycus figure, the night-time stalker, the seedy disreputable, the rural renegade, a petty nuisance rather than a criminal, and so reference to the law regarding the keeping and working of lurchers may seem a shade superfluous. Nevertheless, the laws and indeed the policing of these islands have changed greatly since the Fen Tigers held sway on the marshlands between Cambridge and the sea and poor simple-minded Frederick Rolfe, the anti-hero of *I Walked By Night*, would have been arrested (and detained awaiting a psychiatric report, no doubt) long before he reached the sanctuary of Manchester after his debacle with the Norfolk constabulary.

Lawless lurcher keepers still exist, and sadly are held in some regard by the less astute rural sportsmen, but today the majority of lurcher enthusiasts are honest, law-abiding people and are responsible enough to be trusted and no longer behave as do the denizens of institutions of the disturbed. Thus it is expedient to conclude a book of this nature with a few comments on the law and the lurcher – or perhaps the law and the lurcherman would be more accurate a title.

Let us begin by stating that every square inch of Britain belongs to someone, and the expression 'common land' is rather misleading. The term does not in fact mean a tract of land where any person has a right to run riot or hunt with his dogs or seek out any game or animals that may choose to reside on the said land; common land is simply land on which certain people and only certain people have the right to graze live-stock, and only certain types of livestock at that.

Likewise, rubbish tips which are often havens for rabbits (they are dry and usually well drained and offer rabbits sanctuary from medium-sized predators) are usually the property of one's local councils, and it is highly unlikely that such councils will take too kindly to someone hunt-ing such refuse tips with lurchers, terriers or ferrets. True, these councils do not jealously guard the rabbits living in such waste and detritus but they do prefer to prevent anyone venturing on and hunting in such places. Rubbish tips are often very dangerous and there is a strong possibility that anyone having permission to hunt such places would sustain an injury and hence rush to seek compensation from the owners of the rubbish tip. So permission to hunt these places is seldom obtainable and there are records of youthful hunters being arrested and convicted for poaching such rubbish tips.

The belief that the ownership of a lurcher entitles a person to wander when and where he will is a ludicrous one, and frankly I would decline giving a lurcher to someone who had nowhere to hunt. The humiliation of standing in the dock after spending a morning in a court waiting room with a band of seedy disreputables should act as a deterrent for any thinking person, and the capture of a rabbit is scarcely worth the risk of acquiring a criminal record. Therefore permission to hunt rabbits on any land should be obtained before venturing on the said land. If permission is not obtained then the lurcher owner should not venture on the land.

Rabbits enjoy no legal closed season in which to produce and rear the young, but hares do receive protection, albeit scant, from the law. The Hare Protection Act 1892, which applies to England, Wales and Scotland, makes it an offence to sell or expose for sale any hares or leverets between the months of March and July inclusive, but the act is a shade unclear about the killing of hares with lurchers or other dogs during this time.

The awful monoculture practised by the Forestry Commission in Britain usually ensures that no game will be found under the shelter of thickly planted trees that shut out the sunlight and prevent the growth of grass. Thus the Forestry Commission Byelaws of 1982, which make it illegal to permit a dog to disturb, worry or chase any animal or bird found on forestry land, is perhaps a little superfluous. It is also an offence for any person wilfully to disturb or destroy a burrow or den, sette or any lair of a wild animal on Forestry Commission land.

Rabbits are now fairly plentiful within large towns and cities and may be seen feeding in gardens and parks in quite large conurbations, and foxes are often abundant in the most unlikely urban areas. However, lest the lurcherman believes that this urban quarry is fair game, it is an offence under an Act of Parliament passed in 1848 to set a dog on any other animal within the confines of a town, though the expression 'town' is badly defined by the Act. This Act was passed to reinforce the anti-baiting Act passed in 1835, but it is perfectly feasible and reasonable for a police officer to arrest anyone setting a lurcher at a rabbit, hare or fox in the midst of a town, and while I know of no conviction for the said offence, in the light of today's public opinion and its antipathy to hunting I feel such a prosecution is likely, particularly as few urban dwellers will willingly sanction a fox or rabbit to be coursed across their gardens. However, even if such sanctions were obtained from the householder it is still illegal to course animals of any sort within the confines of a town.

Lamping, or at least the lamping of rabbits and hares, is not illegal but few police officers seem conversant with the law regarding country pursuits. Hence it may be policy for the lamper to call at a police station adjacent to the land he or she intends to lamp to inform the officer in charge of his or her intentions for the night lest the heavy tread of a police officer's feet across the field not only disturbs the game, but also sours the evening for the lamper who has to explain and possibly argue the legality of lamping with a police officer who is not *au fait* with the laws of the countryside.

It is good sense for the hunter, be he a lamper or daytime hunter, to obtain hunting permission in writing from the landowner and to carry the said written permission with him during the time he is hunting. It is irksome for a ferreter to be forced to leave his ferret to ground while he accompanies a police officer to the house of the landowner to prove he has permission to work the land. It is even more irksome for the landowner to be woken up in the early hours of the morning by an over-zealous police officer. Should this happen more than once, it is not unlikely that the landowner may withdraw his permission.

On the subject of lamping, it is illegal to hunt deer with a lamp and lurcher. Section 2 of the Deer Act 1963 makes it an offence to take or wilfully kill deer or take any carcass of any species of deer between one hour after sunset and one hour before sunrise, which effectively makes the lamping of deer an offence. It is also an offence to pursue and catch any species of deer with dogs of any sort in Scotland.

Lurcher owners should always be aware of the laws covering dogs worrying livestock, particularly sheep which usually inhabit the dry terrain that is favoured by rabbits. If a lurcher worries, disturbs or frightens sheep not only is the owner of the lurcher guilty of an offence, but the person who is handling the lurcher at the time of the offence may be deemed equally guilty, but the Dogs (Protection of Livestock) Act 1952 was simply the initial stage of a move to protect livestock from the ravages of dogs.

The Wildlife and Countryside Act 1981 extends the definition of dog 'worrying' to include a situation where the dog is at large (not on the leash or under close control) in a field where there are sheep. Hence the lurcher that courses its hare or pursues a rabbit through a flock of sheep without harming the sheep may also be said to be sheep worrying, and farmers may be justified in shooting a dog to protect livestock. However, even if the dog is destroyed the stock owner may still make a claim for damage through a civil court whether or not the lurcher owner has been found guilty of the offence of owning a stock-worrying dog in a magistrates court.

The responsible lurcher owner will not only obey the letter of the law, but will also follow the unwritten code of good sportsmanship, and be aware of field sport's public image at a time when it is under ever-closer scrutiny by opponents of hunting.

Thus the lurcher, its quarry, its training, its care in sickness and health and the laws that govern the ownership of such a dog. No dog offers its owner a more rewarding and entertaining lifestyle, and no dog asks so little in return. What a pity many of these useful dogs are swapped, changed repeatedly, sold and often badly treated. Indeed, the more I see of men the more I like my dogs!

Index

Index

warrener, historical 11, 18, 19
Waterloo Cup 164
weight 113–14, 117–18, 169
Weston Park Show 173–4
Whaddon Chase Lurcher Show 30, 173
Wheaten terrier 192
  lurcher 28
whelping 227–8

whippet 11–12
  hybrid 32, 79, 104, 147, 210
    Bedlington 32, 213, 215
Wildlife and Countryside Act 1981
  251–2
worming 50, 168, 221, 226, 229–30
worms 49, 242, 246–8
wrist damage 87–8